THE PERILS OF PARTNERSHIP

The Perils of Partnership

INDUSTRY INFLUENCE, INSTITUTIONAL INTEGRITY, AND PUBLIC HEALTH

Jonathan H. Marks

OXFORD
UNIVERSITY PRESS

OXFORD

UNIVERSITY PRESS

Oxford University Press is a department of the University of Oxford. It furthers
the University's objective of excellence in research, scholarship, and education
by publishing worldwide. Oxford is a registered trade mark of Oxford University
Press in the UK and certain other countries.

Published in the United States of America by Oxford University Press
198 Madison Avenue, New York, NY 10016, United States of America.

CIP data is on file at the Library of Congress
ISBN 978-0-19-090708-2

In memory of my father Ronnie Marks,
and for my daughter Miranda

Contents

Preface

A general explanation of the world and of history must first of all take into
account the way our house was situated.
—ITALO CALVINO[1]

YOU MIGHT SAY that I suckled at the breast of industry. A few days before I was
born, a sales "rep" gave my father twelve months' supply of "baby milk." My father
was a family doctor, and the rep believed that if physicians were giving the company's
formula to their own babies, they were far more likely to recommend it to their
patients. So mother's milk was SMA: "simulated milk adapted." In childhood, I continued to benefit from industry largesse. My father gave me the pens, pads, rulers,
and other small gifts that reps from various drug companies left with him after they
had told him about the benefits of their latest drug. By the time I was seven years old,
diuretic, beta-blocker, and *anti-hypertensive* had entered my lexicon. I didn't know
what these words meant. But I knew they referred to the pills my father prescribed
for patients in his NHS practice on the other side of Glasgow.

In time, I weaned myself. I left Scotland to study law at Oxford, where I became accustomed to paying for my own pens and notepads. In London, I qualified
as a barrister. Although I learned about conflicts of interest in legal practice, for
many years I had no cause to reflect on the relationships between pharmaceutical
companies and physicians. In 1999, after a fortuitous conversation in the parking lot
at the European Court of Justice, I was retained to represent a Canadian physician,
Dr. Nancy Olivieri, in a case arising from her dispute with the industry sponsor of
her clinical drug trials.[2] This experience triggered my enduring interest in the ethical

implications of the complex web of relations between industry, academy, and government. Dr. Olivieri had sought a commercial sponsor for the drug trials because the Canadian government made this a condition of *its* financial support for her research. This decision proved fateful when the company tried to prevent Dr. Olivieri from informing the trial participants of her concerns about the drug's efficacy and safety. A report by the Canadian Association of University Teachers found that Dr. Olivieri's university and associated teaching hospital had failed to defend her academic independence.[3] The authors pointedly observed that when the dispute arose, the drug company was negotiating what would have been the largest-ever matched donation for the university and the hospital.

In the wake of this case, I decided to explore the systemic ethical implications of the pharmaceutical industry's interactions with medical researchers and their institutions. However, my arrival at Georgetown and Johns Hopkins Universities in 2004 to take up the Greenwall Fellowship in Bioethics and Health Policy was swiftly followed by reports of health professionals' complicity in torture and aggressive interrogation in the "war on terror." So I put aside the ethics of academy-industry relations to work on interrogation, medical ethics, and human rights.

When I completed the fellowship, I took up a new position as director of the bioethics program at Penn State and decided to return to issues of industry-sponsored research. However, by this time, many scholars were working on the ethics of industry-sponsored *medical* research. Another fortuitous conversation, this time with a food science colleague, Donald B. Thompson, revealed an area of mutual interest: the ethics of industry-sponsored nutrition research. In March 2008, we put together our first workshop at Penn State to explore the topic.

A couple of years later, while I was working on the interrogation project at the Edmond J. Safra Center for Ethics at Harvard, I was invited to join the Center's new "Lab on Institutional Corruption" to explore the ethical issues raised by industry funding of food and nutrition research and by the food industry's influence on public health policy. I had been watching with growing concern the increasingly complex webs of relationships involving universities (including my own) and corporations across a variety of industry sectors and academic units. But many other scholars had written books critiquing the academy's relationships with industry. I decided to focus instead on the ways in which industry actors influence governments and intergovernmental organizations. At the same time, I recognized that this influence occurs both directly and indirectly, and that academic institutions and civil society organizations often provide avenues for indirect influence.

In recent years, I have learned a great deal from my discussions with policymakers at national and international levels. I have had the opportunity to participate in meetings on public-private partnerships and conflicts of interest—among them, events organized by the National Academy of Medicine and the World Health Organization. While a visiting researcher at the Brocher Foundation in the Spring of 2015 (and during subsequent visits to Geneva), I spoke with a number of staff at the World Health Organization who have been wrestling with the ethical challenges presented by public-private partnerships and so-called multistakeholder initiatives—including the fall-out when they do not go according to plan.

These experiences inform the views I express here. Although conflict of interest is an important concept, it cannot fully address the systemic ethical implications of industry relations. Focusing on public health, I will show how relations with industry actors may still be ethically problematic even when they do not create conflicts of interest. Other scholars have drawn on critiques of neoliberalism in an attempt to capture some of these concerns. But many policymakers find this concept too academic or politically charged. I have long believed there are firmer foundations on which to build practical guidance for policymakers. The search for these foundations led me to focus on the implications of industry relations for the independence, integrity, and credibility of government bodies, and for public health.

Industry actors develop close relationships with government bodies to protect their commercial interests. From industry's point of view, these relationships make perfect sense. I recognize the economic pressures that lead governments and intergovernmental organizations to enter close relationships with industry. But these relations threaten the independence, integrity, and credibility of public health agencies, as well as their fidelity to their public health mission and purpose. Corporations have honed highly effective strategies of influence. Government bodies have a responsibility to develop their own counter-strategies. It is my profound hope that this book will help them discharge that responsibility.

Acknowledgments

THIS BOOK COULD not have been completed without the assistance of many, many people.

Audra Wolfe was the first to read the manuscript in its entirety, and her comments were invaluable. Several colleagues read parts of earlier drafts and provided helpful comments: Don Thompson, Julie Kleinman, Jim Dillard, Steve Ross, Adam Muchmore, Jud Mathews, Larry Cata Backer, Javi Lopez, Ben Jones, Jeremy Engels, John Christman, Leland Glenna, and Mike McNamee. Guidance or comments on a number of topics came from others whom I did not burden with the text, in particular, Stephen Marks, Kadri Simm, Shirin Garmaroudi, Peter Aeschbacher, Michele Kennerly, and Andrew Stark. Judith Richter and Lida Lhotska provided invaluable insights on global health policy from NGO perspectives. The book is better because of a conversation with Margaret Atwood. She raised an objection to my thesis. Thanks to a glass or two of merlot, I was not quick-witted enough to respond to her immediately. But within half an hour of walking home, I had penned a rejoinder that found its way into chapter 8. Many people generously took the time to offer their advice on the writing and publication process: Chloe Silverman, Robert Vitalis, Dorn Hetzel, Gabeba Baderoon, Christopher Campbell, Nancy Locke, Susan Squier, Sajay Samuel, Samar Farage, Russell Frank, Sarah Clark Miller, Rosemary Jolly, Charlotte Eubanks, Greg Eghigian, Eric Hayot, Ben Schreier, Sarah Koenig, Geoff Scott, Emily Tarconish, Klaus Keller, Marc Rodwin, Julia Kasdorf, Steve Rubin, and Jud Mathews. I am especially grateful to a number of people on that list who responded to my queries on multiple occasions.

The book benefited immensely from fellowships and research residencies at the Edmond J. Safra Center for Ethics at Harvard, the Hastings Center in New York, and the Brocher Foundation in Geneva. I am grateful for sabbatical and administrative leave from Penn State that allowed me to take advantage of these opportunities. During my two years at Harvard, I benefited immensely from the insights of several faculty, among them, Larry Lessig, Dan Wikler, Nir Eyal, Mahzarin Banaji, and Max Bazerman. I also benefited from the insights of several fellow fellows, especially Lisa Cosgrove, Susannah Rose, and Sunita Sah. In various ways, Francesco Branca, Gauden Galea, Hala Boukerdenna, and Andreas Reis all gave me opportunities to share my work and perspectives with WHO staff, and to receive invaluable feedback. I also spent several days trying to navigate the Borgesian archives of the WHO. It left me with the sense that, as in "The Library of Babel," everything is there, if only I could find it. I did not always succeed. But the small victories I had would have been impossible without the assistance of the library's sympathetic and attentive staff. While at the Hastings Center, I received invaluable feedback from many people, especially, Millie Solomon, Dan Callahan, Greg Kaebnick, Laura Haupt, Nancy Berlinger, Michael Gusmano, and Josephine Johnstone. I am immensely grateful for the research assistance of Adam Banks at Penn State and Stephanie Woods at Harvard.

I obtained extremely helpful feedback on this project from a variety of seminars and presentations at several venues, among them, the Edmond J. Safra Center for Ethics at Harvard; the Bioethics Colloquium at Penn State; the Faculty Seminar at Penn State Law; the Berman Bioethics Institute at Johns Hopkins University; the Hastings Center in New York; the Brocher Foundation in Geneva; and the Global Ethics Group at the WHO. I am also grateful to the Kennedy Institute of Ethics Journal for permission to draw on my 2014 article, "Toward a Systemic Ethics of Public-Private Partnerships in Food and Health."

A special thanks to Sigrid Sterckx and Julian Cockbane for organizing (and catering!) a discussion of my book proposal at the Brocher Foundation as the sun set on the banks of Lake Geneva. I am also grateful to Peter Ohlin for his unflagging editorial support. Tom Campo and Skylar Yuen gave me the opportunity to present the broad argument of this book in a TED talk at Penn State (http://ted.com/talks/2730). Peter Miraldi generously gave far more time than I could have reasonably expected. He helped me hone the talk for a general audience, as did Terri Vescio and Lori Miraldi. The book, as well as the talk, benefited greatly from this feedback.

Lisa Sternlieb's generosity knows no bounds. I sought her guidance far more often than I should have. I am so grateful for her patience, and I appeal for her forgiveness. Miranda Marks—to whom this book is dedicated—is a young fearless writer whose countless talents never cease to surprise and delight me. Many other family and friends on both sides of the Atlantic had no direct input on the book. But they were invaluable simply because they offered pleasurable distractions from my labors.

Since I have no expectation that they will ever read this book (although my mother insists she will!), I shall do my best to reciprocate in other ways.

I have debts to the dead, as well as the living. I had many conversations about this book with the late Tony Kaye. He was a man of profound intellect, compassion, and generosity. His untimely death has left a void in so many lives, including my own. This book would have benefited from the wisdom and insights of my late father, had he been alive to read a complete draft. Although the seeds of the book were planted long ago—perhaps, as the preface suggests, in the days of my childhood—I regret that the final product came far too late for him to hold it in his hands.

Abbreviations

ABA	American Beverage Association
BINGO	business interest NGO
BMGF	Bill and Melinda Gates Foundation
CDC	Centers for Disease Control and Prevention (US)
CoI	conflict of interest
CSO	civil society organization
CSR	corporate social responsibility
DHHS	Department of Health and Human Services (US)
FAO	Food and Agriculture Organization
FDA	Food and Drug Administration (US)
FENSA	Framework of Engagement with Non-State Actors
FTC	Federal Trade Commission (US)
ICN	International Conference on Nutrition (1992)
ICN2	Second International Conference on Nutrition (2014)
IGO	intergovernmental organization
ILSI	International Life Sciences Institute
IoM	Institute of Medicine (US)
MDG	Millennium Development Goal
MSI	multistakeholder initiative
NAM	National Academy of Medicine (US)
NCD	noncommunicable disease
NGO	nongovernmental organization
NIH	National Institutes of Health (US)
PAC	political action committee (US)

PAO	patient advocacy organization
PHA	Partnership for a Healthier America
PHRD	Public Health Responsibility Deal (UK)
PINGO	public interest NGO
PPP	public-private partnership
RDN	Responsibility Deal Network (UK)
SCN	Standing Committee on Nutrition
SDG	Sustainable Development Goal
SSB	sugar-sweetened beverage
SUN	Scaling Up Nutrition
UN	United Nations
UNGA	United Nations General Assembly
USDA	United States Department of Agriculture
WHO	World Health Organization

THE PERILS OF PARTNERSHIP

1

Introduction

There are these two young fish swimming along, and they happen to meet an older fish swimming the other way, who nods at them and says, "Morning, boys, how's the water?" And the two young fish swim on for a bit, and then eventually one of them looks over at the other and goes, "What the hell is water?"
—DAVID FOSTER WALLACE[1]

"PUBLIC-PRIVATE PARTNERSHIPS," "MULTISTAKEHOLDER initiatives," "shared governance," and "inclusiveness." This language dominates the way we think about major public health challenges—and how we address them. It is the water in which policymakers have learned to swim. At first glance, these terms might seem harmless enough. Who could be opposed to partnerships? Why should we not all work together to solve some of the world's most intractable problems—among them, obesity and diet-related noncommunicable diseases (NCDs)? Proponents of public-private partnerships (PPPs) contend that these arrangements pool resources, facilitate the exchange of information and expertise, and promote understanding by each party of the objectives of the others.[2]

When critics object that some industry partners are contributing to the very problems that governments are trying to solve, they are met with some common responses. *Governments cannot solve these problems alone. Industry needs to be part of the solution. Public officials can use these relationships to exert "leverage" over the private sector.* In this book, I challenge that deceptively appealing narrative. I invite the reader—and policymakers—to pay attention to the water and to ask if something might be wrong with it. I explore whether the paradigm relationship between government and the private sector should be "hand in hand," as one UN official put it,[3] or *mano a mano*—involving tension, struggle and, at times, direct conflict.

Public-private partnerships are not entirely new. For several decades, governments have employed these arrangements for building and maintaining infrastructure, including transportation systems. But recent years have seen the emergence of partnerships and so-called multistakeholder initiatives as the paradigm for public health interventions. A distinctive feature of these arrangements is collaboration with corporate actors that are causing or exacerbating the very problems that public health agencies are trying to solve. The United Nations recently endorsed the partnership paradigm as a means of improving nutrition and promoting well-being (among other UN Sustainable Development Goals).[4] This suggests that, if unchecked, the practice will continue with renewed vigor.

I recognize the powerful structural incentives for close relations. In the face of declining funding, public officials feel compelled to look elsewhere for financial support. The private sector is the obvious first stop. Companies are more than willing to "step up," particularly when collaboration with government bodies can burnish corporate reputations and promote leading brands. Public officials feel pressured to show they are accomplishing something during their often relatively short time in office. CEOs are even more motivated by "short-termism," an orientation exacerbated by quarterly returns and annual bonuses.[5] When institutions reward people, whether CEOs or ministers of health, for certain behaviors, we should not be surprised to find them engaged in those behaviors. As the novelist Upton Sinclair once observed, "[i]t is difficult to get a man to understand something when his salary depends upon his not understanding it."[6]

Some people respond to powerful incentives less readily than others. But few are immune. Such incentives often lead to what is sometimes called "moral blindness" or "ethical fading."[7] Both terms describe a failure to recognize the ethical dimensions or issues raised by a problem or practice. This can occur when the problem is framed primarily as a legal or political one. In the case of partnerships, efficacy is the dominant frame. Even when public officials recognize ethical concerns, they often suppress or downplay them. This should not be surprising. If water is scarce and someone else controls the spigot, discussions about water quality may seem, at best, futile.

1.1 WHAT WE DO NOT SEE, AND WHAT WE DO NOT SAY

We cannot speak of things we do not see. And we may not even see them if we do not possess the language to capture them. We have developed a rich lexicon to promote and describe the purported benefits of interactions between the public and the private sector: "partnership," "engagement," "stakeholders," and "inclusiveness." However, we often lack language to describe the problems resulting from such interactions. The traditional lens for addressing these kinds of issues has been "conflict of interest." This term is most commonly used in relation to individuals. A physician who receives speaking fees from a pharmaceutical company has a conflict of interest when she conducts research on, gives lectures about, or prescribes the company's drug. As we now know, interactions with drug companies can and do subtly influence the professional judgment of physicians—even when the personal gain to the physician is not substantial.[8]

Policymakers less frequently apply the concept of conflict of interest to *institutions*. In such cases, the principal hazard is not direct personal gain. Institutional interactions may be ethically problematic for other reasons—especially when they result in the promotion of private interests at the expense of the public interest or the common good. A public health official who accepts money from a soda company for the construction of a playground does not do so on her own account (unless, of course, she is also being bribed!). She accepts on behalf of her institution and does so to support the work of that institution. The same may be said of an academic administrator who accepts millions of dollars from one or more companies to build a center supporting research that is expressly designed to promote industry interests. In this case too, the administrator is unlikely to receive direct financial gain. She is doing her job, she would argue, by building a center to support the work of her faculty, postdoctoral fellows, and graduate students. In order to address the ethics of these interactions, we need an additional set of conceptual tools.

The purpose of this book is to help us "see" *and* help us "say." We will explore the ethical hazards of public-private sector interactions and develop a language to describe those hazards. We will draw on a more demanding account of institutional integrity (one I began in earlier work).[9] The term is commonly used in the context of compliance. There, the emphasis is on ensuring an institution acts in accordance with laws and regulations, especially those concerning illegal activities such as bribery and corruption (in the traditional sense of the word). But integrity can and does have broader ethical implications that should guide public institutions in their interactions with industry.

Close relationships with industry can create subtle reciprocities and influence that undermine the integrity of government bodies, as well as public trust in those institutions. Once we can see the potential ethical problems and explain them to others, we can begin the work of developing the tools to address them. This book is intended to help people *both within and outside* public health agencies (among other institutions) recognize these concerns, articulate them to others, and develop potential remedies. These remedies may range from small changes in internal policies to more fundamental structural reforms.

1.2 WHY YOU SHOULD READ THIS BOOK

If you are not concerned about PPPs and other close relationships between industry and public bodies, then this book was written for you. If you are troubled by these arrangements but have difficulty explaining why, then this book was also written for you. And if you are a public official who already recognizes the ethically problematic dimensions of these arrangements (and you wish to address them and explore alternative approaches to public health interventions), there is much for you here too. In the pages that follow, I attempt to show how the prevailing forms of industry interaction are problematic for government bodies (among others). I explore several common forms of interaction—whether framed as public-private partnerships, multistakeholder initiatives, alliances, or in some other way. I show how they create subtle influence and reciprocity; undermine the integrity of government bodies, academic institutions, and civil society organizations (nonindustry partners); and erode trust and confidence in nonindustry partners, as well as the research and policies they produce. Toward the end of the book, I offer some practical guidance to help policymakers and public officials assess the systemic ethical implications of their institutions' interactions with industry. Much of that discussion is also relevant to academic administrators and leaders of civil society organizations who are exploring closer institutional relations with industry.

1.3 THE PERSPECTIVE AND APPROACH OF THE BOOK

The views expressed here are not premised on a Manichaean view of the world that frames government, the academy, and civil society organizations as inherently good, and industry as inherently evil. On the contrary, my argument rests on the idea that there are fundamental differences between the mission, purpose, and function of public sector bodies on the one hand, and corporations and trade associations on the other hand. These differences are especially acute in the case of a public health agency, and a soda company whose products are exacerbating major public health problems (obesity and diet-related NCDs). Public officials and administrators frequently emphasize a *convergence* of interests with industry, and downplay or ignore the *divergence*, in order to foster collaboration and "get things done." This approach comes at a price. Not least, it provides industry actors with additional opportunities to influence public health policy and research in ways that are most consonant with their commercial interests.

I resist the notion that one can point to an interaction between an industry actor and a government (or academic) institution, and discuss the ethical implications of the interaction in isolation. To fully appreciate and address the ethical issues, we must examine the systemic effects of industry interactions. I do this from the perspective of *public sector* institutions. These institutions and their leaders are the focus of my ethical critique, *not* corporations. Although there is a vigorous debate about the existence, nature, and content of the ethical obligations of corporations, I do not address those questions here. Whatever the ethical obligations of corporations in general, and whether or not any particular corporation may be satisfying those obligations, public institutions have inherent ethical obligations tied to their mission and purpose and to the public good. We depend on these institutions for the protection of our health and well-being.

This book is informed by many disciplines, among them philosophy, law, political science, anthropology, and psychology. It also draws on some interdisciplinary fields, including behavioral law and economics, and institutional corruption studies. As a result, the book addresses many topics, each of which has been the subject of lengthy scholarly analysis. These include the distinction between public and private, notions of the common good, the doctrine of separation of powers, antitrust (or competition) law, and the psychology of gift-giving and reciprocity. There are many scholars who have devoted entire books to each of these topics. What you will find here is a novel approach that draws together disparate strands to help us acknowledge and address a crisis in public health policy. I hope that the reader will find value in such an approach and forgive the author for any oversight resulting from the ambitious scope of the project. Given what economist A. O. Hirschman would have called the "boundary crossing" nature of the book,[10] I have tried to employ language accessible to a wide variety of readers including policymakers and staff in public health agencies and civil society groups. To keep the main text short, I have moved some analysis to the appendices.

I.4 THE SCOPE AND ARGUMENT OF THE BOOK

Partnerships with industry actors are widespread across a variety of sectors—from pharmaceuticals to energy. In many of these sectors, products and practices have profound implications for health. I could have surveyed several sectors. But instead, I decided to focus here on one particular sector, food and beverages, and to address the impact of its companies on public health, especially obesity. It would also be possible to write one book about government relationships with industry, another about universities and industry (as many scholars have done), and a third about civil society organizations' relations with industry. However, industry actors interact with all three categories of institutions as part of their strategies of influence. To counter these strategies, public officials and policymakers must keep all industry interactions in view. Industry funds research to influence policymakers. Industry support of civil society groups also creates avenues for indirect influence of government agencies. For these reasons, I address industry relations with universities and civil society organizations in chapter 5.

My account challenges the prevailing view that government, the academy, civil society, *and* corporations "need to agree upon finding effective and efficient policies."[11] It does not follow that because industry is contributing to a global health problem, governments have to agree with industry on how to develop and implement solutions. On the contrary, such an approach limits potential solutions to those likely to garner industry support. I will argue that partnerships—and other collaborative relations with industry that promote reciprocity and influence—are ethically problematic. In other spheres, we recognize the need for institutions to remain at arm's length. Separation of powers characterizes a quintessential dimension of the relationship between the executive, legislative, and judicial branches of government. We would and should be especially troubled by a partnership or other close relationship between the judiciary and either of the other branches of government. In order for the judiciary to perform its core functions and to maintain trust and confidence in its ability to do so, the judiciary must remain at arm's length from the other branches. It is time for us to consider whether a similar distance between government agencies and industry actors is also necessary to protect the core functions of those agencies, as well as their independence, integrity and credibility.

Any shift will require—and be promoted by—the development of new norms. The absence of norms to address interactions involving the public and the private is a conspicuous lacuna in ethics, policy, and law. We have developed bodies of norms to constrain the exercise of power, protect institutional function, and address reciprocity and influence within each of the public and private sectors. The doctrine of separation of powers constrains collaboration between the judiciary and the other branches of government—what might be called *public-public* interactions. Antitrust and competition laws constrain collaboration among corporations, what might be called *private-private* interactions. I argue that a necessary complement to (and natural corollary of) the norms within each of these two domains is a third body of norms addressing *public-private* sector interactions. These new norms could help us better address the ethical issues raised by the kinds of scenarios set out in the two cases studies included in this chapter.

The first example explores an industry interaction with local government (figure 1.1). The second involves a university department (figure 1.2 on page 8). The academic partnership case study should also be of interest to public officials, since it

> You are the public health official for the city of Blankton. Budgets are tight, and have been for some time. Rates of childhood obesity are rising steadily. There is no playground in your poorest neighborhood. A journalist writes a piece in the *Blankton Gazette* about the "desperate need" for a playground. She describes children playing in a parking garage—a location also used by drug dealers to conduct their business. Shortly after the story appears in print, a national fast food chain, SoTasty Inc. offers to come to the rescue. The company has three popular restaurants in the center of town. Its vice-president for nutrition and public policy calls and offers to give you $100,000 to build an all-natural wooden playground.
>
> The VP emphasizes that the money will not come directly from the company, but from Healthy-Kids-Leap, a charitable foundation that the company recently established. There are only two conditions, and the VP assures you that neither is onerous. First, there will be a bronze plaque at the gate of the playground informing visitors that the facility was constructed with a donation from the foundation and with the support of the company. Second, you will be asked to smile and pose for a photograph with the VP, the executive director of the charitable foundation, and a Latino/a child chosen by the local school. Each of you will pose for the photograph while holding one corner of a greatly enlarged image of the donation check.
>
> As a well-trained public health official, you know the academic literature on childhood obesity. You know that exercise is important, especially for children in the town's poorest neighborhood. And you are certain that a new playground will be a far safer place for children to play than the drug-dealers' parking garage. But you also know that public health experts believe that the fast food sold by SoTasty, and other companies like them, is a major contributor to the rise in childhood obesity. You feel uncomfortable about the proposal, but you also find it hard to resist.
>
> What do you do?

FIGURE 1.1 Case Study: Playing with Industry

is likely to generate health-related research that will influence policymakers and the public more broadly. Although these case studies are hypothetical, they draw from reports of real interactions illuminated by informal discussions with public officials and academic administrators.

Case study analyses often neglect the broader systemic ethical implications. Industry interactions should not be viewed merely as discrete or isolated cases. They are parts of complex webs of industry relations. As figure 1.3(a) on page 9 illustrates, it is tempting to view a public body's relationship with a corporation as a dyad, a relationship that simply involves two entities. We may broaden our view by recognizing the relationships that one public body has with a variety of industry actors or that one industry actor has with a variety of other entities. This is the hub-and-spoke perspective in figure 1.3(b). But a truly systemic perspective, as in figure 1.3(c), should encompass the webs of relationships that multiple industry actors create with a variety of other entities including government bodies (at all levels), the academy, and civil society groups.[12] I say more about these webs of influence in chapter 5.

You are the chair of the food science department at Melamed University. A former alumna is now the CEO of a fast food company, QuickBite Inc. She feels extremely loyal to her alma mater, and she also believes in her company. Although many of the company's products—especially its leading brands—are high in salt, fat or sugar, the CEO and her team of nutritionists are working to reduce these components. She believes her company is as committed to this goal as any other fast food company, perhaps more so. Although she remains unconvinced that sodium is as much of a health problem in the American diet as some of the mainstream media outlets suggest, she would like to explore ways of reducing sodium while formulating other additives to preserve taste. The "holy grail," the CEO says, is "the stevia of salt": something that will give food a salty flavor without the sodium. The company has some of the equipment, but not the in-house personnel, to pursue this groundbreaking research. The university has faculty and postdoctoral researchers who could do the research, but it lacks the necessary equipment and financial resources. The CEO proposes that the company and the university establish a partnership—the "SoLo Tasty" Research Initiative—to address this problem. The CEO makes a very tempting offer. She is willing to commit $5 million dollars per year for the next three years, with the possibility of renewal. She would like to explore this with you.
　　What do you do?

FIGURE I.2 Case Study: The Department of Tempting Offers

I.5 ON TERMINOLOGY
1.5.1 *Public Institutions and Private Institutions*

The language of public and private is deeply embedded in Anglo-American law and society.[13] The word "public" appears in the names of five of the titles of the US Code: public buildings, property and works; public contracts; public health and welfare; public lands; and public printing and documents.[14] But the public and the private are increasingly conflated, especially due to the rise of hybrid institutions.[15] These hybrids are often created by collaborations between entities that are clearly public or private in the traditional sense. In such cases, their very creation falls within the scope of my critique here. But, no matter how hybrid institutions are created, their existence does not undermine the importance of the public-private distinction—just as, for example, the existence of the duck-boat and other amphibious vehicles does not nullify the distinction between vehicles and vessels. (Driving a bus and piloting a boat remain distinct skill sets, and safety requires that the operator of a duck-boat should be trained and licensed to do both.) In any event, the institutions on whose responsibilities I focus here—public health agencies—are indisputably public. And the entities that imperil the integrity of and trust in these public institutions are primarily corporations and industry groups.

　　The term *public partner* is not uniformly defined in the literature on public-private partnerships. I focus here on government agencies and intergovernmental

(a) Dyad

(b) Hub and Spoke

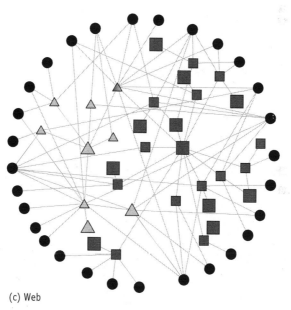

(c) Web

FIGURE 1.3 Three Views of Industry Relations

organizations. Although my discussion draws heavily on examples of partnerships involving the federal government in the United States, these arrangements are increasingly common at all levels of government and occur in many other countries too.[16] Consistent with common practice, I use *private partner* primarily to refer to corporations—often, multinational food and beverage companies—and trade associations (or industry groups) such as the US Chamber of Commerce, the Grocery Manufacturers of America, and the Corn Refiners Association. I use the term "industry" to encompass companies and trade associations more broadly, and "industry actor" to refer to any member of this group.

The terms civil society organization (CSO) and "nongovernmental organization" (NGO) are commonly used to describe a wide range of organizations from health professional associations and community groups to organizations deliber-ately created to promote industry interests. Whether these organizations are better understood as, or akin to, public or private entities will depend on their mission and purpose, and on their relations with industry. The closer these relations are, the more likely that the groups will be promoting the commercial interests of industry rather than the public good. Some analyses focus on how much of a group's funding comes from industry. They often draw a line between organizations that get more than half their funding from industry and those that do not. But this may be too simplistic: even absent financial dependence, close relations with industry may still be highly influential. Others employ the term "public interest NGOs" (PINGOs) and distinguish them from "business interest NGOs" (BINGOs) that primarily rep-resent the interests of industry actors.

Sometimes I discuss specific government agencies, industry actors, and academic institutions. At other times I use government, industry, and the academy as a form of shorthand. In the latter case, I do *not* mean to suggest that governments, industry, and the academy are monolithic in the sense that each is an undifferentiated whole. I acknowledge that these are categories with a broad range of actors in each category. At the same time, some multinational companies have arguably become monoliths (in one sense of the word). As figure 1.4 demonstrates, just ten multinationals control almost every major food brand sold anywhere in the world.[17] Some multinationals are primarily known as "soda companies" (a term I employ here) because of the leading brands with which the company is primarily associated. The word "soda" commonly refers to carbonated, sugar-sweetened drinks.[18] But soda companies usu-ally sell a variety of other sugar-sweetened beverages (SSBs), including so-called en-ergy drinks, sports drinks, juice drinks, and vitamin waters (usually sweetened with high-fructose corn syrup in the United States). They also sell other soft drinks, ar-tificially sweetened or unsweetened, in addition to soda and noncarbonated SSBs. And they often own brands across a variety of categories, for example, snack foods and processed foods, as well as soft drinks.

Multinationals usually market both "healthy" and "unhealthy" foods. As we shall see, there is some evidence that they acquire "healthy" brands to deflect or mini-mize critiques of their "unhealthy" brands.[19] Although the term "unhealthy foods" is not ideal, it serves as a useful shorthand. To be clear, I am not arguing that it is "unhealthy" for an individual to consume the occasional can of soda or snack food. When I speak of unhealthy foods, I am referring to classes of foods and beverages that public health experts believe are contributing to a serious public health chal-lenge: obesity, diabetes, and other diet-related NCDs. These are usually processed, energy-dense products with low-nutrient content. When I use the terms "healthy" or "healthier" foods, I am generally referring to items that do not fall within the

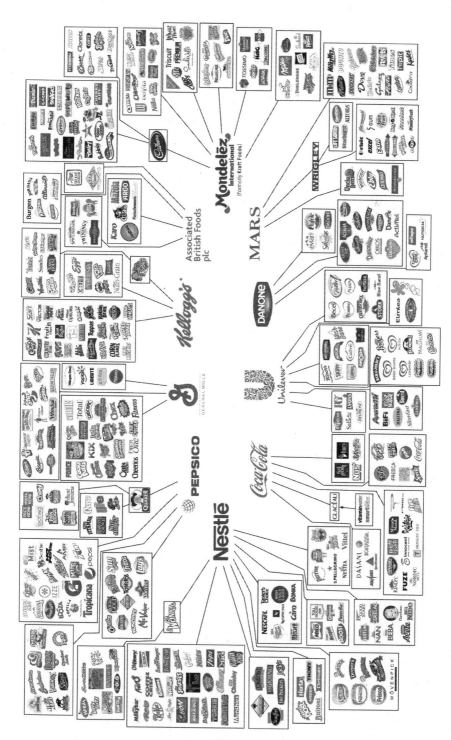

FIGURE 1.4 Behind the Brands

category of "unhealthy" foods. However, I am not endorsing any company's claims about the potential health benefits of its products or ingredients. As I have shown elsewhere, such claims are often spurious or unsupported by evidence.[20] (In chapter 5, I also highlight evidence of adverse effects on consumption patterns when fast food chains position themselves or their "menu items" as "healthy.")

1.5.2 Public-Private Partnerships

There is no universal definition of *public–private partnership* (PPP). The World Health Organization (WHO) has defined the term to encompass "a wide variety of ventures involving a diversity of arrangements, varying with regard to participants, legal status, governance, management, policy-setting prerogatives, contributions and operational roles."[21] These "ventures" may include research collaborations and public health interventions, both of which may employ a product that has been or is being developed by a private "partner."[22] There are a variety of taxonomies of PPPs. The UN Standing Committee on Nutrition (SCN), a body created to harmonize food and nutrition policy, has classified partnerships based on four categories of engagement: (1) direct funding, (2) contributions in kind (whether goods or services), (3) dialogue (including information exchange), and (4) joint delivery.[23] Notably, the SCN's 2006 policy took financial and in-kind contributions from industry "off the table." The policy, apparently no longer in effect (according to a recent communication from the SCN),[24] stated that "to protect against institutional conflict of interest, the Steering Committee will ensure that the SCN does not accept financial or in-kind contributions from food-related PSOs [private sector organizations] for any of its activities."[25] Partnerships can, of course, raise serious ethical concerns even when money does not change hands. For example, they may confer unwarranted "health halos" on companies' products.

Other classification systems focus on the relevance of the relationship to the partners' missions, rather than on the product or nature of their contributions. James Austin, an emeritus professor at Harvard Business School, has characterized "philanthropic partnerships" as single gifts that involve low levels of engagement between the parties; are "peripheral" to the mission of the parties; and are of "minor" strategic value. He contrasts a second phase or level of partnership, which he terms "transactional," involving greater mutual benefit than a philanthropic partnership. His third level is termed "integration." It has been described less transparently as "transformational" by Vivica Kraak and others who apply Austin's framework to obesity-related interventions.[26] The central feature of integrative partnerships is "mission mesh." I consider this feature highly problematic given the fundamental divergence in the obligations and functions of government bodies on the one hand and corporations on the other hand. But even one-off gifts may be ethically problematic. They may be much more central to the missions of both parties, and have greater strategic value than Austin appears to recognize. As we shall see, the soda industry has used one-off gifts with some success in its efforts to stave off soda taxes.

A number of scholars have been critical not only of the practice of PPPs but also of the language of "partnership" and the rhetoric used to justify these partnerships.[27] Perhaps as a response to these criticisms, we have recently seen a proliferation of arrangements with other names, most notably, "multi-stakeholder initiatives" (MSIs). These initiatives tend to involve government agencies, intergovernmental organizations, industry actors, academic institutions, and CSOs. These collaborations, often justified on the grounds of "inclusiveness," may not be very different from "partnerships," and raise similar ethical concerns. We should not assume that the presence of nonindustry participants will counteract industry influence, particularly when corporations bring considerable resources to the initiative. Moreover, the need for agreement among all "stakeholders" will inevitably take off the table measures that have the potential to promote public health if those actions are perceived by industry participants as inimical to their commercial interests. We should keep in mind that the term stakeholder was originally used to highlight the impact on the public interest of corporate practices, the private sphere. But MSIs now threaten to "smuggle" private or commercial interests into the public sphere.

A final note on language: as you will have observed from the discussion thus far, I often use the first-person plural. Sometimes I do so because I hope that "we," the author and reader, are engaged in a shared enterprise to recognize and address the systemic ethical issues identified in this book. At other times, I employ "we" when I discuss social practices involving communities of which the author, reader, or both may be a member. The context should make clear which usage is intended.

1.6 THE CONTRIBUTIONS AND LAYOUT OF THIS BOOK

Industry actors engage in various kinds of interactions with other institutions as part of broader strategies of influence designed to protect and promote their commercial interests. These interactions include lobbying, campaign finance, and revolving doors through which employees move back and forth between government and industry. I do not address those issues here since they have received considerable media and scholarly attention. Instead, I focus on public-private partnerships, which have received far less critical scrutiny. Many commentators assume partnerships are inherently beneficial. The question for them is not whether to partner, but how. Government agencies and intergovernmental organizations have also been proactive in developing partnership strategies. But they have neglected and need to develop, now more than ever, comprehensive strategies to insulate themselves from all forms of industry influence—including partnerships and MSIs. These defensive strategies are essential if public health agencies are to protect their independence, integrity, and credibility—and, of course, public health. This book makes the case for strategies to counter industry influence and provides a framework to inform their development.

The book also seeks to enrich our understanding of the systemic ethical, policy, and legal implications of industry interactions. In chapter 2, I develop a working definition of institutional integrity that policymakers can readily apply to their own agencies. Institutional integrity requires consistency among what an institution does, what it says it does, and what it is obligated to do. This provides a foundation from which policymakers can assess whether a proposed interaction might threaten their institution's integrity.

In chapter 3, I argue that the drive to achieve common ground with industry in public health, especially obesity policy, can undermine rather than promote the common good. The pursuit of common ground with industry necessarily puts off the table certain measures that would promote public health. Executives will not agree to measures that appear to undermine the commercial interests of their company. In other cases, industry could not agree to certain measures even if they wanted to do so. Although governments can impose taxes on products that exacerbate obesity or other public health problems, corporations cannot collectively agree to raise the prices of these products without violating antitrust or competition laws. Public officials should not conflate *common ground* and the *common good*. Officials should also keep in mind that corporations may contribute to the common good, but they cannot be *guardians* of the common good. That is the solemn responsibility of governments and intergovernmental organizations.

In chapter 4, I develop a critique of reciprocity. This chapter draws on the ethnography and behavioral science of gifts. It then goes beyond that literature to address the ethics of reciprocity. I argue that reciprocity is not inherently good. If reciprocation by a public health agency undermines the well-being of third parties (in particular, vulnerable communities that the agency has an obligation to protect), it is ethically problematic.

In chapter 5, I describe the "webs of influence" woven by industry actors involving government agencies, intergovernmental organizations, academic institutions, and civil society groups. I also articulate the systemic effects of these webs of relationships—including framing effects and agenda distortion. I build on this work in chapter 6 by providing both individual snapshots and systemic perspectives to show the ways in which partnerships and other collaborations with food and beverage industry actors create reciprocity and influence. I highlight ethically problematic features of a variety of high-profile PPPs. But more importantly, I argue that, even absent such conspicuous features, partnerships have cumulative and synergistic effects that are also ethically problematic.

In chapter 7, I argue that the law has long recognized the perils of reciprocity between different branches of government (public-public reciprocity) and of reciprocity in industry (private-private reciprocity). But it has yet to appreciate and fully address the perils of reciprocity between public and private bodies. The doctrine of separation of powers speaks not only to the need for the distribution of government functions among different branches. It also speaks to the need for arm's length relationships between those branches—especially, between the judiciary on the one hand and the executive and legislative branches on the other hand. Courts cannot perform their core functions—determining the constitutionality of laws, and holding the other branches of government accountable—if they collaborate with those branches in making or executing laws. We prohibit such collaborations in order to protect the public good. The law similarly prohibits certain forms of anticompetitive collaboration among private sector bodies. Corporations cannot agree to fix prices or divide markets without violating antitrust laws. These legal norms are designed to protect the relevant publics who might be harmed by increased prices resulting from the elimination of competition in the marketplace.

What we lack, however, is a rich body of norms to protect the public from harms caused or exacerbated by collaborations between the public and the private sector. There are pockets of laws, rules, and codes that address some of the hazards—for example, judicial ethics codes, public procurement laws, and (most relevant for our purposes) conflicts of interest policies. But they are far from comprehensive. Conflicts of interest policies are an important tool for addressing industry influence. But they are not, and should not be considered, the only tool. I unpack the principles that inform conflicts of interest policies and argue that these principles can provide the foundations for a more comprehensive set of norms governing public-private interactions. I believe the book makes a compelling case for arm's length relationships between government agencies and industry as the default. Although I provide some guidance in chapter 8 for public institutions currently contemplating or reassessing partnerships, we should not lose sight of the more ambitious challenge: the development of comprehensive strategies to counter industry influence and of alternatives to the PPP paradigm.

2

Institutional Ethics and Integrity

WHEN WE TALK about ethics, we commonly speak of individuals: what John should have done, what Jane ought to do. But ethics offers perspectives and tools that can help us think more clearly about institutions, as well as the individuals within them. Lawrence Lessig, former director of the ethics center at Harvard, argues we "help ethics grow up" when we shift the focus of our ethical attention toward institutions.[1] Although the field has been around too long to be considered an adolescent, Lessig is right that many ethics scholars have neglected institutional perspectives. One notable exception is Dennis Thompson, Lessig's former mentor and predecessor at Harvard. Thompson encourages us to "look for reforms that change structures and incentives rather than increase punishments and denunciations of individuals."[2] In this book, I place a similar emphasis on institutions and structural incentives. But an emphasis on institutional ethics and reforms need not preclude a discussion of the responsibilities and accountability of individuals. On the contrary, exploring institutional ethics can help us address the responsibilities of individuals who are in a position to change institutions.[3]

The obligations of corporations and their employees have received much attention in the business ethics literature. I focus here on other institutions with which corporations interact—in particular, government bodies and intergovernmental organizations. This requires us to address some basic questions: What is an institution? And how should we think about the ethical obligations of institutions? In order to address the second question, we need to explore a third: What are institutions for? Once we can say what an institution (such as the United Nations or a government agency) is for, we can better understand the ethical implications of its interactions with corporations and industry groups. Our inquiry will also explore what it means for an institution to possess integrity.

2.1 WHAT IS AN INSTITUTION?

There is a rich literature in sociology,[4] and in political science,[5] addressing the definition of an "institution" and exploring various taxonomies. This literature often defines institutions to include rules, policies, or norms. But I use the term here in a sense closer to the common understanding: an "establishment, organization, or association, instituted for the promotion of some object."[6] As we shall see, this object or objective—what an institution "is for"—is a key factor in determining the ethical obligations of an institution, as well as the individuals who are members of or operate within the institution.

Rather than attempt to hone a definition of "institution," I will provide examples of the kinds of institutions I am concerned with here. They include government agencies and intergovernmental bodies whose mission, purpose, or function is related to the promotion of public health.[7] The Centers for Disease Control and Prevention (CDC) in the United States and the World Health Organization (WHO), a UN specialized agency, are obvious examples of these kinds of entities. Although I focus on government and intergovernmental bodies, I also consider academic institutions and civil society organizations, such as health professional associations and health-related nongovernmental organizations (NGOs). I do so because industry actors often seek to influence policymaking by funding—and shaping—research on which policymakers rely. In addition, the private sector gives money to professional associations and other civil society organizations to influence these groups and the representations they make in policy forums.

We should keep in mind that smaller institutions are often nested within larger ones. For example, in the United States, the Center for Nutrition Policy and Promotion is housed within the Department of Agriculture, and the Center for Food Safety and Nutrition is part of the Food and Drug Administration. As we shall discover, there may be tensions between what the "parent" and some of its "subsidiary" institutions are for, and conflicts may be exacerbated when a parent or subsidiary develops close relations with industry actors.

2.2 WHAT ARE INSTITUTIONS FOR? A TAXONOMY OF ENDS

How do we determine what institutions are for? Do we look to their founding documents, to their mission statements, or somewhere else? Should we look at what they do, or what society needs them to do? And who gets to determine what institutions are for—people in the institution, people outside the institution who may be affected by what the institution does (or fails to do), or a combination of "insiders" and "outsiders"?

Aristotle argued that the *telos* (or end) of medicine is health; the end of military science, victory; and the end of architecture, a building.[8] Some scholars argue that "purpose" is the institutional analogue of *telos*.[9] Others contend that "function" is a better analogue for institutions.[10] But more important than the words we use to describe the ends of institutions is how we go about defining and determining those ends. We can answer the question what is an institution for, in different ways. And the answers are not mutually exclusive. Some responses are easier to discern than others. Some are more stable than others. But they are all part of what we might call *institutional diagnostics*. When we talk about what institutions are for, we tend to use the words "mission," "purpose," and "function" interchangeably. I offer a distinct meaning for each term to provide some diagnostic clarity. These are summarized in Figure 2.1 and explained in sections 2.2.1 to 2.2.3. For aesthetic reasons, I prefer to use "mission," "purpose," and "function" in the singular. But I recognize there may be multiple dimensions to (or components within) each category and that there may be conflicts or tensions among these components.

2.2.1 Institutional Function: What Society Needs the Institution to Do

We rely on institutions to perform important social functions. Courts of law are a good example. We need courts to perform several distinct but related functions. They adjudicate disputes between private parties, determining, for example, whether Jon Smith & Co. has broken its contract with Jane Doe, or whether Sarah Brown has negligently injured Jamie Jones, and, in either case, what the appropriate remedy should be. The courts administer criminal justice, finding the guilt or innocence of those accused of crimes and determining appropriate sentences. They often rule on whether the other branches of government have exceeded their powers or acted inappropriately. Courts must interpret the laws (constitutional provisions, statutes,

Function	What does society need the institution to do?
Purpose	(a) What are the obligations of the institution, as articulated in the institution's constitutive (or founding) documents? (b) Has the institution acquired other obligations?
Mission	What does the institution say it does?
Practices	What does the institution actually do?

FIGURE 2.1 Institutional Diagnostics

and regulations) in order to dispose of cases before them. How this works varies from one legal system to another.

In some jurisdictions, courts have the power to strike down statutes on the grounds they are unconstitutional; in other countries, they do not. In some jurisdictions (most notably, those with a common law tradition), earlier decisions bind the same court or lower courts when they face a similar decision; in other countries, they do not. In some jurisdictions, judges wholly determine disputes between private parties in civil actions (such as a claim for breach of contract); in other countries, juries make findings of fact in civil cases. In most legal systems, guilt or innocence are the only possible verdicts in a criminal trial. But you need look no further than Scotland to find a system that permits verdicts of "not proven." Some legal systems are adversarial; others, inquisitorial.

Societies need institutions to address and resolve disputes. But they do this in different ways. We may not be able to say that one particular country or community needs an institution of a particular kind to resolve their disputes. But we can usually point to a particular institution that has evolved or been created to resolve disputes peaceably, and we might convincingly say (having considered coexisting institutions) that the relevant society *needs* that institution to perform that particular function.

Although we have long realized the importance of mechanisms for the resolution of disputes, it has taken longer for us to recognize other societal needs—such as a coordinating body for global health. Since the creation of WHO in 1946,[11] this need has grown, especially in the face of pandemic diseases that do not recognize national boundaries and are exacerbated by international travel. Changes in environment and food systems involve transnational actors and have transnational effects on health. When we try to address the causes and health impacts of climate change and obesity, a global coordinating body becomes all the more necessary.

There may be genuine disagreement about the societal need a particular institution fulfills or ought to fulfill.[12] However, as I explain in the next chapter, the function of government bodies and intergovernmental organizations—what we need them to do—is tied to the notion of the public good. In addition, many institutions have an express obligation to pursue a particular purpose, and this can often be discerned with some clarity by looking at the institution's constitutive or founding documents.

2.2.2 Institutional Purpose: What the Institution Has an Obligation to Do

Most institutions have an *obligatory purpose* in the broadest sense.[13] This purpose may be specified in the constitution or other founding document, such as a federal statute. In the case of the US Supreme Court, the relevant document is the US

Constitution. Article III of the Constitution established the Supreme Court and vested the judicial power of the United States in that Court and "in such inferior courts as the Congress may from time to time ordain and establish." Article III, Section 2 specifies in some detail what the Supreme Court is for. But, of course, it does not fully articulate the answer to this question. Figuring out the details can often be a complex process. One of the many issues left open by Article III of the US Constitution was whether the Supreme Court had the power to declare an act of Congress void on the grounds that it was unconstitutional. Early in its life, the Supreme Court answered this question in the affirmative in *Marbury v. Madison* (1803),[14] one of the first of many "tussles" between the Court and the other branches of government regarding the proper function of each. In addition, the Court is frequently called upon to adjudicate questions regarding what other government bodies are for.[15] In common law jurisdictions, judicial review is the legal process ordinarily employed to determine the scope of a government agency's authority.[16]

Turning from these domestic examples to international health, the WHO's Constitution provides that the objective of the organization is "the attainment by all peoples of the highest possible level of health."[17] The Constitution spells out in some detail the ways in which it should achieve this objective—for example, coordinating international health work; assisting governments to strengthen health services; and promoting cooperation between scientific and professional groups that contribute to the advancement of health. However, the WHO's Constitution also provides that the organization should "take all necessary action to attain the objective of the organization."[18] The founding document thereby leaves some discretion to the director-general and the governing bodies of the organization, the World Health Assembly, and the Executive Board about how to fulfill the institution's mandate.

In the case of a disagreement regarding the interpretation or application of the WHO's Constitution—including questions about the purpose of the WHO—the Constitution provides that the International Court of Justice may resolve the dispute.[19] The Constitution also provides a mechanism for its own amendment,[20] and this procedure could be invoked to amend the provisions articulating the WHO's purpose.

As these domestic and international examples make clear, an institution's founding document may set the parameters of the institution's purpose, and provide mechanisms for the resolution of disagreements about purpose and for adjusting the purpose.

In addition to its *constitutive purpose*, an institution might acquire obligations to pursue certain ends. For example, it might commit to a particular purpose in exchange for some form of privilege that it would not otherwise possess. If a nonprofit institution in the United States wishes to receive tax-exempt status, for example, it must commit to pursuing—and in fact pursue—one of the exempt purposes specified in section 501(3)(c) of the IRS Revenue Code.[21] The designated purposes include charitable, religious, educational, scientific, and literary purposes. Charitable purposes, in turn, include the relief of the poor, the advancement of education and science, and defending civil rights.

An institution might also find itself under an obligation to pursue a particular purpose because its statements have given rise to a legitimate expectation on the part of others that it will, in fact, pursue that purpose. Courts can and do uphold legal complaints against public bodies based on legitimate expectations. This can occur when a government agency makes an express promise or other statement on which the complainant reasonably relies to his detriment.[22] But the ethical significance of institutional statements is not confined to reliance on those statements.

2.2.3 *Institutional Mission: What an Institution Says It Does*

Institutions (or their staff) often make express statements about what the institution does or will do. These statements may take the form of a communication to others within and/or outside the institution. One may find these kinds of statements in a variety of places. Today, they are most commonly posted as a "mission statement" on an institution's website. But they may be found elsewhere too, imprinted in brass or chiseled in marble at the main entrance to the institution's head office. Such statements are ethically significant.[23] Employees may join an institution relying on what it says about itself. Third parties may also develop other kinds of relationships with the institution while relying on these statements. But what an institution says about itself has ethical significance even when we cannot show that someone relied on its statements to their detriment. If an institution says it does X but, in fact, it does Y, and Y undermines or is inconsistent with X, the institution's integrity will be in peril.[24] The institution may also lose integrity if its internal and external communications directly conflict with each other.

* * *

There is no reason why we must be interested in only the mission, the purpose, or the function of an institution. We can and should consider all three: (1) What is the mission of an institution? Simply put, what does the institution say it does? (2) What is the purpose of an institution? To what extent have the ends of the institution been specified by a founding document, governing body, or some other means over which the institution does not have complete control. Has the institution also committed itself to a particular purpose? (3) What is the function of the institution? That is to say, what does society need it to do, whether or not this function is also addressed by (or included in) the institution's mission statement or its constitutive document. For anyone concerned about the systemic ethics of institutions, all three kinds of ends are ethically significant.

If an institution says one thing but does another, those who reasonably rely on its statement may be wronged. If an institution does not do what it is required to do by its founding documents, it may find itself in violation of legal and ethical norms. And if an institution does not do what the relevant society or community needs it to do, a profound social need may be left unmet. Moreover, inconsistency or tension either (a) among these categories of ends or (b) within any category is cause for concern. If the mission and purpose of an institution are aligned with each other but not with the function (what society needs the institution to do), we will need deliberative processes to reconsider the institution's mission and purpose and/or to explore the creation of a new institution to fulfill the function currently not being met adequately or at all.[25]

A simpler problem arises from any tension between the practices of an institution and its mission or purpose. Although perfect alignment of the mission, purpose, and practices of an institution may not occur as often as we might like, any fundamental inconsistency among them is likely to undermine the integrity of an institution. I explore these kinds of concerns further in the remainder of this chapter. In short, I argue that institutions should look for and take steps to address any inconsistencies, divergences, or tensions in what they do (practices), what they say they do (mission), and what they are obligated to do (purpose). I also argue that partnerships and close relations with other institutions whose mission, purpose, or practices are at odds with one's own are ethically problematic. But before doing so, I will say more about integrity and what it means for institutions.

2.3 INTEGRITY: A SHORT HISTORY

We have been speaking about "integrity" for more than half a millennium. You will find the word in the writings of Sir Thomas More and, among others, a seventeenth-century treatise on Christian ethics by the English poet and theologian Thomas Traherne.[26] For centuries, the word has commonly been used to denote an attribute possessed by individuals. Political candidates are often described as having or lacking integrity, depending on who is paying for the advertisement! But the term can be also employed in relation to institutions. Although corporations are institutions, I do not address corporate integrity here. My principal concern is the impact of corporations on the integrity of *other* kinds of institutions—especially government bodies and intergovernmental organizations. Even if a corporation arguably possesses integrity, it may still undermine the integrity of the public institutions with which it interacts.

Scholars often invoke integrity to express concerns about the impact of industry on the academy. For example, in his seminal article on the systemic effects of industry-related conflicts of interest in biomedical research, Canadian philosopher Arthur Schafer uses the term "integrity" on more than thirty occasions. In addition to invoking popular concepts such as professional integrity, scientific integrity, and research integrity, Schafer also employs the term "university integrity," and—most notably for our purposes—"institutional integrity." Alas, Schafer does not define this term in his article.[27]

Professional associations have employed similar terminology when discussing the ethical implications of their members' interactions with industry.[28] In the spring of 2014, the American Association of University Professors (AAUP) published a report on university-academy relations.[29] In addition to discussing six other variants of integrity (academic, scientific, research, personal, professional, and scholarly integrity), the report expresses concern about "[i]nstitutional integrity and the appearance of integrity."[30] The AAUP also warns that "[t]he credibility and integrity of our nation's universities are now at stake."[31] Although the report does not define institutional integrity, the context indicates that the term is being used more broadly than in international contexts, where it is commonly used to denote an absence of corruption, narrowly defined as bribery, graft, or other illegal practices.[32] Building on my earlier work,[33] I address the definitional lacuna here by developing a working definition of institutional integrity that can enrich our understanding of the integrity of government and intergovernmental agencies.

2.4 INDIVIDUAL INTEGRITY: A QUICK REVIEW

As a number of scholars have noted, the word integrity has the same Latin root as "integer."[34] In mathematics, the latter term is used to denote all positive and negative whole numbers. So -12, 3, and 97 are all integers. The number 3.1415926536 (π expressed to ten decimal places), on the other hand, is not an integer. It is a fraction, a term derived from the Latin *frangere,* to break. Integrity, Stephen Carter observes, "has much the same sense [as integer], the sense of *wholeness*: a person of integrity, like a whole number, is a whole person, a person somehow undivided."[35] At some level, the idea of being "undivided" may seem to fly in the face of human experience.[36] This was the view of two great French writers living, respectively, in the sixteenth and seventeenth centuries. Montaigne observed that "a man's deeds . . . commonly contradict one another in so odd a fashion that it seems impossible that they should all come out of the same shop."[37] This observation led him to conclude: "given the natural inconstancy of our behavior and opinions . . . even sound authors are wrong in stubbornly trying to weave us into one invariable and solid fabric."[38] In a flourish of frustration and admiration, Blaise Pascal wrote: "What a chimera then is man! What a novelty! What a monster, what a chaos, what a contradiction, what a prodigy!"[39] The political scientist Andrew Stark has argued more recently that integrity in the sense of "wholeness" presents a problem for individuals "whose lives display any kind of self-critical revision, changes in course, or discontinuities over historical time, or for those who compartmentalize, differentiate, and assume conflicting roles across social space; in other words, for all of us."[40] Some scholars offer guidance about how individuals can address those challenges.[41]

Before taking up the analogous challenge for institutions, I distinguish two kinds of integrity problems: consistency at any moment and constancy across time. If I sit down to eat a filet mignon while requiring my child to eat a vegan meal then, absent a persuasive justification, I have a problem with consistency. If I declare myself a vegetarian one day, a pescetarian the next, and an omnivore the following day, I may have a problem with constancy. We see an emphasis on consistency in the work of a number of contemporary scholars.[42] For Deborah Rhode, the notion is important in two different ways.[43] First, she argues that "[a]t a minimum, persons of integrity are individuals whose practices are *consistent* with their principles, even in the face of strong countervailing pressures" (emphasis added).[44] Second, she contends that one's values themselves should "satisfy certain minimum standards of consistency." (Rhode's definition of integrity also has substantive requirements. These include, for example, respect for others.)[45]

Rhode also addresses the challenge of constancy, particularly in the wake of situational influences on behavior.[46] She observes, "When faced with a misalignment of ethical principles, peer pressures, and workplace incentives, many individuals unconsciously readjust their principles or develop strategies of moral disengagement that enable them to rationalize misconduct."[47] Similarly, philosopher David Luban contends that it can be hard to distinguish integrity from its "evil twin," rationalizing one's actions.[48] Institutions arguably do something analogous when they change their mission statement in an effort to legitimate ethically problematic practices that undermine the institution's purpose.

2.5 INSTITUTIONAL INTEGRITY

We can build on the literature exploring individual integrity to develop a framework for assessing institutional integrity.[49] In the case of individuals, if our actions are inconsistent with our commitments, statements, values, or beliefs, our integrity will be called into question. Similarly, *if an institution's practices are inconsistent with what it says it does (its mission) or what it is obligated to do (its purpose), the institution may be said to lack integrity.* As with individuals, institutional integrity involves both consistency at any moment in time and constancy over time.[50] Of course, institutions can and do change over time, and these changes may be legitimate. But changing a mission statement to address a dissonance between an institution's mission and its practices may, in certain cases, be analogous to an individual changing his beliefs so that he can carry on doing what he was doing before, even though the latter may be ethically problematic. For example, to attract industry funding, an academic research institution may state that its mission is to conduct research that will promote the interests of industry. We should be concerned about an academic institution ceasing to conduct research that might advance our knowledge simply because that knowledge could undermine the commercial interests of industry actors. We should be all the more troubled when other institutions are also failing to conduct such research for similar reasons. But the problem will be most acute when there is only one institution that can or should do the work of this particular body. This is why maintaining the integrity of the WHO is particularly crucial.

2.5.1 *Internally Conflicting Mission or Purpose*

An institution with an internally conflicting mission or purpose will soon face ethical challenges.[51] One part of the US Department of Agriculture's (USDA) mission is to promote the consumption of American agricultural products; another is to promote nutrition guidance.[52] It is not hard to see how these might conflict. And, in fact, they have conflicted—as evidenced by the Department's endorsement of efforts to increase the amount of cheese in pizza, tacos, and other fast food chain "menu items."[53] When the *New York Times* revealed the role of the USDA in the promotion of cheese, the story ran with the headline, "While Warning About Fat, U.S. Pushes Cheese Sales."[54] The article demonstrates how an internally conflicting mission can jeopardize trust in, as well the integrity of, an institution.

Internally conflicting missions should be avoided, and where conflicts exist, they should be addressed. How to address conflicts depends on the circumstances. If only one part of the conflicting mission is also part of the institution's purpose (as defined in its founding document), the simplest response may be to jettison the other part of the mission or cede it to another entity.[55] Sometimes an institution's purpose will also have two conflicting components. In that case, it may be necessary to amend the institution's founding document. To determine what kind of amendment is required, we would need to examine the function of the institution—that is, to explore what society needs the institution to do. In the case of the USDA, this might result in transferring all nutrition promotion responsibilities to the Department of Health and Human Services or possibly creating an additional government agency to take over the task.

2.5.2 Practices Inconsistent with an Institution's Mission or Purpose

When one's actions are inconsistent with one's statements, this may be what Stephen Carter calls "the easiest example of unintegrity to spot."[56] Similarly, a mismatch between the mission of an institution and its practices starkly reveals a problem with its integrity. If the practices of an institution predictably undermine the mission—the goals that the institution invokes to justify its existence—then we can say that such an institution lacks integrity.[57] Not all cases will be this clear. But nor need they be so clear for institutional integrity to be in peril. There is a spectrum: at one end, an institution all of whose practices promote the mission; at the other end, an institution all of whose practices undermine its mission; and, in between, an institution some of whose practices promote its mission and some of whose practices neither promote nor undermine its mission.[58] It may well be more common to find examples of this "in between" case than of institutions at either end of the spectrum. Public officials and other institutional leaders should also conduct another comparison to diagnose integrity problems within their institution—one that is analogous to comparing an individual's commitments and actions. If an institution's practices are not in line with its purpose (what it is obligated to do)—a fortiori, if its practices undermine its purpose—that institution will lack integrity.

2.5.3 Institutions in Transition

Institutions are, of course, not static. Nor are the societies in which they exist. The important question is: How does the institution respond to changes in its environment? If the practices remain static, the institution may no longer fulfill its mission, purpose, or function. An institution may change its mission in response to external forces. This will be problematic if the new mission is inconsistent with the institution's purpose or the institution no longer performs its function (what society needs the institution to do).

In order to address the ethical implications of institutions in transition, it may be helpful to draw on recent taxonomies of institutional change.[59] Political scientists employ the word *drift* to describe the failure of institutions to adapt to a changing environment. As a result, there may be "slippage" in the practices of the institution. *Layering* describes the ways in which institutions take on new functions in addition to existing ones—a process that may gradually alter the institution's status and structure. *Conversion* refers to the process by which an old institution becomes redeployed for new purposes. In addition to these three processes (which political scientists describe as forms of adaptation),[60] there are two forms of change said to mark the decline of an institution. *Exhaustion* or *erosion* occurs when an institution gradually breaks down or undermines its "external preconditions." *Displacement* results from the emergence of a second institution that challenges the dominance of the first and may ultimately replace it.

One form of changing environment is a decline in public funds. When an institution revises its mission or practices in response to such a change, it will be important to explore whether the revised mission and new practices are consistent with the purpose and function of the institution. If an institution changes its mission and the revised mission is inconsistent with its purpose (what it is obliged to do), the institution is likely to find itself in violation of legal norms. If the change in mission renders a public institution unable to fulfill its function, there may be a profound societal need that is no longer being met. Imagine an institution that has a mission "to promote research that enhances our understanding of the relationship between food and health." Someone points out that the institution is only funding research designed to demonstrate the health *benefits* of consuming X, Y, and Z—arguably, a conversion. The institution responds by changing its mission: "To promote research that enhances our understanding of the health benefits of consuming certain foods." This change may create a legal problem if it violates the institution's founding document and associated obligations. But even if the new mission is consistent with the institution's purpose, the change may create or exacerbate an unmet social need. There may be a dearth of institutions exploring the potential *adverse effects* of consuming X, Y, or Z in order to obtain the purported benefits. This example is not hypothetical.[61] Some nutrition journals are committed to reporting studies on the purported health benefits of foods and ingredients.[62] But there are no comparable resources devoted to adverse effects.

There are many examples of partial *displacement*—for example, contract research organizations (CROs) and commercial institutional review boards (IRBs) taking over the conduct and approval, respectively, of clinical drug trials from universities and academic medical centers in the United States.[63] But one phenomenon arguably more insidious than actual displacement is the *threat* of displacement. The prospect of displacement can lead institutions to change their practices to preserve their dominance or status. For example, in the face of potential threats to their research portfolios from CROs, academic medical centers may create more industry-favorable research environments to attract additional support from corporate sponsors.[64] Similar threats confront underfunded public health agencies, including the WHO, whose financial resources are dwarfed by the multibillion-dollar endowments of philanthropic foundations.

A core function of the WHO is the coordination of global health. But the WHO's program budget is smaller than each of the following: the budget of CDC in the United States (despite the latter's much more limited geographic scope);[65] the combined advertising budgets of the two leading multinational soda companies;[66] and the combined annual grants awarded by just a handful of foundations, with the Bill and Melinda Gates Foundation at the top of the list.[67] The threat of the WHO's displacement by philanthropic foundations (as the coordinating body for global health)—and the fear that the WHO will be seen as irrelevant—is fueling the WHO's partnerships with industry actors, as well as collaborations with these foundations.[68]

2.6 INTEGRATION AND DISINTEGRATION IN PUBLIC-PRIVATE PARTNERSHIPS

The words integration and disintegration are, of course, related to integrity. Integration is the bringing together of disparate parts to make them whole. Disintegration is the opposite—the fragmentation of the whole. This is important not simply as a matter of etymology. In his work on public-private partnerships, James Austin identifies "integrative" partnerships as the third and most advanced phase of interaction between public and private actors.[69] This relationship involves what Austin characterizes as "mission mesh" between the public and private partners.[70] But "meshing" can be ethically problematic, especially when the public institution has a mission to promote public health, and the corporate partner's leading brands undermine public health. Austin acknowledges that achieving integration will involve distorting the mission of at least one of the parties to mesh more fully with the other. Public officials may hope that partnerships will put them in a position to influence the mission of the private actor. They may believe that if they partner with a multinational food company, they can encourage the company to market products that are less energy-dense and more nutritious. But there is a dearth of evidence to support that optimistic view.[71] Public officials are also far less inclined to recognize the ways in which interactions with industry partners may influence their own institution's policies and practices. As I explain below, the flow of funds or resources from a corporate "partner" makes it far more likely that the company will exert influence on a public health agency (or other public partner) than the other way around.[72]

"Integration" is not inherently good. On the contrary, there may be sound reasons for a public health agency to "dis-integrate" its collaborative relationship with an industry actor. (The same may also be said for universities partnering with industry.[73])

In some cases, the disintegration of the relationship may be necessary to prevent the disintegration of the public body in both senses: to preserve its integrity and to ensure its survival.

2.7 INSTITUTIONAL INTEGRITY, INSTITUTIONAL CORRUPTION, AND PUBLIC TRUST

2.7.1 The Relationship Between Integrity and Corruption

I should say a few words about the relationship between institutional integrity, as I employ the term, and the literature on trust, trustworthiness, and institutional corruption.[74] Although my concerns about industry partnerships predate the launch of the research initiative on institutional corruption at Harvard, my thoughts have greatly benefited from exchanges with Lawrence Lessig, who launched the initiative, and several other scholars. Lessig has written that institutional corruption is "manifest when there is a systemic and strategic influence which is legal, or even currently ethical, that undermines the institution's effectiveness by diverting it from its purpose or weakening its ability to achieve its purpose, including, to the extent relevant to its purpose, weakening either the public's trust in that institution or the institution's inherent trustworthiness."[75] Lessig further contends that this diversion from an institution's purpose, which he also calls "deviation," is "in a literal sense a kind of corruption."[76]

There is, of course, no consensus on the precise definition of institutional corruption, and several scholars have developed their own working definitions or approaches.[77] These disagreements are the sign of a vibrant and evolving field of inquiry, and they do not undermine the role that institutional corruption studies can and do play in helping scholars and policymakers compare issues and institutions that seem disparate but have similar characteristics. The impact of campaign contributions on health-care reform, for example, is different from the impact of pharmaceutical company interactions on biomedical research and patient care in academic medical centers. Until recently, ethics scholars working on either of these issues had rarely considered the impact of the food industry on nutrition research and obesity policy. However, there are common features—notably, potential effects on the exercise of judgment and decision-making related to both individual and public health. Identifying common features—as well as ethically significant differences—may enhance our understanding of ethical problems and help us think creatively about potential interventions and solutions.

That said, I mention a few differences in emphasis. First, Lessig stresses the external influences on an institution.[78] In my discussion of institutional integrity,

I focus on the corresponding *practices* of the institution—an approach that places greater emphasis on the agency of the institution and individuals within it. The internal practices of an institution are always, to some extent, responses to external influences. But we should not shy away from interrogating those practices directly. An institution may be able to eliminate or reduce external influences by changing its internal practices. In recent years, for example, many academic medical centers have introduced policies to prohibit or reduce interactions between physicians and sales representatives from pharmaceutical companies.[79]

While institutional corruption is an extremely helpful framework for analysis, the advantage of addressing policymakers in terms of *institutional integrity* is that the term is less likely to put them on the defensive. This will be helpful when (as is so often the case) we need the support of these individuals for institutional reform. In addition, the concept of *institutional integrity* can help keep public officials and policymakers focused on the ethical implications of their institutions' practices in a way that the language of effectiveness (in Lessig's definition of institutional corruption) may not.

There is, of course, a relationship between integrity and corruption.[80] Peter Euben argues that the word corruption implies an ideal of integrity, and corruption connotes a loss of integrity.[81] But many international organizations take a narrow view of corruption. The World Bank defines corruption as "the abuse of public office for private gain."[82] Transparency International similarly defines it as "the abuse of entrusted power for private gain."[83] In my view, definitions tying institutional corruption to private gain are too narrow. I favor a broader view of institutional corruption—one that encompasses the promotion of private interests at the expense of the public good. (This view is also more compatible with my account of institutional integrity and my claim that the function of a public institution, in particular a public health agency, is tied to the public good.)

2.7.2 *Integrity, Trustworthiness, and Trust*

Trust and trustworthiness are related but distinct.[84] The latter concept, like integrity, might be characterized as an attribute of an individual or institution. The former is an attitude toward (related to perceptions of) an individual or institution.[85] Identifying whether the former, the latter, or both are implicated by the practices of any given institution is essential. If loss of trust tracks the institution's loss of integrity or trustworthiness, it would be problematic to seek to restore trust without addressing the underlying loss of integrity or trustworthiness.[86] Put simply, when a perception is justified, it is misleading to try to change it without tackling the practices that led to it.

Integrity and trustworthiness, both attributes of an institution, are arguably siblings.[87] (Trust, an attitude rather than an attribute, is arguably cousin to both integrity and trustworthiness.) Although policymakers should find it simpler to focus on integrity, as I define it here, rather than trustworthiness, an institution that lacks integrity will almost invariably be untrustworthy. Such an institution may still *in fact* be trusted. But the lack of integrity makes it rightly vulnerable to a loss of trust. Given my emphasis on integrity and the many scholarly volumes (and series of volumes) devoted to trust,[88] I address only briefly the kinds of trust that may be imperiled by partnerships with industry.

When we speak of trust, we require some level of specificity. When you say, "I trust Frank," you are telling me much less about your attitude toward Frank than you might think. If Frank is a close friend, you might trust him to give good financial advice. But you might not trust him to give sound relationship advice. Perhaps Frank has been listed by *Fortune* magazine as one of the best financial advisers in the country, but he has been divorced three times. In such a case, your attitude toward Frank involves a *competence* trust in one context (finances). But in another context (relationships), you possess no competence trust. If you have competence trust in someone, you believe that they possess the requisite (a) knowledge and skills, and (b) capacities and resources to perform the function or task that you trust them to perform. Scholars often distinguish this kind of trust from other kinds of trust—notably, *reliability* trust.[89] If you have reliability trust, you believe that a person does (or will do) what they say they do (or will do). This kind of trust ties in neatly with a core dimension of integrity—the relationship between an institution's mission and practices. If an institution's practices undermine its mission (what it says it does), the institution jeopardizes reliability trust that others repose in it.

Although trust may be parsed in this way as a matter of theory, public officials should recognize that different kinds of trust may bleed into one another. There may be different types of bleeding—both among categories and within categories. An institution that loses competence trust (because it is an underfunded government agency) may similarly lose reliability trust. The loss of competence trust in one area (for example, food regulation) may also undermine competence trust in another area for which the institution is also responsible (for example, pharmaceutical or cosmetics regulation).

Core trust concerns for public and private sector actors partnering with each other are not exactly the same. From the private sector body's point of view, the main trust concern is usually competence trust.[90] Corporations often perceive public sector organizations as lacking competence. They are concerned that, by partnering, competence trust in their company will also be undermined. However, such concerns are arguably a reflection of a more fundamental problem. The increasing dependence of public institutions (including international organizations) on funding from and partnerships with the private sector in order to perform core functions may be exacerbating the lack of competence trust in public institutions. Partnering reinforces the view that public institutions, such as the WHO, lack the capacities and resources to perform their core functions.[91]

Public and private partners may each have concerns about the impact of their relationship on the competence trust of third parties. But the partnership is more likely to generate reliability trust issues for the public body. If a local public health agency is partnering with a fast food industry actor to address obesity, for example, this is likely to imperil reliability trust by casting doubt on whether the agency can be relied on to place public health concerns ahead of the commercial interests of its industry partners.

In many cases, lack of trust will have profound implications for the public institution. If the CDC does not garner competence trust, for example, people will not heed its calls to vaccinate their children. That, in turn, will undermine the mission of the CDC to "protect America from health, safety and security threats."[92] This is an instrumental account of the significance of trust: the institution cannot perform its core functions absent the trust and confidence of the relevant publics. Although political philosophers might ask whether trust is important per se and why,[93] for public officials the instrumental account of trust is likely to be sufficient.

2.8 CONCLUSION

It may be difficult to achieve perfect alignment between what an institution does, what it says it does, and what it is obligated to do. But recognizing the difficulty, perhaps the impossibility, of attaining absolute integrity should not prevent institutions from acculturating institutional integrity as an ideal and constantly striving to achieve it.[94] Public officials should resist throwing up their hands in the wake of fiscal constraints and saying, as a precursor to entering into a partnership with industry: "We don't have the luxury of being pure!" They may tell themselves that they can "align" the practices of corporate "partners" more closely with their own public health mission through these "engagements." But there are practical and ethical hazards in downplaying the divergences between public institutions and corporate donors in order to rationalize an industry partnership. These relations can undermine the integrity of a public institution, pulling its mission, purpose, and practices even further out of alignment than before.

Although I have emphasized consistency in my analysis of institutional integrity, I acknowledge that integrity in its fullest sense has a substantive component above and beyond consistency. In the case of public bodies, I argue that the substantive component of integrity is tied to the notion of the public good. In the discussion that follows, I argue that government agencies should possess an orientation toward—and pursue—the public good.[95] This is the function of government bodies—what society needs them to do.

3

The Common Good and Common Ground

A Senator shall strive to promote the public interest and the common good of all the people of the United States. Senatorial office is a public trust requiring that a Senator shall not subordinate the public interest to the particular interests of any individual, party, region, class, or group.
—MODEL CODE OF ETHICS FOR THE US SENATE[1]

WHEN I TOLD a colleague that I was writing a chapter on corporations and the common good, she replied, "How oxymoronic!" But the relationship between corporations and the common good is more complex than this emotive response suggests. Corporations may well contribute to the common good. They can provide employment that is economically and psychologically rewarding. They may also sell goods or services that improve the economic and social well-being of the community. However, corporations are not guardians of the common good. That is the responsibility of government agencies and intergovernmental bodies. We should not conflate the commercial interests of a corporation with the common good. And policymakers should not assume that achieving common ground with industry actors will promote the common good.

Before exploring the implications of these observations for public-private partnerships, we must examine a cluster of related concepts: the common good, the public good, and the public interest. Each term has a slightly different etymology, history, and emphasis.[2] But they all gesture toward a related set of ideas about government, society, and the relations between them. Which term is employed, what each means, and the concerns it addresses or evokes may vary depending on time and context. Although we cannot and need not reach a universally accepted definition of these terms, we should recognize what is at stake when these concepts are used—or abused.

3.1 THE COMMON GOOD

The notion of the common good has a long history in both theology and philosophy.[3] That history is too lengthy to recount here. Even scholars who devote entire books to the topic shy away from attempting a comprehensive review.[4] In political philosophy, the work of John Rawls has been particularly influential. Rawls argued, "Government is assumed to aim at the common good, that is, at maintaining the conditions and achieving objectives that are similarly to everyone's advantage."[5] He also described the common good as "certain general conditions that are in an appropriate sense equally to everyone's advantage."[6] Drawing on Rawls, Amy Gutmann and Dennis Thompson define the common good as "the goal of 'maintaining conditions and achieving objectives' that benefit all members of society."[7] Some key elements of the common good are articulated by the preamble to the US Constitution, among them, "a more perfect union," "justice," "domestic tranquility," "the common defense," and "the general welfare."[8] Arguably, the institutions established by the US Constitution are part of *and* a means for achieving the common good,[9] since they facilitate collective decision-making and the implementation of those decisions.[10] (Of course, it does not follow that every decision resulting from this process promotes the common good.[11]) Gutmann and Thompson identify a "robust" economy and universal health care as key components of the common good. They acknowledge that not all components are necessarily shared by everyone. But they argue that "the goal is to secure these goods for all, and to maintain a democratic process that is valued by all."[12]

The common good tends to provoke a variety of questions and concerns. How do we define the community (and its limits, if any) within which the principle of commonality applies?[13] The US Senate Model Code of Ethics (quoted at the beginning of the chapter) defines community as "all the people of the United States." Depending on how it is construed, this contested category may be more or less inclusive.[14] Consider current debates about undocumented workers, many of whom play a central role in the US economy. They pay taxes while being denied benefits accorded to citizens and permanent residents.[15] As Harvard psychologist Howard Gardner has observed, "it is easy to scapegoat immigrants and . . . narrow the scope of what is 'common.'"[16] Other concerns arise from apparent conflicts or tensions between the good of individuals and that of the community—however the latter is defined. What if the benefits and burdens of a policy fall primarily on different groups within a community? And how should we characterize and address potential tensions between different components of the common good?

We need not attempt to resolve these questions in the abstract here.[17] But a few brief observations might be helpful for policymakers considering partnerships with industry actors.

First, although there are disagreements about the definition and content of the common good, the term has long captured—and continues to capture—core ethical concerns in political discourse in disparate societies and cultures.[18] We may recognize a lack of consensus about what constitutes or promotes the common good, and still argue that public officials have an obligation to consider how they might best promote the common good. Many questions regarding the content of the common good—and how to address the tensions that I identified in the preceding paragraph—are the very questions that policymakers should address when formulating policy and that the members of a community or society should consider when assessing those policies.[19]

Second, we should resist the temptation to think about the common good solely in utilitarian terms.[20] We should be especially wary of the temptation to reduce everything to a simple cost-benefit analysis (utilitarianism's most popular contemporary incarnation). As we shall see, such an approach has come to dominate the way public officials approach policy development and implementation—including public health policies and partnerships. We should avoid focusing on economic value at the expense of other values.[21] Policymakers frequently address economic well-being while neglecting physical, psychological, social, and community well-being.[22]

Third, as Adam Smith recognized,[23] certain facets of the common good cannot and will not be promoted by the activities of the private sector. Sometimes, there will be insufficient economic incentives for the private sector to act.[24] (At other times, the incentives will be perverse: extremely profitable activities can simultaneously undermine the common good.) Smith argued that the "duty of the sovereign or commonwealth is that of erecting and maintaining those public institutions and those public works . . . of such a nature that the profit could never repay the expense to any individual or small number of individuals, and which it therefore cannot be expected that any individual or small number of individuals should erect or maintain."[25] The narrow incentives of the private sector have broad implications for health policy. On a recent visit to the doctor's office, I noticed a poster instructing prediabetic patients to ask their doctor whether they should start taking medication now. None of the large print mentioned any prescription drug or the name of its manufacturer. But the very small print at the bottom of the poster revealed that it had been created and provided to the physician's office by a pharmaceutical company. Better diet and increased exercise might also prevent prediabetic patients from becoming diabetic—without the potential side effects of medication. Unsurprisingly, the poster did not say this. The company's profits are boosted by prediabetic patients who take the company's medicine, not by patients who exercise. Similarly, a snack food or soda company might have an interest in promoting exercise, but not dietary changes—especially when the latter would have an adverse effect on its short-term profits. In contrast, a government agency could enhance the common good by promoting both exercise and better diets. It might do so by creating or enhancing public parks and spaces, reconfiguring agricultural subsidies to promote the production and consumption of healthy foods, and improving public transport (especially bus services between low-income residential areas and supermarkets selling fresh produce).

Fourth, the concept of "the common good" is often misused or abused. How this occurs varies across time, societies, and cultures. Hundreds of years ago, the "subjects" of a European monarch might worry that he would invoke the "common good" to deprive them of their property through the exercise of "eminent domain."[26] Recently, eminent domain has returned in another form—to support private sector enterprise and the construction of gas pipelines.[27] This example raises similar concerns to those at the heart of this book. Public officials can and do invoke the common good while primarily promoting the commercial interests of corporations. This often occurs when these officials are making the case for public-private partnerships.

3.2 WHEN WE CONFOUND THE COMMON GOOD AND COMMON GROUND

The *common good* should not be confused with *common ground*.[28] Policymakers, whether local, national, or international,[29] often assume that the common good will be promoted when they find common ground with industry. A central aim of this book is to challenge that assumption. In order to achieve common ground with industry, governments will almost invariably need to take some policies "off the table." These would include increased regulation that might promote the common good by improving health but could threaten the short-term profits of the private sector. I recognize that corporations can and do contribute to the common good. An institution may do so even when (as is ordinarily the case) that institution's mission or purpose does not require it to pursue the common good. An analogy might help illuminate this point. The law firm that represents the defendant who has been indicted for a mass shooting contributes to the common good by facilitating the administration of justice in an adversarial system. The fair trial of the accused depends upon his having access to the assistance of legal counsel. But the lawyer is not "aiming" for the common good. On the contrary, his objective is to defend his client to the best of his ability. Government agencies, on the other hand, have a duty to "aim" for the common good in the development and implementation of policy. The performance of that duty may be undermined when public bodies collaborate with corporations. Multinational corporations may contribute to the common good in the course of their business activities but they are not—and should not be mistaken for—guardians of the common good.

3.3 THE PUBLIC GOOD AND PUBLIC GOODS

The term the "public good" is often used interchangeably with the common good.[30] However, some scholars prefer to invoke "the public good." For example, sociologist Craig Calhoun distinguishes "public" and "community" as "two different modes of organizing social life."[31] In his view, "Community is present in the familiarity of dense networks of social relationships," while "[p]ublic life, by contrast, requires us to engage and care about the needs of strangers." Calhoun argues that "the public must be an institutional arena within which we not only live with but cherish difference" and that the "language of community is too often used either to evoke a spurious unity of the whole or to describe those categories within which people are 'like us.'"

For some political scientists, the use of the word "public" instead of "common" serves other helpful purposes. Jane Mansbridge acknowledges the contested nature of the public good, and the dangers of its manipulation and abuse (echoing other scholars' concerns about the common good.)[32] However, she argues strongly that we should preserve the term because it serves as "a site for contest over what is public and what is good."[33] As Mansbridge observes, the word "public" has a normative function, serving to distinguish private interests and the public good, and encouraging approbation for those who promote the latter over the former.

Although I take the view that "the public good" and "the common good" can be used interchangeably (and I use both in this book), there are reasons to favor "the public good" when discussing the ethics of public-private partnerships. In particular, the term may serve as a mild antidote to the tendency of policymakers to confound the common good with common ground—and, in particular, to assume that common ground with industry actors will promote the common good. Corporate interests are often unthinkingly folded into the "common good." By employing the language of "the public good," public officials may become better attuned to the distinction between the public good and the private interests of corporations, and we may more readily call them to account for blurring that distinction.

We should distinguish *the* public good from *a* public good—a concept from the argot of economics. In short, public goods might be considered constituents of, or as contributing to, the public good. For economists, a public good has two characteristics: it is "nonrivalrous" and "nonexcludable." These mean, respectively, that "the consumption of one individual does not detract from that of another," and that "it is difficult if not impossible to exclude an individual from enjoying the good."[34] The economist and Nobel Laureate Joseph Stiglitz puts it another way, arguing that nonrivalrous means "no one *should* be excluded from the enjoyment of a public good (since the marginal cost of benefiting from it is zero)" while "non-excludability implies that no one *can* be excluded."[35] Stiglitz describes knowledge as an example of a global public good. Public health infrastructure for the control of pandemics is also a global public good. Private goods such as sports utility vehicles and smart phones, on the other hand, are rivalrous and excludable. Policymakers—and, for that matter, academic administrators[36]—should be careful not to conflate *nonmaterial public goods,* such as knowledge, with *material private goods,* such as commercial products developed as a result of that knowledge.

3.4 PUBLIC INTEREST

Some scholars argue that the public interest has different connotations from the common good and draw on historical analysis to support this claim.[37] They contend that the common good refers to the well-being of the community and is tied to shared values, goals, and cooperation. The public interest, on the other hand (they argue), refers to "the aggregation of private interests of individuals."[38] Although this distinction has some historical foundations, contemporary policymakers (as well as some philosophers[39]) tend to treat both terms as interchangeable.[40]

The word "interest" can create confusion because it is open to a variety of interpretations. As the political philosopher Jock Gunn has observed, the word may "suggest that its possessor subjectively feels a concern, and may thus actively promote it." Alternatively, it may "convey the claim of some observer that the welfare of the party addressed is objectively affected by certain factors whether or not the situation has promoted any felt need."[41] Tensions may arise when subjective and objective interpretations conflict—for example, when governments intervene to promote the interests of a certain public, and its members do not believe the intervention serves to promote their interests or what they perceive to be their own interests.[42]

Another conflation of different senses of the word "interest" arises in the context of public-private partnerships (and relationships with industry more broadly). Government agencies (and, for that matter, academic institutions) often search for donors or partners that have an "interest" in a particular project or public health challenge. Instead of looking for a donor that has expressed concern about (one way of being "interested in") a particular problem, government agencies often actively seek donors with a *vested economic interest* in the problem or the manner of its resolution. As we shall see, this approach creates serious ethical challenges.

The term "public interest" flourished during the twentieth century due, in no small part, to the ways in which the term was operationalized in the law. In that context, too, there is risk of conflation. Judges are often tasked with distinguishing disclosures of information that are truly "in the public interest" and those that are merely "interesting to" the public.[43] Laws designed to safeguard the former include provisions protecting employees who make "public interest disclosures" about practices of their employers that cause environmental damage or create health hazards.[44] The public interest also plays a role in international human rights law. Some rights, such as the prohibition on torture, are absolute and "nonderogable"; no violations of these rights are permitted in any circumstances. But states may justify interference with several other rights in order to protect "public health," "public safety," and "public order,"[45] All these grounds are different specifications of "the public interest." While human rights law and practice is premised on recognition that protecting human rights promotes the common good,[46] the law also recognizes that the public interest may sometimes take priority over certain individual rights. The tension between the public interest and individual rights is *not* resolved using a simple balancing exercise. The law is more demanding. In the example most relevant for our purposes, states may restrict certain rights and freedoms if they can show that this is "necessary" to protect public health.[47] Necessity has been authoritatively interpreted to require that interference with the relevant human right is in response to a pressing public or social need; in pursuit of a legitimate aim; proportionate with that aim; and the least restrictive means of achieving that aim.[48] Notably, this analytical framework from the law has also been influential in public health ethics.[49] And, as I explain in chapter 8, it offers an alternative to cost-benefit analyses (including so-called risk-benefit balancing) that prevail in the context of public-private partnerships.

It is possible, of course, for two or more different "specifications" of the public interest to be in tension with each other. There may be public interest in *both* national security and in the disclosure of information about unlawful government practices intended to promote national security.[50] For the purpose of the discussion here, I focus on the public interest in the protection and promotion of public health which may be further or more finely specified. For example, we may speak of the public interest in promoting access to clean sanitation facilities *and* in reducing obesity and diet-related noncommunicable diseases. As we shall see, a collaboration between public and private sector bodies designed to promote the former public health goal may, in the longer term, undermine the latter.[51]

In this book, I refer to "the public interest" when it provides a helpful contrast to "private interests," especially the commercial interests of corporations. My use of public interest is consonant with contemporary usage in law—where the term is employed to assess specific policies and practices.[52] To be clear, I am not endorsing an aggregative approach that frames the public interest simply as the sum of the private interests of individuals. Some scholars rightly worry that such a view can lead to "tyranny of the majority." In the context of public-private partnerships, it creates another ethical hazard. It tends to promote a cost-benefit analysis of partnerships, one that simply asks whether a collaboration helps more people than it harms.

3.5 THE COMMON GOOD, THE PUBLIC GOOD, AND THE PUBLIC INTEREST AS ORIENTATIONS

The most important task for public officials is not to get caught up in fine academic distinctions among the common good, the public good, and the public interest. Rather, it is to focus on how attention to these related concepts might orient them in the discharge of their official functions.

The US Senate Model Code of Ethics acknowledges that senators are "faced with the difficult tasks of balancing the different and sometimes conflicting interests of various groups in the society and of assessing the differential impact of laws and policies on various segments of the population."[53] Its authors also recognized that "an injunction to promote the public interest provides neither a formula for simplifying these judgments nor a substantive definition of what 'the public interest' requires." However, the Model Code provides that each senator has an "obligation to be constantly attentive to the broadest implications and the wide-ranging impact of his or her official acts," and that this "frame of mind" requires senators to "be on guard against legislative decisions that are consistently and systematically biased in favor of some narrow interests or some particular group."[54] To characterize the common good as a frame of mind or orientation is not to say that it is merely aspirational. On the contrary, the Model Code expressly frames the common good in terms of legislators' *obligations*. As the authors of the Code also recognized, an orientation toward the common good is necessary but not sufficient.

Public officials should be sensitive to the possibility that they are promoting or being induced to promote private interests in the name of—*and* at the expense of—the common good. The political scientist, Jock Gunn, has observed that for hundreds of years "proponents of private concerns aligned themselves with the supposed interests of the great mass of people." "Far from discarding the familiar injunctions to prefer the common good," Gunn notes, "they tried to bring themselves within its terms."[55] Today, public officials should be especially wary of conflating the commercial interests of multinational corporations with the common good—especially given popular narratives about corporations, collaboration, and the common good.[56]

3.6 CORPORATIONS AND THE COMMON GOOD

3.6.1 Shareholders and Stakeholders

One popular narrative holds that the so-called stakeholder view of corporations was dominant in the United States after the Second World War. Corporations began to recognize that they had obligations to a broad set of "stakeholders," not just shareholders. The Johnson & Johnson "credo," drafted by Robert Wood Johnson in 1943, is often cited as evidence for that view. The credo, revised several times in the last seven and a half decades, articulates the company's obligations to the health professionals and customers that use its products; to its employees, and the communities in which they live and work; and to the "world community" and the environment. Notably, the credo describes the company's obligations to shareholders as its "final responsibility."[57]

In 1953, Charles Wilson, then the chief executive of General Motors (GM), was tapped to be secretary of defense for President-elect Dwight Eisenhower. In a closed Senate hearing, Wilson was asked whether he could make a decision as secretary of defense that might harm the interests of GM, given that he owned $2.5 million worth of investments in GM (equivalent to $20 million today). Wilson replied: "I cannot conceive of one, because for years I thought what was good for our country was good for General Motors and vice versa. The difference did not exist. Our company is too big. It goes with the welfare of the country."[58] Wilson subsequently divested his shareholding in GM in order to secure his Senate confirmation. But his response reflects a persistent elision of corporate interests and the common good.

There was (and is) undoubtedly a relationship between the commercial interests of GM and the common good—particularly in the states with GM factories. In the 1950s, GM had more employees at this time than the combined populations of Nevada and Delaware.[59] But it is possible to imagine a variety of legislative reforms (such as increased safety or environmental regulation) that might reduce the profit margins of corporations such as GM in the short term but would clearly contribute to the common good. Conversely, a number of corporate practices, such as outsourcing of jobs, might improve profitability but destroy local economies.

Nearly thirty years after Charles Wilson's Senate testimony, the Business Roundtable, an organization of business executives in the United States, echoed his view, asserting, "the well-being of society depends upon profitable and responsible business enterprises."[60] The roundtable also claimed that the "long-term viability of the corporation depends upon its responsibility to the society of which it is a part." But, by this time, a different view had already begun to take root. In 1970, Milton Friedman wrote a piece for the *New York Times* arguing that the "social responsibility of business is to increase its profits."[61] Although others tried to champion the stakeholder view of corporations,[62] Friedman's view prevailed. When the Business Roundtable published a statement on corporate governance in the late 1990s (more than a decade and a half after the one just quoted), it asserted that "the principal objective of a business enterprise is to generate economic returns to its owners."[63] One purported advantage of this approach was that it would be simpler for corporate executives to focus on share price than to try to balance profits with the interests of workers, consumers, and society more broadly.[64]

Two professors at New York University's Stern School of Business, Ralph Gomory and Richard Sylla, recently argued that, contrary to popular assumptions, maximizing profits and shareholder value is *not* a legal requirement.[65] Drawing on provisions of the Model Business Corporation Act (adopted in many US states), they contend that company directors owe fiduciary duties not to the shareholders but to the corporation. However, they acknowledge "the dominant motivation of the American corporation is to maximize profits and raise stock price in the interest of shareholders." Simply put, their view is: things don't have to be this way, but they are now.[66]

It is tempting to see the tension between corporate interests and the common good as simply a consequence of recent shifts in business practices and prevailing theories of the corporation, and to frame the divergence between corporate interests and the common good as principally the result of profit-maximization and bonus packages for executives. But there are more fundamental tensions between corporate interests and the common good that this narrative downplays. Gomory and Sylla assert, "*We cannot ignore the possibility that the interests of our global corporations and the interests of our country may have diverged*" (emphasis in original).[67] They pose the question: "*How do we align the actions of corporations with the broader interests of the country?*" In my view, the complete alignment of the commercial interests of industry actors and the public interest is not possible, and we imperil the public good by pretending otherwise.

The divergence may be most conspicuous when a corporation's products are harmful to health or the environment—especially when the company's profits accrue primarily to company executives and shareholders, while the burdens of the company's activities fall on other communities. But even companies whose products or services are designed to promote health and well-being have the potential to undermine the public good. One does not have to look far for an example of this. Pain management is a major health challenge. A company manufacturing pharmaceuticals that can alleviate pain symptoms may contribute to the public good, in particular by promoting individual and community health and well-being. But the current opioid crisis—or epidemic, as some characterize it—demonstrates the ways in which the interests of the company and its major shareholders diverge profoundly from the public interest.[68] Several companies promoted oxycodone for patients who do not have a terminal illness and downplayed the risks of addiction. This generated substantial revenues for the companies and increased shareholder value. But many patients became addicted to oxycodone and were driven to the black market when they could no longer obtain prescriptions from their physicians. (Drug dealers commonly "cut" heroin with cheaper synthetic opioids such as fentanyl and carfentanil—drugs that are many times more powerful than heroin and greatly increase the risk of accidental overdose.) Recent analyses suggest that 72,000 Americans died in 2017 from drug overdoses, and that the total societal cost of the opioid crisis in the United States alone exceeds half a *trillion* dollars per year.[69] This cost is being borne primarily by families, communities, and government bodies (local, state, and federal). The opioid crisis starkly reveals that even when a corporation engages in an enterprise with the express aim of promoting health, there may be a fundamental divergence between the company's commercial interests and the public good.

When considering potential interactions with the private sector, public officials should not ignore or downplay these *divergences*. They may be more acute in some cases than others. But officials should scrutinize any actual or potential divergence—just as they should scrutinize divergence between the mission and purpose of their institution, and those of a potential "partner." Even when there appears to be a first-order convergence in a collaboration between government and industry—for example, the development of a product to improve health—there is inevitably a second-order divergence between the orientation of public bodies toward the public good and the private sector's dependence on profit generation.

3.7 CORPORATE SOCIAL RESPONSIBILITY (CSR) RECONSIDERED

The term "corporate social responsibility" is used in at least two different ways. Although they are not mutually exclusive, they should not be conflated. The first sense is corporate philanthropy—what might be termed "doing well, *then* doing good." This form of CSR does not address the impact of companies' business activities on their communities, the environment, their consumers, or their employees. Corporations commonly "donate" a portion of their profits to civil society organizations (such as community groups) and to academic institutions. These profits may or may not be generated by socially harmful activities. But CSR as "corporate philanthropy" does not address such concerns. The second use of the term might be characterized as "doing well *by* doing good." Proponents of this kind of CSR exhort corporations to be attentive to the impact of their business practices on their communities, the environment, their consumers, and their employees. Companies can pursue corporate social responsibility in both senses. But, commonly, corporations embrace the first sense (philanthropy) while neglecting the second. Not surprisingly, there is some evidence that companies engage in philanthropy to "morally compensate" for—and restore goodwill after—revelations of business practices that are not socially responsible (in the other sense).[70]

When Milton Friedman called on business executives to resist exhortations that they engage in CSR, the majority of his comments were directed at what I call "doing well by doing good." But he also spoke out against corporate philanthropy—as did Robert Reich, former secretary of labor under President Clinton. Friedman and Reich are hardly political allies, but they are equally skeptical of corporate philanthropy. While Friedman argues that executives should not engage in such activities, Reich argues that they cannot do so, and we should not be seduced by their claims to the contrary. The commercial and political climate, Reich argues, "does not permit acts of corporate virtue that erode the bottom line."[71] But, more fundamentally, corporations are "not set up to be public charities."[72] He argues that the "only legitimate reason for a corporation to be generous with its shareholders' money is to burnish its brand image," and such a rationale "will only go so far." When WalMart's CEO turned down a request for 2,000 blankets in the wake of Hurricane Katrina, he explained: "We can't send three trailer loads of merchandise to every group that asks for it. We have to . . . have a viable business."[73] A recent spate of hurricanes since Katrina—including Hurricane Harvey in 2017—have resulted in numerous corporate donations and pledges.[74] These donations are small when compared with both the revenues of the donor and the overall costs of the damage. But they serve to burnish the reputation of donors. Donations are frequently designed to be "matched gifts" that are only triggered when a customer makes a donation "at the point of sale."

A former vice president at Kraft Foods, Michael Mudd, has written candidly about corporate philanthropy. Its intended function, in the words of a former colleague, is to make the company "look angelic while making consumers feel good about the brand and drawing attention away from the unhealthful nature of the company's products."[75] (This is what Friedman meant when he wrote forty years ago about "the cloak" of social responsibility.[76]) But recognition of the ethical challenges presented by corporate philanthropy does not depend on such a cynical view.

Multinational corporations strive to increase profits—and, in turn, shareholder value. They understandably distribute a small portion of profits for charitable or public purposes in ways that burnish the company's reputation and increase brand loyalty for its products. But, as we shall see, corporate philanthropy creates reciprocity and influence that promote the commercial interests of the donor. So-called philanthropic partnerships can also have a chilling effect on governments' willingness to exercise their regulatory powers—even when the exercise of those powers would promote "responsible" business practices by reducing the adverse effects of commercial operations on public health and the environment.[77] Philanthropic contributions are used to reduce companies' tax liability. This creates another potential peril: companies may withdraw—and partnerships may collapse—in the wake of an unexpected downturn in corporate profits, leaving the public body scrambling to sustain a vital initiative.[78]

Corporations are also constrained in their ability to engage in practices that might be described as "doing well *by* doing good." When PepsiCo's shareholders complained that the marketing of the company's (purportedly healthier) "good for you" products led to loss of market share for its "fun for you" products, the company increased marketing of the latter.[79] If a corporation can take into account the interests of employees, consumers, and the environment without impairing profitability, we might hope it would do so. But we would be naive to expect companies to do this if profitability might be impaired, and executives are rewarded for procuring increases in short-term profits.[80] Time will tell whether we can expect more from new forms of corporation known as "benefit corporations," for-profit entities that commit to the promotion of the common good in some way or other. But partnerships with such institutions still raise ethical concerns.

3.7.1 Benefit Corporations

J. Haskell Murray, a prominent scholar of benefit corporations, has described a "social enterprise" as "an entity that uses commercial activity to drive revenue with the common good as its *primary* purpose."[81] Close readers will immediately note the constraints here: the entities are still revenue based, and they engage in commercial activity. Before discussing the ethical implications of government collaborations with these entities, I briefly review the relevant law.

A corporate securities lawyer in private practice in Philadelphia, William H. Clark, Jr., has drafted an influential model law for benefit corporations (the Model Law).[82] This law requires benefit corporations to have a "general public benefit" purpose, defined as a "material positive impact on society and the environment, taken as a whole, assessed against a third party standard, from [its] business and operations."[83] The Model Law permits—but does not require—companies to articulate a specific benefit—such as providing low-income communities with beneficial products or services, protecting the environment, or improving human health. But the law calls on directors to consider seven sets of interests:[84] the interests of shareholders;

employees of the corporation, its subsidiaries and suppliers; customers; community and society; the local and global environment; the short and long-term interests of the corporation; and its ability to accomplish general (and any relevant specific) benefit.[85] Companies must post an annual benefit report that will help readers determine whether a company is living up to its claims—a requirement expressly intended to reduce "greenwashing."[86] The law also provides for a "benefit enforcement proceeding" if the corporation fails to pursue or create a public benefit.[87] But only a limited set of actors may avail themselves of this enforcement action: the corporation, shareholders with 2 percent or more stock, a director, the owner of at least 5 percent of the parent company, or persons listed in the bylaws or articles of the corporation.[88] There is no provision for members of the public to bring such enforcement proceedings, even if they suffer special harm or loss as a result of the corporation's failure to fulfill its public purpose.

At the time of this writing, thirty-four US states have passed some form of legislation that recognizes benefit corporations, and six states are "working on it."[89] Although many states have adopted the Model Code (with variations), the Delaware law has attracted particular attention because so many national and multinational corporations are registered there, and its law departs from the Model Code in important respects.[90] In many ways, the Delaware law is less demanding than the Model Code.[91] It does not require third-party assessment standards;[92] benefit reports need to filed biennially rather than annually;[93] benefit reports need not be made public;[94] and there is no requirement for a "benefit director." In one notable respect, the Delaware statute is more demanding than the Model Code: it requires the company's charter to state one or more specific public benefits that the corporation will promote.[95] However, an initial review found several corporations had successfully registered in Delaware without specifying the benefit.[96]

Under the Delaware law, the directors of a public benefit corporation must manage the corporation in a manner that *balances* shareholders' pecuniary interests, the best interests of those materially affected by the company's conduct, and the public benefit(s) identified in the company's certificate of incorporation.[97] If the directors fail to do this, shareholders who own at least 2 percent of the shares may bring a "derivative" lawsuit.[98] Like the Model Law, the Delaware statute has been criticized for failing to give nonshareholders a role in "governance."[99]

Within a few months of the Delaware law coming into force, roughly three-quarters of registered public benefit companies were "conversions." In other words, these companies existed before the law came into effect, and they subsequently converted from traditional to public benefit status.[100] One scholar estimates that over a third of public benefit companies could have obtained tax-exempt status as nonprofits under section 501(3)(c) of the Inland Revenue Code had they chosen to do so.[101] Just under a third of the companies appear to be professional services companies (defined broadly to include business consulting, architectural design, and legal and financial entities).[102] But it is the remainder—the companies that could not have obtained nonprofit status and do not provide professional services— that are of particular interest and relevance.

One of the most profitable public benefit companies to be registered under the Delaware law is Plum Organics. It had sales of $93 million for the year prior to its conversion, and sales surged in the wake of its conversion.[103] Notably, the company obtained public benefit status with the help of Campbell's, a large multi-national food company that acquired Plum in the same year.[104] The acquisition of public benefit corporations by multinational corporations—including food and beverage companies—should raise concerns.[105] Large parent companies can use "benefit subsidiaries" to burnish their reputation; increase brand loyalty for the parent's unhealthy leading brands; provide "moral compensation" for pro-motion and sale of these brands; and undermine support for regulation directed at those products. Public benefit subsidiaries may be unjustifiably burnishing their own and their parents' reputations. Reinforcing continued concerns about "greenwashing," a recent study found that many benefit reports are "self-promotional and do not provide much value to a reader looking for a full, fair evaluation of the business."[106]

R. Edward Freeman, a strong proponent of stakeholder theory, once observed that the theory is "a genre of stories about how we could live."[107] When readers of stories engage in what Samuel Taylor Coleridge called "the willing suspension of disbe-lief,"[108] they enhance their own pleasure. But when policymakers suspend their dis-belief in order to partner with corporations and engage in so-called multistakeholder initiatives, they may expose their institutions—and us—to harm.

Lawmakers can create structural incentives that reward directors for taking the interests of a broader range of stakeholders into account and punishing them for failing to do so. Legislation providing for the establishment of benefit corporations (or public benefit corporations) may go some but not all of the way toward doing this. However, even if requirements become more robust, it would be a mistake to assume that the interests of corporations are perfectly aligned with the public good or with the interests that public bodies have obligations to protect.

Benefit corporations are still for-profit enterprises, and by definition players in the market. Although their purpose is purportedly tied to the public good, they are required to achieve that purpose by a particular *means*. They *sell* goods or services. Even if directors consider other interests and do not focus solely on making a profit, the company's existence still depends upon profit generation. Companies have a special interest in the individuals or entities that purchase their goods and services; they depend upon the loyalty of their customers. (Consumer confidence may be analogous to, but is not the same as, public trust in public bodies.)

Public officials should also keep in mind that for-profit entities tend to focus on certain kinds of public health problems, to frame those problems in particular ways, and to develop particular kinds of solutions.[109] They are more likely to pick problems that can be addressed (demonstrably reduced, if not solved) in the short term. Those problems are often viewed through a narrow biomedical or behavioral lens—one that masks social and environmental factors. And the solutions proposed are usually technological "fixes" that are most readily commercialized.

Finally, democratic accountability is not the same as corporate accountability.[110] Governments are accountable to the electorate who may sanction them in several ways, notably by voting. Corporations—even benefit corporations—are not so broadly accountable. Only a small subset of those potentially affected by the actions or omissions of a benefit corporation may bring proceedings under the Model Law, leaving many affected by its failure to provide a public benefit without recourse. Fewer still may bring a derivative suit in Delaware. The broader public(s) cannot determine who may or may not be appointed director of a benefit corporation. Directors of benefit corporations are not public officials, and benefit corporations are not public bodies. Public officials should keep this in mind when considering relationships with benefit corporations.

3.8 THE PERILS OF PARTNERING FOR THE PUBLIC GOOD

Corporations may contribute to the good of a community. A corporation that provides residents of a small town with rewarding employment for a decent wage and creates affordable "healthets" (widgets that promote human health) may be described as contributing to the public good. However, policymakers should not conflate the promotion of the public good with the sale of private goods; and they should be attentive to actual and potential inconsistencies, divergences, and tensions between the public good and the commercial interests of proposed collaborators. They should not simply echo, or take at face value, claims that partnerships with industry are a "win-win-win" or that they will promote the public good.

In the case of the partnership to improve sanitation in public schools in India (which I explore in detail in chapter 6), the goal was the promotion of public health. But the means to achieve this, a partnership with Coca-Cola, imperils public health by promoting consumption of sugar-sweetened beverages, a key factor in obesity and NCDs. It is tempting to approach this problem by conducting a simple balancing exercise. (What are the expected benefits of improving school sanitation? What are the risks—the potential harms of conducting this endeavor in collaboration with a soda company?) But this is not the only way of thinking about the problem. Nor is it the best way of doing so. A simple cost-benefit analysis cannot address concerns about the integrity of public partners, and the breach of their obligations to protect the health of populations (including, but not limited to, schoolchildren). We need to develop a more sophisticated ethical framework (which I propose in chapter 8) to address these problems.

Public-private partnerships also raise other less obvious concerns. When public bodies seek out or are approached by private sector institutions as potential collaborators, the former may (often unwittingly) adjust their priorities by doing only what makes most sense for corporate partners and in a way that makes most sense to them too. I call the resulting phenomenon *agenda distortion*.[111] It is most evident when public bodies adjust the priority of initiatives by directing energies to those favored by industry. More subtly, public bodies may cede to nondemocratic actors the determination of what constitutes the public good, and how best to achieve it.

Policymakers are far less likely to consider measures that will promote the public good if those measures are inimical to the interests of their industry partners. And industry will only partner on initiatives that they perceive as being likely to promote their commercial interests. As one academic has wryly noted, market-based approaches to global health problems neglect long-term challenges that call for nontechnological solutions: "All the financial incentives in the world will not create a vaccine against poverty, racial and gender discrimination, and inequality."[112]

I began by identifying periodic concerns about wrongs that may be perpetuated or masked by the invocation of the common good. The twenty-first century concern is the conflation of the common good and the commercial interests of powerful corporations and trade associations. (Although these concerns may appear especially acute during President Trump's administration, they have clearly arisen in prior administrations, and they will do so again in future administrations.) Much of the literature on partnerships assumes that if collaborations involve multiple actors—including multiple industry actors—these initiatives will promote the common good. This view is informed by at least two mistaken assumptions. The first is that all entities participating in a partnership or collaboration will possess the same degree of influence. Institutions and organizations that have the greatest financial resources—whether or not they bring those resources to the table—are far more likely to possess disproportionate influence.[113]

The second problematic assumption is that the inclusion of multiple corporate actors in what are often called multistakeholder initiatives will ensure the common good is promoted. This assumption fails to recognize the many ways in which the interests of competing corporations may be aligned with each other but in tension with the public good. For example, soda companies share a commercial interest in added sugars *not* being identified on food labels—as do manufacturers of high fructose corn syrup and cane sugar. Close relationships with multiple corporate actors can undermine the public good by influencing the framing of public health problems and their solutions in ways that are least threatening to industry interests.[114]

If public health agencies need to collaborate to protect or promote public health, they would be well advised to look for other institutions that also possess a public health mission and purpose and that are similarly oriented toward the public good. A city health official trying to develop a new initiative could avoid several ethical challenges by collaborating with state and federal governments, as well as other city health departments, instead of partnering with a soda company.

3.9 CONCLUSION

Although corporations may contribute to *the common good*, they cannot and should not be considered *guardians* of the common good.[115] The pursuit of the public good is the responsibility of public officials, government bodies, and intergovernmental organizations. (I believe research universities have an analogous responsibility[116]—one that may similarly be undermined by their relations with industry actors.[117]) Public officials should be highly skeptical when the common good is framed in ways that appear to render it entirely consonant with the commercial interests of powerful industry actors. There are inevitably inconsistencies, tensions, and divergences that should not be ignored. Policymakers should not confound the common good and common ground—especially when the latter is interpreted as achieving consensus with industry. Multinational corporations subtly shape the way we think about the common good,[118] as well as the ways in which we think about our society and ourselves. We are commonly characterized as consumers rather than citizens, residents, or communities.[119] This is, understandably, how corporations see us. But public bodies, the guardians of the public good, should avoid industry interactions that might also lead *them* to characterize us in this way.

4

The Perils of Reciprocity

There is nothing more productive of joy than the repayment of kindness, or the sharing of interests and exchange of favors.

—CICERO[1]

IF YOU COOK dinner, you might reasonably expect your partner to wash the dishes. If you cook *and* wash the dishes tonight, your partner may be inclined do likewise tomorrow. When domestic partners share tasks in these ways, they engage in balanced reciprocity. We consider this the hallmark of a great relationship, especially when reciprocity is tacit and fluent, when there is no need to say: "If you cook tonight, I'll wash up." Economists call this kind of reciprocity (and similar forms among friends and co-workers) "positive" to distinguish it from retaliation and other forms of "negative reciprocity." But positive reciprocities may have negative effects. Some are obvious, others less so.

Reciprocal relations between industry actors and public bodies, whether characterized as partnerships or in some other way, may be attractive to the parties involved. But these relations can have negative effects that imperil both the public institution and the publics that the institution has an obligation to protect. Few policymakers consider the ethical implications of reciprocity in the context of public-private partnerships. I offer some insights from ethnography and behavioral science to show how the forms of reciprocity inherent in public-private partnerships imperil the institutional integrity of public bodies.

Governments and intergovernmental organizations enter partnerships with multinational corporations, often food and beverage companies,[2] because of the resources these companies bring to the table: funds, in-kind contributions, or both. Civil society organizations and academic institutions frequently participate in these collaborations and when they do, the arrangements may be called "multistakeholder initiatives." These collaborations have become the paradigm for addressing public health challenges.

Partnerships with corporations tend to resemble gifts rather than commercial contracts. Often, partnership is the vehicle for a gift. The industry donor can claim its contribution as a tax-deductible donation,[3] and the directors can report it to shareholders as part of the donor's corporate social responsibility activities.[4] Commercial contracts generally specify reciprocal obligations in the agreement. In the case of public-private partnerships, the agreement may only lay out what each party owes the other with regard to the partnership initiative. (For example, a soda company might agree to foot the bill for thousands of mosquito nets in Zambia if the public health department creates teams to distribute the nets to local communities.) But corporations often hope to receive something entirely outside the partnership initiative, something not specified in the agreement—such as a more favorable regulatory environment. Companies may also expect reciprocal returns from third parties who do not directly participate in the partnership—for instance, consumers who reward the company for its apparently generous participation in public health initiatives by demonstrating brand loyalty. Corporations have long recognized the power of reciprocity as a tool for influence and persuasion.[5] They participate in partnerships and multistakeholder initiatives as part of broader strategies of influence. A deeper understanding of reciprocity can help policymakers recognize the ethical perils of these relationships and take steps to anticipate and address industry influence.

4.1 RECIPROCITY: A BRIEF INTRODUCTION

Scientists have found evidence of reciprocal behavior in various nonhuman animals (including primates,[6] birds, and fish[7]) as well as humans. The writer, Margaret Atwood, claims that reciprocal altruism (the term used by primatologists and evolutionary psychologists) is our "inner module," providing us with our sense of fairness and the desire for "balancing out."[8] Reciprocity plays a central role in both Jean Piaget's and Lawrence Kohlberg's psychological theories of moral development.[9] Contemporary social and moral psychologist Jonathan Haidt considers reciprocity to be a "universal moral sense."[10] The philosopher Lawrence Becker contends that reciprocity is a "fundamental" moral virtue.[11] He argues that we "ought to be disposed . . . to return good in proportion to the good we receive."[12] There are, of course, disagreements about the definition of reciprocity. For some, it is simple "tit-for-tat." For others, it includes indirect exchanges that need not be in kind. There are also scholarly disputes about whether reciprocity is an obligation or an ideal, and whether it includes retaliation.[13] In my analysis, I focus on reciprocity as returning good for good. This includes not harming—or undermining the interests of—those who have been good to us.[14]

We should distinguish two different ways in which the term reciprocity is used: the first is descriptive (how we *in fact* reciprocate), the second normative (when we *ought* to reciprocate). The former is the terrain of anthropologists, sociologists, psychologists, evolutionary biologists, behavioral scientists, neuroscientists, and primatologists. They tell us when they observe reciprocity in the field or in the laboratory, and they offer theories to explain the behaviors they observe and to predict future behaviors. Whether and in what circumstances human beings or bonobos demonstrate reciprocity are empirical questions. Similarly, when scientists explore the role of brains, genes, culture, and environment in reciprocal behaviors, they are attempting to answer empirical questions. But only ethics can address the normative question: When is it right or wrong for human beings—and, by extension, institutions, organizations, and communities—to reciprocate? To answer this question, we must address the ethical implications of reciprocity when it has adverse effects on third parties. This issue has received insufficient attention—especially in the context of public-private partnerships.[15]

4.1.1 *Institutional Perspectives*

Few would dispute that reciprocity has important cognitive, affective, and behavioral dimensions. Reciprocity can profoundly, yet subtly, influence the way individuals think, feel, and behave. But you might reasonably ask whether it makes sense to talk about reciprocity in the context of institutions. In a word, my answer is: yes. Denying that such reciprocity is possible blinds us to serious ethical hazards. Writing about industry influence in medicine, the philosopher Arthur Schafer observes:

> What the drug companies understand is that much of social life is based on reciprocity. The need to return benefit for benefit, kindness for kindness, and favour for favour is a basic motivator in virtually every human society, past or present. It behoves us, therefore, to consider that every dollar of the hundreds of millions of dollars which the companies invest in grants and gifts to researchers, hospitals and universities, doctors, and medical students is viewed by the companies as an important part of their corporate strategy.[16]

A report by the American Association of Medical Colleges also expressed profound concerns about reciprocity in a medical context. Its authors noted that at the time of the report (2007) the pharmaceutical industry was spending between $12 and

15 billion annually on gifts and related strategies to market drugs to physicians.[17] They modestly concluded: "It is unlikely that the industry would invest that kind of money in an activity if it did not expect to receive something worthwhile in return." [18]

Schafer argues that "whether intended or not, every grant and gift from a pharmaceutical company to scientists or to their university or hospital comes with strings attached."[19] These strings, he adds, are "sometimes as heavy and oppressive as lead chains." I share Schafer's concerns but doubt his metaphor. Subtle reciprocity is like gossamer: incredibly strong but with strands so fine, they may almost be imperceptible.

4.1.2 Attitudinal Reciprocity

When we think of reciprocity, we often have in mind *calculated reciprocity*—that is, mental scorekeeping, and "quid pro quo."[20] But the perils of public-private partnerships also involve *attitudinal reciprocity*: "the general social predisposition rather than precise costs and benefits of exchanged behavior."[21] When philosopher Lawrence Becker writes that we should be "disposed" to reciprocate, he uses the term "disposition" to mean "a persistent readiness to respond and a propensity to act" that "does not require explicit or exact accounting."[22] He argues accounting is "rarely even necessary once the habit of reciprocating is well ingrained, any more than sounding out the syllables is necessary for fluent readers."[23]

Fluent reciprocity may be ideal among lovers, friends, and family. But reciprocity should worry us when it occurs between our physician and a drug company sales rep; between the officers of an energy company and environmental regulators; or between public health officials and a soda company.[24] We might rightly commend domestic partners for anticipating and responding to each other's needs. But, in public-private interactions, reciprocity can be hazardous to the integrity of and trust in the public institution, and to the well-being of individuals that the institution has an obligation to protect. The subtlety and fluency of reciprocity that are hallmarks of laudable personal relations should serve as warning lights in these institutional contexts. In particular, public officials should be wary of reciprocal obligations to corporations whose activities they have a responsibility to regulate.[25]

4.2 RECIPROCITY AND GIFTS

Partnerships with industry are often vehicles for gift-giving, and to better address the ethical implications of reciprocity arising from such relationships, we need to draw on some of the central themes in the literature on reciprocity and gifts. Much work in the field now known as economic anthropology focuses on gift-giving in what were once called "primitive societies"—most famously, *The Gift* (1925) by Marcel Mauss.[26] As anthropologist Mary Douglas has observed, a central theme in Mauss's work is that "[t]here are no free gifts; gift cycles engage persons in permanent commitments that articulate the dominant institutions."[27] These cycles result from three distinct but related obligations identified by Mauss: the obligations to give, to receive, and to reciprocate.[28] For Mauss, "the unreciprocated gift . . . makes the person who has accepted it inferior," and charity is "wounding for him who has accepted it."[29] Contemporary ethnographers have applied this work to our own society—including "gifts" from corporations.[30] But we may also draw lessons from traditional work in the field, corroborated by recent research in psychology, behavioral economics, and related disciplines.

4.2.1 Donor Perspectives

Rarely is giving purely altruistic. There are usually other motives involved. Several motives may be at play simultaneously.[31] We may give out of duty, propriety, or for the resulting self-satisfaction. We may give for the social effects—to have an impact on the views of others (for example, to elicit praise, gratitude, esteem or the "liking" of others.) Our gifts may be intended to establish or alter hierarchies and social status, to initiate or transform social relations. Gifts may be given to promote self-interest by eliciting a return gift or reward. A gift might also promote self-interest as a result of the social effects, such as the change in the donor's status or social relations. Sometimes the central motive is to induce the continuation of relations that promote self-interest, whether or not this motive is expressed.[32]

Motives for gift-giving by corporations and trade associations may well be mixed. We need not argue (as do some critics from within as well as outside industry[33]) that CEOs are being disingenuous when they claim that their gifts are intended to promote the public good. Nor do we need to show that the gifts are motivated by a desire to enhance the status and reputations of the corporations that give. For our purposes, it is sufficient that industry gifts can and do have these effects.

4.2.2 Recipient Perspectives

Gifts can create a "gratitude imperative," compelling reciprocity and controlling (or, at least, influencing) the behavior of the recipient.[34] This imperative may be especially strong when the staff of a recipient institution know the identity of the donor, and the gift seems central to the recipient's survival or the success of an important project. As journalist Robert Wright puts it: "Gratitude is an IOU," and "the more desperate the plight of the beneficiary, the larger the IOU."[35] In the face of intractable public health problems, underfunded public health officials might understandably feel desperate.

Gratitude can induce "liking."[36] And it can also influence our appraisals of others' performance.[37] Gratitude toward a donor and liking its representatives are particularly problematic when the recipient has responsibilities to regulate the donor and hold it accountable. It may be impossible for a government agency to make a credible and impartial judgment about the performance of its industry donor.

Gifts may create influence without dependence. Although a doctor does not "depend" on a drug company to supply her with pens, these and other small gifts can and do still exert influence.[38] But we should also keep in mind that gift exchange can create or exacerbate dependence.[39] When a government agency relies on a corporate donation to fund a public health initiative, this may result in dependence, "moral indebtedness," and a sense of "inferiority" that undermines the status of the recipient.[40] Status is a function of the perceptions and attitudes of others. Anthropologists have long observed the status effects of gift-giving and reciprocity. As Stephen Gudeman recently noted, "reciprocity is *part of a system of practices in which participants express, constitute, lose and gain position in the sphere of human value.*"[41] The status effects of industry gifts are frequently exacerbated by the ritual of the gift—in particular, rituals of promotion.

4.2.3 The Ritual of the Gift

Three years before Mauss published *The Gift*, Bronislaw Malinowski wrote about the *kula* exchange among Trobriand islanders in the Western Pacific. He observed that the exchange involved gifts given in public and ostentatiously, "accompanied by the blowing of a conch shell."[42] Mary Douglas later noted that such "[g]ifts are given in a context of public drama with nothing secret about them."[43] Anonymous donors—and, to a lesser extent, identified donors who eschew public promotion of their gifts—may give primarily to enhance the well-being of others whom they may never meet and whose identities they may never discover.[44] (Donors may also experience an increased "warm glow" effect when they give anonymously.[45]) In contrast, the aim of ceremonial gift exchange is "public reciprocal recognition."[46] The exchange must be "known" to achieve its goal, "reciprocal and public recognition . . . to create or reinforce the social bond."[47]

Gifts from industry are usually well publicized. They almost invariably involve press releases with photographs of representatives of the donor organization, the recipient organization, and some of the purported beneficiaries of the gift—especially children. A popular ritual is the photo shoot with a grossly enlarged image of the donation check (or fictionalized check in the case of electronic funds transfer) with various parties holding the corners of the check.[48] These kinds of rituals are analogous to the blowing of a conch in *kula* exchange, and they help soda companies (among others) broadcast their corporate philanthropy. But these rituals may have adverse effects for gift recipients and public health—particularly when they promote consumption of unhealthy products.

4.2.4 The Poison in/of the Gift

Some anthropologists describe the gift as a "Trojan Horse."[49] Others characterize its ethical perils as "the poison of the gift."[50] In the case of *dana*, a form of gift-giving to priests, observed in parts of India in the 1970s and early 1980s, the gift presents a peril because it is believed to "embody and transmit the sins of the donor to the priestly recipient."[51] Although the gift is supposed to be reciprocated by the donor's "liberation from sin," anthropologist Jonathan Parry argues that the "profligate priesthood" cannot deliver liberation because they themselves are sullied by these transactions, "dragged down into hell by the bonds which the gift creates between them."[52] This language may seem melodramatic and the context far removed from gifts by multinational corporations. But there are parallels between the priestly perils of *dana* and ethical concerns raised by industry gifts. Recipients in either case may appear "sullied."

Corporations try to build close relationships with public health agencies and other government bodies to enhance their credibility and burnish their reputations. Governments often encourage industry actors to partner with them by *expressly invoking this rationale*.[53] But gifts from and partnerships with industry can undermine the credibility of public bodies. When a public health agency loses the trust of certain communities, this makes it more difficult for the agency to work effectively to promote public health. There are also striking parallels between the "obsequious sycophancy" of *dana* priests toward their benefactors,[54] and the self-censorship of government agencies (and academic institutions) when they are worried about jeopardizing industry funding.

4.2.5 The Tyranny of the Next Gift

This brings us to another important issue—what I call the tyranny of the *next* gift. Sociologist Renee Fox and historian of medicine Judith Swazey coined the term "the tyranny of the gift" to describe the onerous psychological and moral burden on the recipients of organ donation.[55] They argue that because the gift has "no physical or symbolic equivalent" and is "so extraordinary," it is "inherently unreciprocal."[56] As a result, the donor, the recipient, and their families "may find themselves locked in a creditor-debtor vise that binds them one to another in a mutually fettering way." I would argue that, in the case of corporate gifts, the public bodies receiving donations are far more likely to feel fettered than the industry donors. But I build on Fox and Swazey's concept here in order to address a more fundamental misconception about gifts.

Policymakers should not assume that the only concern is what we might call *responsive reciprocity*: subtle influence and obligations arising *after* receipt of a gift. They should also recognize the hazards of *anticipatory reciprocity*. When I anticipate your potential gift, I may be more inclined to confer benefits on you and not act in ways that could harm your interests. In a well-documented case, the president of a prestigious Canadian university lobbied his prime minister to oppose patent reform. The proposed laws threatened to reduce the revenues of the drug company contemplating the largest-ever matched donation to his university.[57] In this case, the drug company asked the university president to intervene on its behalf. But other examples may be more subtle or tacit.

A public health official might prioritize one obesity initiative (such as an exercise program) that is not threatening to food and beverage industry donors or partners, while demoting another initiative that might well be threatening (such as increased regulatory oversight). A dean might provide support for research that could advance the commercial interests of a potential industry sponsor while not supporting research that might threaten those interests. Anticipatory reciprocity arising from a potential future gift may be even more powerful than responsive reciprocity in the wake of a gift. The next gift might appear to be a benevolent dictator. But, more likely, it is a charming tyrant.

Imagine that you run a public health agency or an academic department, and my company offers you $10 million. I inform you that your institution may do whatever it pleases with the money. I may also tell you that there is more where that came from. But even if I do not tell you this, you have good reason to believe that future gifts are also possible. Would you do anything that might undermine my company's commercial interests—or that I might perceive as threatening to the company's interests?

4.3 GIFTS, PARTNERSHIP, AND COMMUNITY

Claude Levi-Strauss argued that reciprocity is "the most immediate form of integrating the opposition between the self and others."[58] He observed that gifts have "a synthetic nature," turning individuals into "partners." Other scholars similarly contend that gifts and reciprocity can be a means of "bringing in new members," "extending the base," and "making community."[59] The language of "integration" and "partnership" is reflected in much of the literature advocating closer interactions between corporations and governments.[60] But companies also engage in gift-giving to extend their "base." When they succeed in doing so, they can more effectively build, exercise, and preserve political and market power,[61] and ensure favorable conditions for their business.

This is why corporations also make gifts to and establish relations with professional associations, public interest NGOs, and community organizations (among others). Ethnographers of corporate philanthropy have observed that when companies contribute to community organizations or projects, they often refer the affected communities as "our community."[62] In South Africa, an international mining company's educational bursaries to disadvantaged students create "permeating ripples of loyalty" to the mine.[63] The obligations of reciprocity implicit in such gifts are crucial for ensuring continued ties between the company and the communities, and the support of these communities protects the company's commercial activities. Gifts allow the company to "co-opt support . . . mitigating and lubricating the harsh realities of the mining business." Oil and gas companies (often described euphemistically as "energy companies") employ similar strategies to promote support for "fracking" and other activities related to "natural gas" production.[64] As we shall see in chapters 5 and 6, soda and snack food companies engage in similar practices to protect their commercial interests in the face of obesity concerns.

It is often claimed that gifts empower communities and civil society groups. But they can empower the giver while weakening the recipient, creating dependence on the part of communities and civil society organizations that remain indebted and "vulnerable to the whims of the donor."[65] Consistent with my analysis of corporate social responsibility in the previous chapter, a mining company CEO notably dismissed the idea that he was "spend[ing] shareholder money on grand philanthropic gestures."[66] Such gifts are intended to "build security for long term business investment" by making the company "a much more attractive partner to a host government or host community." In order to appreciate the countervailing hazards for both government and community "partners," we must look briefly at the literature on negative and asymmetric reciprocity.

4.3.1 Negative Reciprocity

Economists tend to employ the term "negative reciprocity" to mean retaliation: "an eye for an eye." However, the term has a different meaning for ethnographers. According to Marshall Sahlins, writing almost half a century ago, reciprocity lies on a spectrum from "sacrifice in favor of another to self-interested gain at the expense of another."[67] He places "generalized reciprocity" ("putatively altruistic" transactions) at one end of the spectrum, "negative reciprocity" at the other end, and "balanced reciprocity" in the middle. Negative reciprocity is "the unsociable extreme . . . the attempt to get something for nothing with impunity."[68] Sahlins describes this form of reciprocity as "the most impersonal sort of exchange." He associates it with haggling, bartering, gambling, and (more problematically) theft: participants "confront each other as opposed interests, each looking to maximize utility at the other's expense." Such reciprocity may involve "one-way flow," with one party's reciprocation arising from the other's "cunning, guile, [or] stealth." But even when there is no evidence of sharp practice, there may still be good reasons not to characterize partnerships with industry as "balanced."

4.3.2 *The Asymmetry of Gifts and Partnerships*

The philosopher Iris Marion Young argued that gift-giving is inherently asymmetric: "I do not return, I accept. If I later give you a gift, it is a new offering, with its own asymmetry."[69] However, in his analysis of blood donation, social researcher Richard Titmuss identified a narrower form of asymmetry. Titmuss observed: "To the giver, the gift is quickly replaced by the body. There is no permanent loss. To the receiver, the gift may be everything: life itself."[70] In corporate philanthropy, the significance of a gift for the donor and the recipient also differ. Industry gifts come from funds that are similarly replaced with remarkable alacrity: profits from the sales of leading brands. But such gifts often seem vital to cash-starved recipients. A gift can be a drop in the donor's profitable ocean, but it may feel like the only thing keeping the recipient afloat.

This *asymmetry* can exacerbate the inequality of bargaining power and shape the terms on which any gift is made. But even when—and perhaps especially when—the terms do not include substantial mechanisms of control by the donor, the asymmetry can magnify the gratitude imperative and obligation to reciprocate. Since public institutions and civil society groups ordinarily cannot reciprocate financially (for obvious reasons), they find other ways of providing economic benefits to corporate donors. When the recipient is a government body, reciprocation may take the form of a more relaxed regulatory environment. When the recipient is an academic institution or a civil society organization, faculty or staff may be more inclined to argue in favor of policies or engage in practices that are favorable to the donor and reject those that are unfavorable.[71]

Asymmetry also occurs when one party experiences the arrangement as a gift, and the other does not.[72] In a public-private partnership, even public officials skeptical about the motivations of a corporate donor may experience the arrangement as a gift and fall prey to subtle influence and obligations of reciprocity. The corporation's executives, on the other hand, may consider reputational benefits and brand promotion to be the expected return. As a result, public officials may experience *attitudinal reciprocity* that influences behaviors outside the partnership, while company executives are not similarly affected.

Some scholars argue that reciprocity can provide regulatory benefits, by inducing corporations to comply not only with the letter but also the spirit of regulations and voluntary agreements.[73] However, there is no compelling evidence that this has occurred in the food and beverage sector. On the contrary, systematic reviews suggest that collaborations with food industry actors have failed to procure compliance despite repeated requests by the WHO and the UN for companies to improve marketing and manufacturing practices—in particular, to produce and promote healthier foods.[74]

Evolutionary psychology may explain why reciprocal relations have generally not improved the business practices of food and soda companies. In his seminal article on reciprocal altruism, R. L. Trivers wrote about *mimicry and subtle cheating*— terms he used without attributing any malice on the part of the cheating party.[75] He observed that apparent acts of generosity may elicit genuine acts of altruism in return,[76] and that one party may knowingly accept "subtle cheating" by the other in order not to jeopardize the relationship, on the grounds that "half a loaf is better than none at all."[77] This may explain why public health officials accept funds from fast food, snack, and soda companies that claim to manufacture healthy products but continue to aggressively market leading brands with a low-nutrient profile and high-caloric content. Half a loaf might well seem better than no loaf at all—even if it has a great deal of added sugar!

4.3.3 The Impact of Reciprocity on Judgment and Decision-Making

Gifts may influence our aesthetic judgments in subtle and unconscious ways. In one notable experiment, participants were asked to report how much they liked or disliked various paintings. They had been told that a fictitious corporation had contributed to the compensation they received for participating in the study. When the logo of the fictitious corporation appeared randomly alongside certain paintings, participants reported liking those paintings more.[78] Gift-giving may have similar effects on other forms of judgment and decision-making, especially professional and scientific judgments.[79] Evidence of the impact of drug company gifts on physicians' judgment has been well-documented.[80] Corporate donations and industry partnerships may similarly influence government agencies, and comments made by former industry executives suggest this is generally the intention.[81]

4.3.4 Reciprocity and Integrity

A core dimension of institutional integrity is consistency among what the institution says it does (its mission), what it is obligated to do (its purpose), and what it actually does (its practices).[82] When two institutions possess fundamentally divergent missions or purposes, reciprocity between them can undermine their integrity. This risk will be greater for one institution than the other when the reciprocity is asymmetric. Public-private partnerships are more likely to promote attitudinal reciprocities that are asymmetric—and, consequently, more hazardous for the public partner—when the public institution lacks financial resources and funds are provided by a very profitable multinational corporation. The sums changing hands may be small from the perspective of the corporate donor, but large from the perspective of the underfunded public body. When a public health agency partners with a corporation whose commercial activities may be exacerbating a public health challenge, asymmetric reciprocity is especially likely to undermine the integrity of the public institution. This occurs when an agency fails to take measures to improve public health because those measures might appear to threaten the commercial interests of its industry partner. Loss of integrity is deeply problematic for a public body that has an obligation to protect the health and well-being of others.

4.3.5 Reciprocity, Third Parties, and Public Health

Although there is some discussion of third parties in the social science literature on reciprocity, few scholars have addressed the ethical implications of third-party effects. Before addressing this lacuna, I draw briefly on the social science literature to help us understand the effects of public-private partnerships—in particular, how partnerships wield influence by means of "extended reciprocities."[83] Examples of such reciprocities are gifts from A to B that elicit a response from B to C, a response from C to A (sometimes called "reverse reciprocity"), or from C to D. Other forms of extended reciprocities include those involving groups or collectives (for example, a gift jointly from AB to C that elicits a gift from C to AB) or, more broadly, transfers to a "society as a whole" (sometimes called "general reciprocity.")[84] Extended reciprocities include "chain reciprocities" where A gives to B, who gives to C, who gives to D, and so forth. These chains may be characterized as "open" or "closed,"[85] depending on whether something comes back to A. The controversial $10 million donation from the American Beverage

Association (ABA) to the Children's Hospital of Philadelphia (CHOP) in 2011, reportedly an effort to "ward off" (temporarily, at least) a Philadelphia soda tax,[86] might be characterized as an exercise in extended reciprocity. Soda companies agreed to donate millions of dollars to the ABA, which established a foundation that, in turn, channeled the gift to the hospital's foundation. A separate entity, the Philadelphia City Council, which was not a direct recipient of the gift, then voted down the tax proposal.

This gift may also illustrate one of the ways in which extended reciprocities can have *multiplication* effects. In the paradigm case, one party, A, expresses a willingness to make a gift, and asks another, B, to identify the recipient, C. In such a case, when A gives to C, *both* B and C may reciprocate. A similar effect may occur when the recipient of the gift, C, is not expressly requested or identified by B, but A knows (or has good reason to believe) that B would want C to receive such a gift. In the case of the donation to CHOP, the soda companies had good reason to believe that members of the City Council would be strong supporters of the city's flagship pediatric hospital, and that they would be grateful for the gift to CHOP.

The concept of extended reciprocity does not address the ways in which positive reciprocity may *adversely affect* others.[87] This is what some economists call "the dark side of pro-social behavior, the presence of negative externalities."[88] These scholars cite business-to-business gifts and lobbying as cases in which an interested party may be "kind" to a decision-maker to influence its decision to the detriment of a third party.[89] Gifts or lobbying that promote the interests of one corporation (or sector) at the expense of another may well be problematic. But I am concerned here with adverse effects on nonindustry actors, especially the relevant public(s). From the point of view of economists, third-party effects, if considered at all, are "externalities." But, from an ethical perspective, adverse effects on so-called third parties are a central concern.

Where one party in a reciprocal relationship has an obligation to protect or promote the interests of third parties, and reciprocity results in behaviors harmful to those parties, this is ethically problematic. The obligation to protect third parties need not be a specific form of legal obligation, such as the fiduciary obligations that lawyers owe their clients, or the obligation of confidentiality that physicians owe their patients.[90] Any obligation (whether legal or ethical) should be considered when addressing the ethical implications of reciprocities that adversely affect third parties. And we should be especially concerned when these adverse effects burden vulnerable individuals or communities.[91]

The concept of stewardship can help us address these ethical concerns. Legal scholar Daniel Hays Lowenstein has argued that the "paradigm of stewardship [is] almost as basic to any non-primitive society as the reciprocity paradigm," and that they exist in a kind of "counterpoise."[92] Lowenstein defines "stewards" as individuals—to which I would add institutions—that are obliged to act in the interests of others, "beneficiaries." Reciprocity between stewards and nonbeneficiaries, Lowenstein observes, can "lose its benevolent character" when benefits accrue to the steward and not the beneficiary.

From the perspective of the reciprocity paradigm, persons who do not participate in the reciprocal arrangements are third parties. But from the perspective of the stewardship paradigm, the term "third parties" denotes those who are neither stewards nor beneficiaries. One can apply this paradigm to institutions that have obligations at a population level (as well as to individuals who possess obligations to other individuals). On such a view, food and beverage companies are third parties whose reciprocal relations with public health agencies (stewards) threaten the interests of, among others, children (beneficiaries).[93] This shift in perspective is not merely semantic. It has profound ethical implications, making central relationships and obligations that might otherwise be minimized or neglected.

Government bodies and intergovernmental organizations may recognize the perils of partnering with corporations whose products may be contributing to a major public health challenge. But they only draw bright lines in the most obvious cases. Although WHO policies call for the avoidance of close relations with the tobacco and arms industries,[94] they do not put relations with food and beverage industry actors off the table. Many national health agencies also have close relations with companies in this sector.

4.4 CONCLUSION

The ethnographic literature on gift-giving and reciprocity helps identify several ethically problematic features of public-private partnerships and other close relations with industry. Industry gifts create asymmetric reciprocities. They are often made at little cost to the donor (coming from substantial revenue streams, and used to offset tax liabilities), but they can be of great significance to the recipient (supporting a key initiative). Such gifts create powerful gratitude imperatives and obligations to reciprocate. Partnerships are often vehicles for and operate in similar ways to gifts. They create subtle, fluent reciprocities that influence public bodies and promote industry interests. Partnerships may also burnish the reputation of the corporate donor, and increase brand loyalty. The public nature of industry gifts and their attendant rituals reinforces these effects. While enhancing the industry partner's reputation, partnerships may promote the public health agency's perceived (as well as actual) dependence on industry and undermine its status, authority, and credibility.

Corporations develop close relations with public bodies to "extend their base" and build "community." These relations fuel support for (and defuse resistance to) companies' commercial activities. Partnerships can undermine the integrity of a public partner with a public health mission and purpose—particularly if the industry partner's products exacerbate public health challenges and the partnership leads to increased consumption of those products. But even absent those concerns, the integrity of the public health agency will still be at stake if reciprocity leads the agency to refrain from taking steps that might promote public health because they would threaten (or appear to threaten) an industry partner's commercial interests. When public health agencies partner with soda, snack, or fast food companies, they imperil the health of vulnerable populations—communities the agencies have a duty to protect. In such cases, reciprocity hardly seems virtuous. On the contrary, it may be better characterized as a vice.[95]

5

Webs of Influence

Research can either serve or subvert the public interest. . . . The capacities and integrity of researchers, and their universities, can be enhanced or corrupted in the process.
—STEVEN LEWIS ET AL.[1]

CORPORATIONS AND TRADE associations routinely provide financial support to academic institutions and civil society organizations. A multinational soda company might partner with several local governments to develop exercise programs; make gifts to dozens of medical professional and public health associations; and sponsor research teams working on physical activity and obesity.[2] These relationships are attractive to industry actors because they burnish corporate reputations, increase brand loyalty, and promote sales of products—often energy-dense low-nutrient products that exacerbate obesity.

Partnerships and analogous interactions present opportunities for industry to exercise *direct* influence on the academy and civil society groups and, through them, *indirect* influence on governments and intergovernmental organizations. These interactions are key components of corporate strategies, creating webs of influence that promote and protect companies' commercial interests. Industry actors seek to influence policy by shaping the research on which policies are based. They also recognize that their policy positions gain credibility and reinforcement when academics and public interest NGOs make apparently independent representations consonant with their commercial interests.

We should expect industry to take advantage of all legally permissible avenues for the exercise of influence to advance their commercial interests. But public officials need to develop their own strategies to guard against such influence. Policymakers should be aware that academics and civil society groups may be promoting (at times, unwittingly) the commercial interests of powerful industry actors under the guise of advancing the common good. Public officials wishing to guard against in-direct industry influence in policymaking will need to be sensitive to divergences between corporate interests and the public good. They should also scrutinize the relationships that nonindustry participants in policymaking have with industry and ensure that public funds are available to support research that might promote the public interest.

5.1 INDUSTRY AND ACADEMIC INSTITUTIONS

Academy-industry partnerships are widespread. In some cases, they occur at the level of a department or program; in others, they involve a college or the entire university.[3] Sometimes industry labs are housed—or "co-located"—on campus.[4] One of the most influential proponents of these approaches, Stanford professor Henry Etkzowitz, argues that universities are undergoing "mission change"; in addition to education and research, there is an "emerging 'third academic mission': to con-tribute to economic and social development."[5] Research universities, he contends, are "expanding" to become "entrepreneurial universities." Etzkowitz lauds the transition, arguing that it "intersects with transition of the government role from regulating separate institutional spheres to encouraging interaction among them." He writes, "Each institutional sphere, *in addition to performing its traditional role*, also 'takes the role of the other,' with government serving as a public venture capitalist, industry taking training to higher levels in company universities, and universities performing increasingly direct economic roles in translating research with technological implications into use" (emphasis added).[6]

Drawing on Archimedes' screw as a metaphor, Etzkowitz describes the entwined relationship of industry with government and academy as a "triple helix," and he argues that "the appearance of conflicts of interest may be taken as a positive sign that a sclerotic system is becoming flexible and that people are taking creative steps, transcending their traditional roles, to put knowledge to use."[7] Conflicts of interest, he argues, should be seen as "confluences of interest," and, in the "entrepreneurial university," the economic development mission should be viewed as supporting the research mission.[8] Although collaborations with industry actors are popular among academic administrators, they have rightly elicited criticisms and concerns from both academics and journalists.[9] Three common themes among these critical responses are worthy of comment here.

Several commentators have warned of the hazards of academic institutions "dancing" with industry.[10] But this metaphor does not fully capture the systemic effects of industry relations. In particular, it reinforces a dyadic image of two institutions interacting with each other. This view can be misleading: many industry actors artfully weave webs of relations with multiple organizations. Only when viewed in that context can the ethical implications be fully addressed.

Other scholars discuss high-profile disputes between industry and academic institutions as "the tip of the iceberg."[11] However, the iceberg metaphor is also potentially misleading. Beneath the visible part of an iceberg, there is just more ice. But the problems we don't "see" in industry-academy relations are very different in kind from those we do see. The latter tend to involve dissent, speaking up, and whistleblowing—often at great personal and professional cost. The former, undoubtedly the majority of cases, are those in which reciprocity and influence work silently, subtly, and powerfully.

Critics of the "triple helix" tend to focus on biomedical research and on individual relationships (for example, the government employee or academic researcher who has a financial relationship with industry).[12] Although academics' and government employees' relations with industry are important, we should not neglect the systemic effects of institutional relationships common in many fields.

* * *

In chapter 2, we explored the "ends" of institutions (what institutions are for) in order to lay the foundations for my analysis of institutional ethics and integrity. When thinking about what universities are for, it is helpful to examine statements made by the professional organizations of the people who work there—among them, the American Association of University Professors (AAUP), and the Canadian Association of University Teachers (CAUT). According to the AAUP, institutions of higher education should operate "for the *common good* and not to further the interest of either the individual teacher or the institution as a whole."[13] The common good, the AAUP contends, "depends upon the free search for truth and its free exposition." The CAUT emphasizes "the public missions of the university" and expresses the concern that the academy's increasing relationships with industry undermine its ability to work in the public interest.[14] Tying integrity to pursuit of the common good, the organization concludes that a university's integrity is "measured by the extent to which it protects [the] necessary context for scholarly work," which is defined to include service to the community and "the public at large."[15] For CAUT, "the very nature of the university" is to be "a place where faculty and students are free [to] teach and to learn as well as to question, evaluate, criticize, analyze, and examine without restriction by established orthodoxy, social custom, conventional wisdom, or the preferences of the most powerful in their society."[16] These organizations do not distinguish between private nonprofits (such as Harvard) or public institutions (such as my university, Penn State). In either case, this is the function of universities—what society needs them to do.

To speak of university integrity is, in a sense, to speak of "the wholeness of the whole." The word "university" comes from the Latin, *universitas*, meaning the whole, the entire number, the sum of things.[17] It is also related to "universality," a word that represents two ideas: "the whole subject," and "the study or contemplation of things from a general point of view." Both ideas map neatly on to two different senses of the "scope" of academic research: what we look at, and how we look at it. Although no institution can explore every research question from every perspective, a university should be open to examining everything from every perspective. Academy-industry relationships threaten both senses of universality by constraining the research questions that are explored and how they are explored. Even in the absence of formal constraints, they may create powerful disincentives to conduct research that might undermine industry interests.

According to the CAUT, "what makes a university a university is that it *pursues and advances knowledge in the broader interests of society*." The organization also contends that "part of what distinguishes it from being a corporate lab or the job shop of another organization," is that "at its core a university produces knowledge for the general public not for any *particular* individual, corporate, or organizational interest" (emphasis added).[18] In short, universities should be *universal* in their outlook, not *particular*. This need not entail a rejection of all research that might promote the commercial interests of corporations. But if universities are to retain their universal rather than particular character, they must be equally prepared to do research that does not promote, and may well undermine, the commercial interests of powerful industry actors.

The enthusiastic endorsement of universities' entrepreneurial roles fails to recognize the ways in which such roles can undermine institutions' "traditional roles." (To make this point more clearly, I will draw on my discussion of institutional integrity and institutional change in chapter 2.) Proponents of closer academy-industry relations, including Etzkowitz, tend to present the transformation as a form of *layering*—a change that involves the acquisition of an additional component to the institution's mission. However, if the transition comes at the expense of certain kinds of research, the change may be better described as a *conversion*—from research that increases knowledge but need not possess commercial potential to research that may be readily commercialized. If such a change undermines public trust in science and, in turn, the preconditions for universities' existence, it may ultimately constitute a form of institutional *erosion*.

The mission, purpose, and function of institutions may evolve over time.[19] But an institution cannot be all things at the same time. This is not simply because institutions have limited resources. Some institutional ends are mutually inconsistent. An institution trying to pursue one such end could find itself undermining the other. As a result, its integrity will be at stake, as will its credibility in relation to one or both ends. The purpose of academic institutions is ordinarily specified in their founding documents. But research universities are increasingly formulating or revising mission statements to attract industry donors and to endorse existing collaborative practices. This can imperil their integrity and their credibility in communities affected by their work. To pick an example close to home, an academic institute will find it challenging to fulfill a mission that requires it *both* to promote research that advances the interests of industry *and* to educate the public about that industry's activities—especially when those activities are controversial and raise serious public health and environmental concerns.[20]

In addition, the emphasis on convergences of interest between industry and the academy is a Panglossian view that can lead administrators to downplay or ignore the ethical perils arising from fundamental divergences in interests. Divergences arise when the generation of some kinds of knowledge (for example, evidence about the impact of certain foods or chemicals on health) might advance industry interests, while other kinds of knowledge might not. In addition to the threat they pose to the integrity of academic institutions, these divergences have important practical and ethical implications for research and policymaking. Before addressing those implications, I discuss civil society organizations—among them, professional associations, patient advocacy organizations, and other health-related NGOs.[21] These groups may have direct financial relationships with industry, often as a result of systemic efforts by industry to engage them in these relationships. They may also be invited to participate in multistakeholder initiatives involving government bodies, academic institutions, and industry actors.

5.2 INDUSTRY AND CIVIL SOCIETY ORGANIZATIONS

The UN Food and Agriculture Organization (FAO) has folded civil society into the concept of the "triple helix" and argued for consensus among members of what it calls the "Golden Quadrant" of government, academy, industry, and civil society organizations.[22] This approach plays into industry strategies of influence. Relationships with civil society organizations can greatly enhance the credibility of corporations' claims about their products—especially their health effects (whether companies are alleging health benefits or disputing allegations of harm). Corporations build these relationships as part of their *credibility management* strategies.[23] These strategies involve both direct and indirect communication. A historical example of indirect communication is a food company influencing consumer groups and health professionals to persuade "housewives" to buy margarine.[24] Today, strategies involve sponsoring sessions—and entire meetings—of major nutrition and dietetics conferences.[25] Industry employs similar approaches in policy processes too, where the strategies can be even more subtle and influential.

When a civil society organization (CSO) has close relations with one or more corporations or trade associations and, in particular, when it receives funding from such entities, the CSO is likely to be influenced by that interaction and, in turn, to exercise influence on industry's behalf. The CSO may do this unwittingly as a result of subtle reciprocity. The organization's staff may not realize that they are exercising self-censorship, and modifying or shaping their views to avoid undermining the short-term commercial interests of an industry sponsor. CSOs may unintentionally serve as proxies for industry or at the very least provide them with "credibility enhancement."

In one notable case, a children's charity that had previously supported soda tax proposals in three states and two cities announced that it would no longer support such initiatives. It did so after receiving a $5 million grant from one major soda company, and while also seeking a second grant from another soda company.[26] Representatives of both companies told the *New York Times* they had not asked the charity to change its position. But, even if true, this claim ignores the subtle influence and reciprocity in the wake of the first gift, and the tyrannous anticipation of the second. The case also calls into question the integrity of the children's charity in two ways. First, in the absence of a persuasive explanation, the charity's volte-face (such a sudden reversal in relation to a major policy position) deprives it of consistency over time. Second, the charity's statement of mission and values declares that the organization will "always act in the best interests of children."[27] It is hard to see (and the charity did not show) how the withdrawal of support for the soda tax might be consistent with that mission. These kinds of interactions leave CSOs vulnerable to claims that they are acting as "inadvertent pitchmen" for industry.[28]

Other examples may not receive such public attention, initially or at all. A patient advocacy organization (PAO) that receives financial contributions from a pharmaceutical company may do so in the belief that the company's new drug (currently awaiting FDA approval) represents the most promising new therapy.[29] The PAO's staff may also accept funds believing it is in the interests of patients, the organization, and the pharmaceutical company that the drug be approved. But the reciprocity and influence that arises as a result of this relationship can compromise the ability of the organization's leaders and experts to evaluate the respective promises and perils of the drug. The close relationship with industry may make the organization less receptive to new evidence that calls into question the safety and efficacy of the drug. It may also lead the organization to advocate on behalf of the drug company during a contested regulatory process.

Policymakers and regulators should be wary when CSOs appear to be promoting the common good in ways that are consonant with the interests of powerful industry actors—especially corporations and trade associations with which those CSOs have close relations. (Policymakers should require that all CSOs making representations to them disclose industry funding and close relations with industry actors, particularly when those actors have a vested interest in the outcome of the policy or regulatory process. This basic requirement, however, is *not* a complete solution to the problem of influence.)[30]

5.3 SYSTEMIC EFFECTS OF INDUSTRY RELATIONS

5.3.1 *From Health Halos to Policy Influence*

Partnerships can fuel positive affective responses to corporate brands and increase consumer loyalty.[31] Put simply, partnerships may make consumers feel good about products that are not good for them! Collaborations can promote consumption of energy-dense foods and beverages that are contributing to obesity and diet-related NCDs. When they do so, they undermine public health and the integrity of public partners whose mission and purpose is to promote public health. Two factors that exacerbate brand loyalty for unhealthy products are "health halos" and "logo effects." Restaurants claiming to be "healthy" can confer unwarranted health halos on their products. One notable study shows that when main dishes are positioned as "healthy," consumers choose more energy-dense beverages, side dishes, and desserts.[32] Investigators also found consumers estimated that fast food menu items contained up to 35 percent fewer calories when restaurants claimed they were "healthy." In addition, consumers chose beverages, side dishes, and desserts with up to 131 percent more calories when the main course was positioned as "healthy." The effect may be even more powerful when the halo is conferred not by the company itself but by a government body or another entity perceived to be independent and trustworthy.

The USDA's Center for Nutrition Policy and Promotion appoints food and beverage companies—including snack food companies—as "national strategic partners," and authorizes them to use the government's "MyPlate" icon on its food packaging.[33] A food company's partnership status and the presence of the icon on its packaging (a kind of health "logo") has the potential to confer a health halo on the company and its brands, and promote less healthy consumption patterns. There is some evidence to suggest that these kinds of icons might also lead consumers to believe the products taste better![34]

When a public health agency permits the private partner's logo to become associated with a public health initiative, it may have the same (or similar) effect as the government's icon appearing on the private partner's product. In another notable study, the use of a sponsor's logo had subconscious effects on the participants' aesthetic judgments. As discussed in chapter 4, research participants reported liking paintings better when a (fictional) corporate sponsor's logo was randomly displayed alongside the painting.[35] One theory for this finding is reciprocity: liking and gratitude toward the sponsor. Another factor at work may be akin to *evaluative conditioning*—the evaluation of one stimulus (the painting) becomes more positive when it is paired with another positive stimulus (the logo of an apparently generous sponsor).[36] This kind of effect and its potential operation in reverse provide another reason to be concerned about the use of corporate logos in public-private collaborations (a common practice, as the examples in the next chapter demonstrate.) A public health collaboration may influence appraisals of and responses to a corporate partner's logo and to the company and brands with which it is associated. If a partnership initiative for the construction of a children's playground confers a health halo on a logo that is also used to market unhealthy brands, the arrangement will imperil the integrity of the public partner especially when it is an agency with a public health mission and purpose.

By burnishing the reputation of corporations, partnerships can also influence public opinion and, in turn, citizens' support for—or opposition to—policies, including increased regulation. It is not only consumers and voters who are vulnerable to influence. Health professionals and public health experts may be influenced too.[37] So may policymakers, regulators, and other officials. Health halos and the reputational benefits of industry partnerships may lead policymakers to interpret the behavior of industry partners more charitably and make officials less responsive to concerns about adverse effects of companies' products or practices. When industry engages in health-related philanthropy (the side dish!), governments may be less critical of the unhealthy nature of its leading brands (the main dish) and marketing practices related to those brands.

5.3.2 Research Outcomes

Several scholars have explored the impact of industry sponsorship on the outcomes of research, especially medical research. For example, a meta-analysis of more than 1,000 pharmaceutical studies conducted in 2003 found that industry-sponsored studies were "significantly more likely to reach conclusions that were favorable to the sponsor than were non-industry sponsored studies."[38] The authors believed that poor trial design was responsible for more favorable outcomes. Examples of poor quality methodology include using an inactive control or a comparator drug that is underdosed or poorly absorbed. In its 2009 report on conflicts of interest, the Institute of Medicine (IoM), since renamed the National Academy of Medicine (NAM), offered an explanation that appears more benign. The report's authors suggest, "for-profit companies may be more risk averse than non-profit sponsors and fund mostly studies that seem likely to produce favorable results."[39] However, this explanation only serves to highlight the concern I discuss further below: if industry sponsors are risk-averse or "select for success," then industry funding is distorting academic research, narrowing what we look at by crowding out (or diminishing the possibility of) more groundbreaking research with the potential to challenge paradigms and create new knowledge. Although much of the work correlating industry funding with findings favorable to sponsors has been conducted in the pharmaceutical sector, there is increasing evidence of this phenomenon in other areas of scientific inquiry—including research on food, nutrition, and health.[40]

5.3.3 The Interpretive Gap

Concerns about the impact of funding on research findings are also exacerbated by what I call the *interpretive gap*—the distance between the data and the meaning attributed to them in the report of a study. A systematic review published in the *BMJ* in 2007 found that 55 percent of meta-analyses conducted by individuals with financial ties to a drug company showed more favorable *results*; in contrast, 92 percent reported more favorable *conclusions*.[41] Using remarkably moderate language, the authors of the review suggest there is "a discordance between the data that underlie the results and the interpretation of these data in the conclusions."[42] Unfounded interpretations of data (interpretive gaps) can be exacerbated by simplified and often sensational media coverage of scientific studies. Universities may not always be able to prevent media hype associated with their faculty's research. But they should not fuel the fire with their own hyperbolic press releases.

5.3.4 Research Agenda Distortion

Industry funding influences the research agendas of individual scientists, as many researchers would readily admit. But funding can also distort the research agendas of academic departments, universities, and entire fields of research.[43] The concept of agenda distortion is not premised on an assumption that we agree (or know) precisely what the research agenda of a particular academic institution should be. Members of Congress spend most of their time fundraising. We need not agree on what they should be doing with their time—whether working on legislation related to gun control, agricultural subsidies, or foreign aid—to agree that there is something wrong with this situation. Similarly, we do not have to agree what kind of research a particular scientist, institution, or field as a whole should be exploring in order to say that there is something amiss when they mainly do research that promotes the interests of industry. In short, when I speak of research agenda distortion I am not arguing that there is one "true" research agenda. The point is simply that industry interactions with the academy and government are shaping bodies of scientific research in subtle but extremely important ways that have a profound impact on knowledge, policymaking, and public health.

Although examples abound in many areas of scientific inquiry, the problem is readily apparent in health-related food and nutrition research—especially research on so-called functional foods. These are foods or ingredients that purportedly confer health benefits above and beyond basic nutrition.[44] Much of this research is funded by industry. Not surprisingly, studies tend to explore *only* the potential health *benefits* of consuming the relevant foods and ingredients. They rarely explore potential chronic adverse effects of consuming these foods for their purported health benefits. Studies tend to involve foods or ingredients in which one or more major industry actors have a significant commercial interest. There are, for example, many studies on the health benefits of consuming various kinds of nuts—often using chocolate as the "delivery device!"[45]

Candy companies (and, for that matter, nut trade associations) do not have a commercial interest in funding studies exploring the chronic adverse effects of consuming chocolate-nut bars for their purported health benefits. (These effects include but may not be limited to weight gain due to increased caloric intake.) Other industry-funded studies have explored the purported benefits of consuming yogurt to improve "regularity." But unsurprisingly, they have not explored the potential chronic adverse effects of consuming three servings of yogurt a day to increase regularity.[46] Industry funding for this one-sided research—what I call *felicific research*—undermines the ability of universities to explore the relationships between food and health, conceived more broadly as both positive *and* negative associations.

There is some debate about whether there has been a shift in recent years from basic to applied research in the academy, and whether industry-sponsored research is responsible for this shift.[47] But the basic/applied research distinction does not fully capture the distortion that may result from industry partnerships. If the amount of applied research stays the same, but an increasing proportion is directed toward developing products that may be readily commercialized, this may still cause research agenda distortion. The important distinction may be less about basic *versus* applied research, and more about research aimed primarily at the promotion of the public good rather than the promotion of the commercial interests of sponsors. As other scholars have noted, two features that distinguish academic health research and contribute to its social value are "*[p]ursuit of knowledge as an end,* which accounts for only a portion of academic research but is a portion unique to the public sector," and "*[s]cience and technology not coupled to marketable products,* but highly relevant to public health, social policy, and other practical uses."[48] The food industry is far more likely to develop a satiety supplement that can be sprinkled on fast food than to engage in a long-term project that addresses the social and environmental factors that contribute to obesity[49]—especially when its current business model depends on the preservation of those factors. Similarly, a multinational seed company is far more likely to participate in the development of a GMO staple crop that is more resistant to pesticides than to address its own (or its sector's) contribution to climate changes that are exacerbating the pest problem.

Some professional associations recognize that industry partnerships can distort the activities of research universities and undermine the integrity of those institutions.[50] The CAUT cautions that "[t]he longer term strategic goals of the department, college, and institution should not be diverted or distorted by the shorter term goals of the collaborative agreements and donor arrangements." The organization views distortion as "a function of the proportion of the department/program/college resources devoted to [such an] agreement relative to the overall resources of the unit in question," and "of the proportion of [its] faculty expected to receive much or all of their funding through the agreement."[51] This approach highlights concerns arising from a substantial partnership with one industry sponsor.[52] But multiple smaller collaborations—and the potential for such collaborations—may have cumulative and synergistic distorting effects on an institution and its research. Academic units can and do alter their mission statements and tailor new strategic plans to make them consonant with the research agendas of corporations. This is done in the hope of eliciting industry funding in the future. Anticipated sponsorship can generate reciprocity and influence in a similar way to anticipated gifts.

Industry funding and partnerships can also affect research conducted outside those relationships. Scientists often have both government and industry funding—sometimes for the same study. But they are unlikely to conduct research with public funds that could jeopardize significant future funding from current or potential industry sponsors. Scientists who are neither funded by industry nor involved in industry partnerships may be discouraged by senior administrators from doing research that is inimical to the commercial interests of industry actors who are sponsoring their colleagues. More subtly, they may be deprived of internal support that would facilitate such research, or they may shy away from that research for fear of being marginalized and labeled not a team player. Government agencies commonly require research institutions seeking public funds to demonstrate their willingness and their ability to collaborate with industry.[53] To get more bang for their buck, these agencies are aligning their research priorities with those of industry. As a result, industry funding can shape—or distort—entire fields of research, not just studies funded by industry. These systemic effects are troubling from a scientific perspective. But they are especially problematic when the relevant research may influence public health policy in addition to dietary trends.

5.3.5 Policy Agenda Distortion

Partnerships prioritize public health interventions that promote the interests of industry sponsors. At the same time, they tend to relegate interventions that do not have this effect and put off the table interventions that might undermine sponsors' interests. Structural incentives, such as quarterly reports and bonuses, promote the pursuit of short-term profits in industry and other successes that are demonstrable in the short term. These incentives can carry over into corporate philanthropy, reinforcing pressures on public health officials to demonstrate the impact of their policies and interventions. Public-private partnerships can lead to the prioritization of public health problems that may be resolved in the short term. As the examples in the next chapter demonstrate, these collaborations often employ quick-fix solutions that neglect or, worse still, exacerbate chronic public health problems. The bias toward technological solutions, especially those that are readily commercialized, can lead to the neglect of social and structural solutions. Policy agenda distortion and research agenda distortion are intimately connected. When governments change funding priorities, research agendas are affected. When research agendas are distorted, the products of that research influence policymaking.

5.3.6 "Philanthropogenic" Distortion

Thus far, I have focused on partnerships with corporations and trade associations. But philanthropic foundations also raise concerns about agenda distortion. One recent analysis offers a historical critique of the Rockefeller Foundation's health-related work. The author finds that the Foundation neglected two widespread causes of death, infantile diarrhea and tuberculosis, because these problems were not amenable to simple technological solutions and required prolonged socially oriented interventions.[54] Nor did the Foundation address broader environmental factors such as clean water and sound sanitation systems. Instead, its work was based on a "technological paradigm" in which interventions were "structured in disease control terms based upon a) biological and individual behavioral understandings of disease etiology, and b) technical tools."[55]

Some argue this legacy has been exacerbated by the Bill and Melinda Gates Foundation (BMGF) because, unlike the Rockefeller Foundation, it does not consider public health to be primarily the responsibility of the public sector.[56] We can recognize the contributions of BMGF to global health (among other areas) while also acknowledging its limitations and the related ethical concerns. Like the Rockefeller Foundation, BMGF has been criticized for bias toward technological solutions to health problems. The emphasis on technology is built into its mission: "We do all of our work in collaboration with grantees and other partners, who join with us in taking risks, pushing for new solutions, and harnessing the transformative power of science and technology."[57]

Several commentators have understandably expressed concern about the substantial shareholdings of BMGF and its trust—both direct and indirect shareholdings (through Berkshire Hathaway) in multinational food and beverage corporations, as well as pharmaceutical companies.[58] (Legitimate concerns persist despite some divestments by BMGF.[59]) But the investment issue threatens to overshadow a more subtle concern, BMGF's influence on the WHO and the global health agenda— what one critic calls the Gates Foundation's "sway and dominance."[60] BMGF has been instrumental in promoting and supporting public-private partnerships in global health. One of the most significant is the Global Fund to Fight AIDS, Tuberculosis and Malaria, established with a $100 million grant from BMGF. Although the private sector and private foundations (represented by BMGF) have voting rights on the Board of the Global Fund, the WHO and UNAIDS do not.[61] Even if these structural concerns are remedied, BMGF and other major donors are still bound to have a profound influence on global health, particularly in light of the reciprocity exacerbated by the size of their financial contributions to public health projects. These contributions may be small in terms of the BMGF's total assets, but they are substantial for the recipients.

5.3.7 Framing Effects

To fully appreciate how industry relations can distort research and policy agendas, we need to understand the framing effects of those relations. Framing is a process in which "communicators, consciously or unconsciously, act to construct a point of view that encourages the facts of a given situation to be interpreted by others in a particular manner."[62] Framing makes certain features of a situation more salient than others. Framing can function in a number of different ways: (1) defining problems, (2) diagnosing causes, (3) making moral judgments, and (4) proposing remedies.[63]

Applying this taxonomy and other insights from framing analysis can help us recognize the ways in which obesity is commonly framed. First, the problem is *defined* at the level of the individual (the *micro* level) rather than as a systemic problem with institutional (*meso*) and social (*macro*) dimensions. This shifts attention away from the very dimensions at which industry actors commonly operate (for example, manufacturing, distribution, and marketing).[64] Second, the principal *cause* is framed as "consumer behavior," with an emphasis on physical inactivity.[65] Even when the framing encompasses food and beverage consumption, the influence of corporate strategies on such behaviors (through labeling and marketing), and the influence of multinational corporations on food systems more broadly are both downplayed. Third, *moral judgments* are directed at individuals for failing to make "healthy choices." This neglects the responsibility of corporations for exerting powerful influences over consumer behavior and for shaping the food system.[66] Fourth, *remedies* focus on changing individual behavior (for example, exercise initiatives in local parks). They rarely include effective measures to address the practices of corporations that may be contributing to or exacerbating the problem. Consistent with and fueling the last of these is the emphasis on working with industry and reaching a *consensus* with, rather than regulating, industry.

Partnerships not only influence the framing of problems and their solutions (often called, respectively, *diagnostic* and *prognostic framing*). They also contribute to *motivational framing*—that is, the rhetoric used to provide a rationale for action.[67] Public officials and policymakers commonly tell us that "industry must be part of the solution," that we cannot solve obesity without industry, and that partnering with industry is a "win-win-win," that is, a win for government, industry, and "consumers" (formerly, the public!)[68]

Framing may, of course, take place at multiple levels—from the framing of the research question in a small interventional health study or a local government exercise initiative to the development of transnational health strategy.[69] In addition to geographic scope, framing may also vary in temporal scope, from discrete interventions to the formulation of longer term policy. Each level of framing may reflect and contribute to the others. Framing at the international level (involving the WHO, the FAO or both) is likely to influence framing at the national and local levels. When national governments frame an issue in a particular way, this may influence not only local governments but also intergovernmental organizations in whose meetings national officials participate.

At all levels, there are indications that the food industry has influenced the framing of obesity as a question of individual behavior, personal responsibility, and physical inactivity.[70] Emphasis on these factors downplays the significance of what some public health experts call "obesogenic environments," in particular, the food system and the role that large multinational corporations play in the creation and operation of that system.[71] We find evidence of these framing effects in both public health research and policy interventions.

Recent archival research revealed that in the 1960s and 1970s, the sugar industry sponsored a research program that successfully cast doubt about the hazards of sucrose while promoting fat as the dietary culprit in coronary heart disease.[72] This strategy clearly prefigures contemporary approaches that focus attention on lack of physical activity. Kelly Brownell and Kenneth Warner have argued that food companies, trade associations, and "political front groups" have been "aggressive in attempting to shape public and legislator opinion" and that "the heart of this strategy is a script built on values of personal responsibility."[73] This emphasis has not only influenced the way research is framed. It imperils trust in studies exploring associations between personal behavior and obesity. The editors of a recent obesity issue of the *Journal of Public Health Policy* expressed concern that "research studies concentrating on personal behavior and responsibility as causes of the obesity epidemic do little but offer cover to an industry seeking to downplay its own responsibility" for the public health crisis.[74]

The work of Nicolas Christakis, who argues that obesity "spreads" through networks of relations between individuals,[75] remains appealing both to industry and to policymakers who wish to collaborate with industry. In 2010, Britain's secretary of state for health summarized this work as follows: "if a friend becomes obese your chances of becoming obese increase by more than half." This work has fueled provocative headlines that ask, "Are Your Friends Making You Fat?"[76] It is not surprising that people who are obese have friends and family who are also obese. Friends and family in low-income neighborhoods are likely to be subjected to similarly inadequate living and working conditions, and to experience poor access to healthy foods. In short, they are likely to be exposed to the same influences on and social and environmental determinants of health.[77]

Food industry actors—especially, soda companies—use partnerships to emphasize inactivity rather than the consumption of their calorie-rich products as the main cause of obesity.[78] We can and should recognize the value of physical activity initiatives in public spaces while also flagging ethical perils that arise when these activities are funded by or conducted in partnership with food and soda industry actors. The emphasis on individual responsibility, and physical inactivity in particular, also promotes what might be called a *nudging bias* in obesity policy—that is, a bias toward trying to influence the decisions and behaviors of individuals.[79] Nudging has been institutionalized in a number of countries.[80] As some critics of this approach have observed, nudging "pitches government action at the soft end of policy interventions," especially from the perspective of corporations.[81] This bias leads to the neglect of interventions directed at changing corporate rather than individual behaviors.

Framing effects are arguably some of the most subtle challenges arising from industry interactions. They are compounded and exacerbated by collaborations with multiple industry actors. And we tend not to see them because they shape what we see.

5.4 CONCLUSION

A scholar of international relations recently asked me, "What are the current priorities in global health?" "The more fundamental question is," I replied, "who gets to determine those priorities?" Critics often raise concerns about the democratic accountability of intergovernmental organizations such as the WHO. But when corporations (and philanthropic foundations) determine public health agendas, there is no democratic accountability whatsoever. In this chapter, I have tried to show how corporations build webs of relations with academic institutions and civil society organizations in order to influence research and policy agendas, and to frame public health problems and potential solutions in ways that protect and promote their commercial interests. Nowhere has this been more conspicuous than in the webs of influence artfully constructed by the soda industry. In the next chapter, I use these and other case studies to tease out some of the finer strands, while keeping in view the webs of which they are an intrinsic part.

6

Case Studies and Caveats

Next time you hear of a big food or beverage company sponsoring an after-school physical activity program in your community, you can be sure they'll say it's to show "our company's concern for our kids' health." But the real intent is to look angelic while making consumers feel good about the brand and drawing attention away from the unhealthful nature of the company's products. "Posing for holy cards," as one of my colleagues used to put it.

—MICHAEL MUDD, former VP, Global Corporate Affairs, Kraft Foods[1]

Unhealthy diets are now a greater threat to global health than tobacco. . . . [O]besity continues to advance—and diabetes, heart disease and other health complications along with it. The warning signs are not being heard.

—OLIVIER DE SCHUTTER, former UN Special Rapporteur on the Right to Food[2]

THIS CHAPTER REVIEWS a variety of partnerships involving corporations and trade associations in the food and beverage sector. As we shall see, snack food and soda companies are frequent participants. The widespread use of partnerships in this sector is shaping a variety of public health interventions, especially in relation to obesity. I outline some of the ways in which they are problematic, drawing on the theories and methods developed earlier in the book. In order to provide a richer context for this analysis, I first discuss the increasing rates of obesity; the associations between obesity and various noncommunicable diseases (NCDs) such as diabetes; and the role of multinational food and beverage corporations in the global food system.

Partnerships occur at all levels—from the local (for example, an exercise initiative in a London borough) to the global (policies of the UN, the WHO, and the FAO).[3] The local, the national, and the global are interrelated. Local and national partnerships reflect international trends, and the support of national governments for these approaches influences the development of global policies (see Appendix A). The examples from the food and beverage sector, while of special importance to public health, are not sui generis. They reflect a systemic problem that should concern policymakers in every domain.

6.1 THE PUBLIC HEALTH PROBLEM AND THE POLICY RESPONSES

In 1992, Dr. Hisroshi Nakajima, director general of the WHO, observed that the International Conference on Nutrition (1992), co-organized by the WHO and FAO, was "the first [conference] of its kind where health and agriculture...joined together to address the nutritional security of all peoples."[4] At that time, the consensus was that undernutrition was the "dominant nutrition problem." But Nakajima recognized that diet-related NCDs were increasing in many developed countries. By the time of the Second International Conference on Nutrition (ICN2, 2014) more than two decades later, overnutrition had supplanted undernutrition as the dominant concern. The 2013 Global Burden of Disease study concluded that rates of overweight, obesity, and NCDs were still increasing and that there had been "no national success story" addressing obesity in the last thirty-three years.[5] The Rome Declaration on Nutrition (adopted at ICN2, 2014) reinforced this distressing conclusion. The declaration acknowledged that "overweight and obesity among both children and adults have been increasing rapidly in all regions, with 42 million children under five years of age affected by overweight in 2013 and over 500 million adults affected by obesity in 2010."[6]

Human genetics may play a role at the individual level. But they obviously cannot explain large changes in weight and health at the population level. If they did, we would be witnessing evolution at hyper-speed! It is also nostalgic, unconvincing, and somewhat insulting to suggest that people today have less "moral fiber" or self-control than previous generations. Far more plausible explanations draw on systemic changes in the environments in which we live, work, and travel, including food systems that affect what we eat and drink. Researchers have found that increased consumption of meals outside the home is associated with increased caloric and fat intake.[7] Recent studies also suggest that the consumption of sugar-sweetened beverages is very strongly associated with increasing rates of overweight, obesity, and NCDs even when controlling for other factors, including lack of physical activity.[8]

It is often assumed that the consumption of soft drinks and processed foods that are high in sugar, fat, salt, or a combination thereof is mainly a problem in high-income countries. However, the greatest growth in the consumption of snacks, soft drinks, and processed foods is in low- and middle-income countries, with "market penetration" in middle-income countries similar to that in high-income countries.[9] This is no surprise given food and beverage companies' efforts to penetrate these markets. (A recent article in the *New York Times* put it rather succinctly: "As growth slows in wealthy countries, Western food companies are aggressively expanding in developed nations."[10]) For several years, Mexico's consumption of soft drinks exceeded that of any other country, with the average person drinking more than 300 liters per year. (The introduction of a soda tax has since helped reduce consumption.[11]) Mexico has the highest rate of childhood obesity among developing countries; and, of all countries, it is second only to the United States. India is also one of the fastest-growing soft drink markets in the world, and soda companies are exploiting commercial opportunities there too.[12]

* * *

In December 2005, an Institute of Medicine (IoM) report concluded that food and beverage marketing practices directed at children and youth were "out of balance with healthful diets and contribute to an environment that puts their health at risk."[13] The report urged the food industry to take action. It recommended that food and beverage companies "use their creativity, resources, and full range of marketing practices to promote and support more healthful diets for children and youth." It also recommended that fast food restaurants chains promote more "healthful meals." These exhortations largely went unheeded. In 2011, another review examined industry marketing of food and beverages to children and adolescents in the United States for the five-year period following the IoM report. The authors of the review concluded that "extensive progress" had *not* been made by "any industry stakeholder" in response to IoM's recommendations.[14]

In 2012, the Federal Trade Commission (FTC) produced its own report reviewing food marketing to children and adolescents for the period 2006 to 2009.[15] Although this report acknowledged that the food and beverage industry had taken "several positive steps," it concluded that many of these steps were minimal or not significant and that much remained to be done. The FTC found that snacks marketed to both children and teens showed "minimal or no improvements in nutrition" in this period.[16] It concluded that nutritional improvements in cereal marketed to children and teens were "generally too small to be nutritionally meaningful in the context of the daily diet."[17] The report's authors also found that, by the end of the period of study, water and juice continued to represent a small percentage of overall youth drink marketing (8 percent and 16 percent of drinks marketed to teens and children respectively.)[18] These findings were consistent with a larger body of research suggesting that industry practices, on the whole, have remained relatively unchanged in the United States; and that government collaborations with industry and attempts at exhorting companies to make their manufacturing and marketing processes healthier have been largely unsuccessful.

Findings at the international level are similar to those in the United States. The 2011 UN Political Declaration on NCDs called on member states to address the marketing of foods high in fat, sugar, or salt to children; to take measures to reduce salt, sugar, saturated fats, and trans fats in foods; and to promote policies that support the production of and facilitate access to foods that contribute to a healthy diet (including local produce).[19] The Declaration also called directly on the private sector to curtail the marketing of unhealthy foods to children; reformulate products to provide healthier options that are affordable and accessible; follow labeling standards; and reduce salt content (para. 44).

Once again, these exhortations urging industry to take voluntary action had little effect. Three years later, the UN High-Level Meeting on NCDs in July 2014 concluded that insufficient progress had been made and that further action was necessary.[20] The authors of the meeting's Outcome Document used far more muted language than the UN Special Rapporteur on the Right to Food quoted in the epigraph to this chapter! They found that the private sector had made only "limited progress" in response to the calls in paragraph 44 of the 2011 Declaration for companies to address marketing to children, reformulation, labeling, and salt.[21] Documents drafted in preparation for the 2018 UN High-Level Meeting continue to exhort the private sector to do more, while reiterating that progress toward the reduction in NCDs has generally been "inadequate" and "disappointing" (see Appendix A).

* * *

Voluntary, collaborative, and consensual approaches for improving food manufacturing and marketing practices have dominated global nutrition and health policy for more than two decades. Several international policies invite and encourage partnerships with industry actors—most recently, the UN's Sustainable Development Goals. I lay out some of the policies of the UN and two of its specialized agencies—the WHO and FAO—in more detail in Appendix A.[22] A few themes emerge. First, whether or not framed as "partnership strategies" or policies of "engagement," these strategies are often adopted without rigorous policies to address the systemic ethical issues they raise. Second, although policies frequently acknowledge conflicts of interest concerns, international agencies have not developed—and are not developing—broader strategies to address industry influence. Third, international agencies often speak with two voices, further imperiling their integrity. One voice acknowledges the threat posed by industry influence. The other *encourages* private sector bodies to partner with them by touting the opportunities for influence that these relationships provide!

International approaches both inform and reflect policies and practices at the national and local level. In the remainder of this chapter, I analyze examples of partnerships involving three countries, the United States, the United Kingdom, and India. This analysis also reveals the ways in which the distinction between partnership at the national and international level is artificial: partnerships and multistakeholder initiatives often involve local and national governments, as well as intergovernmental organizations.

6.2 PARTNERSHIP CASE STUDIES

The danger in looking at individual partnerships or other close relationships with industry in isolation is that this neglects the cumulative and synergistic effects of these arrangements. However, some partnerships are clearly ethically problematic when considered in isolation. I present these case studies with two caveats. First, I do not purport to examine each case study exhaustively. That would require a thorough assessment with access to documents not in the public domain, as well as interviews of participants and other parties affected by these arrangements. Instead, I flag the most ethically problematic features based on materials currently in the public domain. Second, partnerships may still raise ethical concerns even if they do not possess the problematic features identified in the collaborations described in this chapter. As we saw in chapter 5, the cumulative effects of partnerships—and, more broadly, the webs of relations woven by industry strategies of influence—are of great ethical significance and should not be neglected.

6.2.1 *The American Beverage Association, a Soda Tax,*
and Children's Hospital of Philadelphia

As we learned in chapter 1, some scholars of philanthropy construe "one-off" gifts as a form a "partnership."[23] Although this characterization may appear counterintuitive to some readers, the following case demonstrates that a "one-off" gift may have enduring effects similar to those involved in an ongoing relationship. In 2011, the American Beverage Association (ABA), the trade association for the nonalcoholic beverage industry in the United States, coordinated a $10 million gift to the Children's Hospital of Philadelphia to fund clinical care, policy research, outreach, and prevention efforts related to childhood obesity.[24] The sum was pledged while the Philadelphia City Council was considering a resolution to introduce a two-cents-per-ounce tax on sugar-sweetened beverages. The donation, which supplemented the ABA's already substantial lobbying expenditures,[25] was made through a foundation established by the ABA.[26] The $10 million came largely from funds provided directly for this purpose by Coca-Cola, PepsiCo, and the Dr. Pepper/Snapple Group.[27] The proposed tax would have raised an estimated $77 million annually.[28] However, the resolution was defeated in 2011. Although the city finally passed a soda tax resolution in the summer of 2016,[29] the trade association's gift may have helped keep the tax at bay for five years—making it rather a sound investment from the point of view of the soda companies.

I understand the temptation for the hospital and its charitable foundation to accept the gift. But the donation imperiled the integrity of the hospital. Its mission statement asserts, "preventing disease is at least as important as treating illnesses."[30] The gift jeopardized the goal of prevention by burnishing the reputation of—and conferring a health halo on—the soda company donors and their leading brands. Given that soda consumption plays a significant role in obesity rates even after controlling for other factors, the mere acceptance of the gift has the potential to exacerbate rather than prevent NCDs associated with obesity. No matter when the gift was pledged, there would be ethical perils. But these perils were exacerbated by the timing of the pledge.

At present, there is no evidence in the public domain of an explicit quid pro quo—one or more city councilors voting against the soda tax proposal in exchange for the donation to the city's flagship children's hospital. But, as we learned in chapter 4, reciprocity and influence does not depend on a direct or explicit exchange. Councilors could still have been influenced by a pledge to an institution they value and support—contributing, in turn, to the failure of a measure that could have reduced rates of childhood obesity and diet-related NCDs in Philadelphia.[31]

The donation led some academics to question the trustworthiness of the soda industry.[32] But I am more concerned about the threats it posed to trust in the nonindustry actors involved. Members of the City Council might have had a variety of reasons for rejecting the soda tax, but the donation inevitably led some critics to call their motives into question. While the hospital could have been criticized for accepting any donation from the beverage industry to fund obesity initiatives, this particular gift was all the more likely to be considered "tainted" because it was pledged when the soda tax proposal was under consideration.[33] (After the gift was received, the hospital offered to fund anti-obesity education through the city's public health centers. However, the city's health commissioner terminated discussions when he learned that the funds would come from the soda industry's donation.[34] This decision reflects legitimate concerns about the potential impact of the gift and its acceptance on trust and confidence in the city government.)

This case is not an isolated example. On the contrary, the ABA's concerted action in Philadelphia was part of a broader soda industry strategy. Faced with the prospect of a soda tax in Chicago, Coke executives announced in 2012 that they would contribute $3 million to Chicago Park District exercise and nutrition classes, and in 2013, its "philanthropic arm" announced a $2.59 million grant for 50,000 recycling bins with images of Coca-Cola products on the lid.[35] This strategy bought the soda companies some time. Berkeley was the first city to pass a soda tax in 2015, and, in 2016, the tide appeared to turn: Philadelphia, San Francisco, Boulder, and Cook

County, Illinois (where Chicago is located) all adopted soda taxes.[36] But the ABA got a good return for its "philanthropic investment." Its efforts arguably staved off the tax in Philadelphia for more than half a decade. We should also expect to see a similar industry strategy going forward in attempts to roll back these city and county taxes and to prevent similar taxes at the state level. (Notably, the Cook County soda tax was rather short-lived—it was repealed at the end of 2017.)

6.2.2 *Coca-Cola, Local Government in Britain, and "ParkLives"*

In May 2013, Coca-Cola launched a "partnership" program with the London borough of Newham, and the city councils in Newcastle and Birmingham. Other public authorities have since joined, and the company now claims that the program operates in forty-five locations including several "disadvantaged areas" across Britain. The initiative was initially called "Coca-Cola Zero ParkLives" (expressly referring to one of the company's leading brands). But the name was later changed to "ParkLives."[37] The program is intended to promote physical activity by sponsoring a variety of exercise initiatives (from yoga classes to boxing) in parks and public spaces. Coca-Cola plans further expansion, and has pledged to spend £20 million by 2020. Despite the name change, the program still uses a logo with at least three devices that tie it directly to Coca-Cola products. The ParkLives logo takes the form of a white bottle cap. Within the cap, the "I" in ParkLives is in the shape of the traditional contoured Coke bottle. The white cap also contains the familiar red Coca-Cola logo. The company's logo and contoured bottle are both registered trademarks. The ParkLives logo (containing the company's familiar registered trademarks) is printed on T-shirts and sweatshirts worn by participants in the program. It also appears on local government and company webpages promoting the program.

Not surprisingly, this initiative has attracted criticism.[38] Concerns include framing effects (which I explained more fully in chapter 5). In particular, public health experts have complained that the food and beverage industry is using these kinds of partnerships "to emphasize that inactivity—not the promotion and consumption of its calorie-rich products—is the prime cause of obesity."[39] The partnership also raises integrity concerns. The use of the company's name and its logo in association with a health-related initiative may create an unwarranted positive health association for Coca-Cola and its products. (I discussed "health halos" and "logo effects" in more detail in chapter 5.) By promoting the consumption of sugar-sweetened beverages (among other Coke products) and increasing loyalty for the company's leading brands, these partnerships imperil public health. That is especially problematic given the public health duties imposed on local authorities in England, pursuant to the Health and Social Care Act 2012. The timing is notable too—these duties took effect from April 1, 2013, the month before the ParkLives initiative was launched. Many local authorities have also incorporated these obligations into their mission statements. For example, the London borough of Newham's website states: "We are responsible for promoting and protecting the health and wellbeing of people who live in Newham. We took over this duty from the NHS in 2013." Alas, the Borough does not seem to have fully appreciated the ways in which ParkLives might undermine its public health mission and purpose, and—as a result—its own integrity. In addition, by promoting Coca-Cola and its products, the initiative could undermine its own purported goal of promoting healthier lifestyles—exacerbating the very problem it is supposed to address.

The initiative is subject to periodic evaluation. But the evaluation process does not appear to explore the extent to which the initiative has increased consumption of Coke products. (Nor does it explore the impact of the initiative on trust and confidence in the local authorities that have chosen to "partner" with the soda company.) The program's 2017 report concluded, "ParkLives is helping to ensure that there are positive corporate perceptions, as those who are aware of ParkLives are more likely to signify positive statements of corporate reputation."[40] The report includes this sample testimonial: "I feel as though a large multi-national company is helping my community." Given what we know about reciprocity and influence, this should not be surprising. In light of what we have learned about industry webs of influence, we should also not be surprised that the soda company used its existing relationship with a national sports charity to help overcome initial skepticism or resistance to this partnership initiative.[41] Since the program was launched, "outreach" efforts have included seeking the support of health professionals by publishing an e-newsletter in the leading medical journal for general practitioners and distributing a promotional video to doctors' surgeries.[42]

6.2.3 The US Department of Agriculture, Cheese Promotion, and "MyPlate"

Although the previous examples involve the soda industry, fast food companies also engage in these kinds of relationships. Investigative reporting by the *New York Times* revealed a vivid example of an arrangement involving several fast food chains and the US Department of Agriculture (USDA). The USDA arguably has an internally conflicting mission. Its strategic plan commits the department to "expanding markets for agricultural products" and "improving nutrition and health by providing . . . nutrition education and promotion."[43] However, these activities can and do conflict—as the case I discuss here demonstrates—when the promotion of certain products might lead to less healthy consumption patterns. In 2010, the *Times* revealed that Dairy Management, Inc.—a corporation created by federal statute and funded primarily by agribusiness through the dairy check-off program—had been partnering covertly with fast food chains to increase the amount of cheese in their menu items.[44] The arrangements, formally approved by the USDA, resulted in one chain's creation of the cheese-stuffed pizza crust, and a new menu item created by another with eight times as much cheese as its average menu item.

These collaborations were clearly in tension with the health and nutrition component of the USDA's mission. They were also at odds with the "key recommendation" in the Dietary Guidelines (issued by the USDA in collaboration with the Department of Health and Human Services) to limit the intake of saturated fats.[45] The *New York Times* highlighted this contradiction with the blunt headline: "While Warning About Fat, U.S. Pushes Cheese Sales." The article understandably called into question the integrity of the USDA. In addition, it raised profound trust-related concerns. These arrangements, which had been approved by the secretaries of agriculture in both the George W. Bush and Obama administrations, were intended to remain confidential. Transparency alone cannot remedy all the ethical challenges presented by public-private partnerships.[46] But this case reveals how trust may be further imperiled when partnerships are conducted behind closed doors.

In June 2011, just a few months after the *New York Times* exposed these collaborations, the USDA launched "MyPlate," a visual aid designed to provide simplified dietary guidance to Americans (http://www.choosemyplate.gov). MyPlate has been criticized on several grounds—among them (a) its failure to distinguish between red meat or processed meat and other sources of protein, such as fish, poultry, beans, and nuts; (b) its failure to distinguish between whole grains and refined grains; (c) its silence on sugar-sweetened beverages; and (d) its recommendation that dairy should be a component of every meal.[47] While any simplified dietary guidance is likely to attract criticism, what unites these complaints is that all the features criticized operate to the benefit of powerful commercial interests in the food and agriculture sector. Walter Willett, chair of Nutrition at Harvard argued, "MyPlate mixes science with the influence of powerful agricultural interests, which is not the recipe for healthy eating."[48]

Whether or not one agrees with Willett's criticisms of MyPlate, public sector entities contemplating public-private partnerships should recognize that these arrangements can undermine trust and confidence in public partners. Loss of trust in one of the public partner's activities or responsibilities can also undermine trust related to another. This problem is illustrated by the USDA's use of its network of (among others) industry partners to disseminate the "MyPlate" icon.

The ChooseMyPlate.gov website offers national and multinational companies the opportunity to become "national strategic partners." (Other organizations may apply, but, if they are not national in scope, they can only join as "community partners.") A company wishing to join must complete a one-page application form and sign a two-page memorandum of intent.[49] The company declares in the latter that it has "a mission consistent with the Dietary Guidelines for Americans; and . . . a health mandate consistent with USDA Food, Nutrition, and Consumer Services," the unit in which the CNPP (the USDA's Center for Nutrition Policy and Promotion) is housed. Both parties to the memorandum attest that they have the "*common goals* of ensuring the *completeness and accuracy* of all information on nutrition disseminated to the public, particularly such information directed at school-age children and their parents" (emphasis added). Current national strategic partners include public relations and marketing firms that represent the food industry, as well as several multinational food, beverage, and restaurant companies, and their trade associations.[50]

The memorandum downplays the obvious divergence in the commercial interests of food companies and the public health mission of the CNPP. According to its website, the CNPP's mission is "to improve the health of Americans by developing and promoting dietary guidance that links scientific research to the nutrition needs of consumers."[51] It is not difficult to identify actual or potential tensions between this mission and the commercial interests of a national or multinational food company.[52] If communicating dietary guidance or nutrition information might undermine the promotion and sale of the company's products—particularly its leading brands—it is not in the company's interests to do so. Nor is it in the company's interests to communicate "complete" information when an incomplete account might be far more effective in promoting sales. Regulators are frequently called upon to take action against food companies for misleading labeling and marketing. These corporate practices are widespread even though there are only a few high-profile cases that attract significant media attention.[53]

The CNPP has actively encouraged corporations to apply to join its "Nutrition Communicators Network" by citing the "credibility associated with federal government partnership."[54] However, the CNPP does not seem to recognize that conferring credibility on food companies may promote products that contribute to unhealthy eating patterns, undermining the CNPP's mission and, in turn, its integrity. Given that some of its partners are food companies that continue to produce and promote foods that are high in sugar, fat, salt, or some combination thereof,[55] and that other partners are public relations and marketing firms that represent food companies, the program may also undermine trust and confidence in the CNPP. The Center has justified the partnership program on the grounds that it is "a way for us to extend our reach."[56] However, an institution's "reach" is a function not only of its ability to communicate and disseminate but also its credibility. (The program may burnish private sector partners' reputations while at the same time undermining the Center's credibility. Such effects are not mutually exclusive. They may occur at the same time but in different populations, or at different times within the same population.)

Finally, it is worth emphasizing that the CNPP's national strategic partners network shows how partnerships may be ethically problematic *even when no money changes hands*. Membership in the network itself provides a valuable service to companies, conferring a health halo on its products and burnishing its corporate reputation. Food companies would have to pay considerable sums of money to public relations firms for comparable services.

6.2.4 Partnership for a Healthier America (PHA)

The Partnership for a Healthier America (PHA) was launched in 2010 by First Lady Michelle Obama. PHA works with individual companies to create voluntary pledges. Echoing language often used by proponents of public-private partnerships, PHA has defended its voluntary approach to improving corporate products and practices by arguing it "has no interest in forcing industry to meet unrealistic benchmarks" and that it wants the private sector "with us because, quite simply, we will not succeed without it."[57] Although it is formally an independent foundation, PHA's 2010 launch was coordinated and publicized by the White House—giving it the imprimatur of the executive branch, and conferring the associated reputational benefits on participating companies.[58] By the end of the Obama administration, PHA's website listed 137 "partners" who had made commitments, including, among others, fast food and confectionary companies. The foundation continues to operate under the leadership of the former First Lady (among others) and has more than 200 partners. They now include, notably, the American Beverage Association (the trade association for soda companies discussed at length earlier).

A recent article authored by directors and staff at PHA asserts the PHA's "guiding principles for commitments are rigorous and hold public companies accountable."[59] The article emphasizes the "*verification of the commitments* through unbiased, independent third party evaluators." But the authors do not make clear what happens when companies fail to meet their commitments.[60] They also acknowledge, "commitments that do not advance the business interests of the company making the commitment are not typically sustainable."[61] (Given this approach, it is not surprising that an important metric of success appears to be *sales*—whether of bottled water or food in hospital cafeterias.) The response to the initiative from some commentators outside PHA has been far more critical.

Despite PHA's claims of success, critics argue, there are no statistical analyses of the causal relationship between either the PHA's strategies or the companies' commitments, on the one hand, and obesity rates on the other.[62] Critics have also pointed out that the pledges involving the creation and promotion of healthier options are relatively modest. The dean of the School of Nutrition Science and Policy at Tufts University has also argued that the voluntary pledge is "a stroke of marketing genius, turning [companies'] steadily declining marketing sales into a novel opportunity for self-promotion."[63] This kind of pledge, he argues, is effectively a "sham" that anticipates and then takes credit for market trends.

One fast food company pledged $41 million in "media value"—that is, marketing and advertising to children to encourage healthy eating, fruits and vegetables.[64] Although a breakdown of this spending is not publicly available, we should anticipate that much of the expenditure is directed at promotion of the company's own products. Even so, this commitment is minimal when compared to the company's total advertising revenue—more than half a billion dollars every year from 2012-2015.[65] Previous studies have also shown that by positioning itself as healthy, the same company has led customers to underestimate the caloric content of meals and to order "energy-dense" dishes and desserts.[66] If this partnership confers a further health halo on the company and its products, it may undermine the very goal it is intended to achieve.

Other critics also highlight the concern I characterize in the previous chapter as *agenda distortion,* and its implications for public health. Voluntary pledges have (what economists call) "opportunity costs" because they "replace and eliminate the space in which other efforts might develop that actually could reduce obesity and public health."[67] In addition, they note partnerships "can degrade the public's trust in the ability of public institutions to competently advance the public's wellbeing on matters of health, nutrition, and quality food access." [68]

6.2.5 Public Health Responsibility Deal Networks, UK

While PHA was negotiating pledges with individual companies in the United States, the British government adopted a "sectoral" approach. Under the Public Health Responsibility Deal Networks (RDNs), voluntary pledges relating to alcohol, food, health at work, and physical activity were established in collaboration with selected industry actors and NGOs. The majority of participants were industry representatives. Once they had formulated the pledges, other industry actors were invited to sign on to the pledges as "partners." Hundreds did so.

The pledges were voluntary, nonbinding commitments, and there was no enforcement mechanism. The networks were heavily criticized for these reasons—and for the leadership role given to industry actors whose products and activities contribute to the problem that the networks were intended to address. As one critic noted, PepsiCo chaired the food subgroup on calories. The company owns Walker's Crisps, the British cousin of Frito-Lay (also owned by PepsiCo).[69]

Critics complained that public interest groups were not adequately represented and warned that "representation alone does not guarantee influence." The Faculty of Public Health—a prominent professional association with a mission to improve public health—withdrew its participation, citing concerns about the prioritization of industry interests over public health.[70] Like many examples discussed in this chapter, these voluntary arrangements risk burnishing the reputation of food and beverage companies while jeopardizing the credibility of a government agency, in this case the Ministry of Health. The reputational gains to the companies were not matched by public health gains. Recent studies found that companies tended to commit to actions they would have undertaken in any event (even absent the pledges.[71]) Some public health experts argue that, to be effective, pledges would need to be accompanied by incentives, monitoring, and effective sanctions; others find their analysis of the RDNs provides strong support for the view that "regulation is the way forward to deliver on public health outcomes."[72]

The RDN approach also illustrates how the pursuit of *common ground* can put off the table measures that might promote the *common good.* When the networks were launched, the secretary of state for health, Andrew Lansley, said that pledges related to price were not on the table. But he did not explain why. European competition law (which regulates industry in similar ways to antitrust law in the United States) prohibits a range of agreements and concerted practices that have as their object or effect the prevention, restriction, or distortion of competition.[73] A consensual pledge between competing companies to raise the price of foods and beverages that are high in sugar or fat (to pick just one obvious example) would violate this prohibition. However, EU law does not prevent national legislatures from imposing a *tax* that seeks to regulate consumption by increasing the price of foods and beverages that might be contributing to obesity and diet-related NCDs. Consensual approaches thus eliminate from consideration a measure (raising the prices of unhealthy foods) that could reduce consumption in the short term and improve public health in the long term.[74] (It would take another six years for the British government to adopt a two-tier soda tax, an approach that induced some manufacturers to reduce the sugar content of SSBs—even before it came into effect in 2018—in order to avoid the higher tax level).[75]

6.2.6 UN Habitat Program: Support My School, India

Industry partnerships sometimes involve international agencies in conjunction with local and national governments. In January 2011, Coca-Cola launched the "Support My School Project" in partnership with, among others, New Delhi Television, the Indian government, and UN Habitat—a United Nations program whose mission is "to promote socially and environmentally sustainable human settlements development and the achievement of adequate shelter for all."[76] The goal of the partnership was to improve access to water, sanitation, and facilities in Indian schools.[77] No one would dispute the value of this goal. It has the potential not only to improve education and health but also to address a gender equity issue. Girls tend to drop out of school before boys when sanitation is poor. However, as an Atlanta-based trade publication succinctly put it: "Coca-Cola is working to change education in rural India through the Support My School campaign. India is a major market for the Atlanta-based beverage giant."[78] For an initial investment in 2011 of approximately $200,000 and a further pledge of $800,000,[79] Coca-Cola was the beneficiary of a high-profile publicity and promotion campaign, thanks in no small part to another major partner, New Delhi Television. The campaign has used the soda company's logo and the color scheme of its leading brand in a variety of activities and events, including a twelve-hour telethon designed to stage the company's second pledge.

The initiative was the subject of a case study in an Indian business journal. The authors of the case study appear conspicuously enthusiastic about Support My School, describing the "[s]parkling spirits and dazzling performances" during the initiative's telethon.[80] However, the authors fail to comment on a photograph they include from the launch. The image shows participants seated behind a giant banner on which the soda company's logo is the largest of all the participants' logos. That logo is clearly visible in at least four different places. In contrast, the logo of UN Habitat appears just once, close to the ground, and partially obstructed by the speakers' chairs. Intentional or not, the positioning and visibility of the participants' logos communicates a powerful message about which partners are important and which are not.

If we simply balance the risks and potential benefits of this partnership, it is easy to see how the calculus might come out in favor of the arrangement. Clean sanitation is essential to retain children in schools, so they can be healthy and educated. If the partnership does influence consumption habits in India, including those of school children, and they drink more sugar-sweetened beverages as a result, there will be adverse health implications. These are chronic effects. Compared to the acute health risks of inadequate sanitation, they might seem less weighty. But I do not believe a simple risk-benefit analysis is capable of addressing the systemic ethical issues raised by this partnership. If, instead, we adopt the approach I advocate in this book, we should quickly begin to see why this partnership is ethically problematic—especially for UN Habitat.

Although NDTV announced with much fanfare that the initiative had reached 1,000 schools by 2017, there appears to have been no independent assessment of the impact of the initiative on soda consumption. If the partnership increased the consumption of Coke products (as Coca-Cola surely intended),[81] it undermined the integrity of UN Habitat. The program's mission is to promote sustainability. But promoting the consumption of Coke products undermines sustainability in three ways. First, the manufacture of the company's beverages serves to deplete already stretched local water supplies in India. Second, the package and sale of these products in plastic bottles is also not sustainable from an environmental perspective. Third, given the contribution of the company's products to obesity and diet-related NCDs, increasing sales of these products is not sustainable from a public health perspective.[82] While this public health concern is most acute in the case of sugar-sweetened beverages and energy drinks, the concerns about environmental sustainability apply to all the company's beverages. For similar reasons, the partnership imperils trust in UN Habitat. Critics may doubt whether the program can be relied on to promote its own sustainability mission.

The partnership also undermines the integrity of the UN more broadly. The Political Declaration adopted by the UN General Assembly following the 2011 UN High-Level Meeting on NCDs emphasized the importance of "whole-of-government" and "health in all policies" approaches. Put simply, the UN was exhorting member states to infuse all policymaking with a concern for the impact of those policies on NCDs—whatever the department making the policy, whatever the subject matter of the policy. However, a public-private partnership that seeks to address sanitation while promoting a soda company seems to reflect just the kind of fragmented policymaking and implementation that the UN strongly discourages.

* * *

All the partnerships discussed in section 6.2 involve government bodies. Sometimes these partnerships include academic institutions and civil society organizations, in addition to government and industry. The Public Health Responsibility Deal Networks in Britain were an example of this. Governments often bring on board universities and public health NGOs to enhance the legitimacy of their partnerships with industry. These arrangements are sometimes described as "multistakeholder initiatives" (MSIs), about which I say more in chapter 8. But sometimes industry actors partner solely with an academic institution or public health NGO. Relationships with research universities deserve special mention not only because they are pervasive, but also because of their impact on science, behavior, public health, and public policy.

6.3 INDUSTRY PARTNERSHIPS WITH RESEARCH UNIVERSITIES

There are a host of individual industry-academy case studies that raise serious ethical and public health concerns. Consider, for example, a study co-funded by a snack food company to demonstrate the health benefits of snacking.[83] Or another study that one journalist described as "thinner-children-ate-candy research." (It was funded by a trade association for candy companies!)[84] Or yet another study funded by a chocolate company that, according to the company's press release, demonstrated that "[c]ocoa flavanols lower blood pressure and increase blood vessel function in healthy people." The company also touted the study's findings in a full-page advertisement in the *New York Times*.[85] This led New York University professor of nutrition Marion Nestle to observe: "Neither the press release nor the advertisement explained that cocoa flavanols are largely destroyed during all but the most careful processing of chocolate.... They didn't have to. Uncritical readers are likely to interpret the statement as evidence that chocolate is good for them."[86] These are just three notable examples among many, many studies.

However, focusing on individual studies fails to capture the ways in which corporations and trade associations have been funding food and nutrition research as part of their strategies of influence—with the goal of shaping policy, as well as influencing consumers. A recent meta-analysis examining systemic reviews of studies that explored the relationship between sugar-sweetened beverages (SSBs) and obesity or weight gain found that reviews disclosing sponsorship or conflicts of interest with food or beverage companies were *five times* more likely to report no positive association between SSB consumption and weight gain or obesity than reviews disclosing no industry sponsorship or conflicts of interest.[87] The authors of this analysis noted that the more favorable findings often contradicted the findings of the original studies on which the reviews were purportedly based. This is especially problematic given that policymakers, as well as health practitioners, rely on reviews and do not have time to verify them by reading the original studies.

Industry actors also recognize the value of not merely sponsoring studies but also funding initiatives that can shape, interpret, and disseminate this research. The University of Colorado recently came under the spotlight because it accepted $1 million dollars from a soda company to launch an initiative called the "Global Energy Balance Network."[88] The network emphasized that lack of exercise rather than poor diet was responsible for increasing rates of overweight and obesity—an emphasis that served the commercial interests of the network's soda company sponsor. The network was rightly criticized for initially failing to disclose its funding source on its website. Then, in August 2015, a public interest group circulated a letter signed by thirty-seven scientists and public health experts, accusing the network of "peddling scientific nonsense."[89] After considerable adverse publicity (much of it directed at the researchers involved), the university returned the money. Although that decision was undoubtedly motivated by the administration's desire to restore credibility, the university's initial acceptance of the gift imperiled its institutional integrity.[90] These kinds of collaborations should also cause—but often fail to cause—serious concerns among public officials. By framing the causes of obesity as lack of physical activity and "energy imbalance," they influence not only diet, but also the policy process. This strategy is not novel.

Recent research has revealed that for over fifty years industry actors have sought to detract attention from the chronic adverse effects of their products (sugar and sugar-sweetened beverages).[91] They did so first by funding research to shift the focus from sugar to fat,[92] a precursor to more recent efforts to deflect attention away from sugar and toward lack of physical activity.[93] Historical documents and recent e-mails between academics and executives provide evidence of long-term strategies of influence. (In some cases, the word "strategy" is expressly used in correspondence between industry representatives and researchers.[94])

Unsurprisingly, strategies of influence have also been observed across a variety of sectors of industry.[95] As some commentators have pointed out, producing and disseminating favorable research has "become a business in itself."[96] Companies and trade associations from many of these sectors have been hiring the same public relations firm that has a reputation for being a leader in this business—a reputation earned from the firm's work on behalf of tobacco companies.[97]

6.4 SHIFTING FROM INDIVIDUAL PARTNERSHIPS TO SYSTEMIC PERSPECTIVES

In this chapter, I have discussed a variety of partnerships and multistakeholder initiatives in isolation. But I have done so with the necessary caveats because these relationships do not occur in isolation. Industry actors, especially multinational corporations, usually have close relationships with a host of other entities—not only government bodies, but also public health NGOs, health professional associations, patient advocacy organizations, and academic institutions.[98] And each of these entities may, in turn, have close relationships with a variety of corporations and trade assocations.[99] One way of looking at these webs of influence is to explore all the relationships that a category of industry actors has with a range of nonindustry actors within a particular geographic region. Recent investigations by the *New York Times* have attempted the latter. Its teams of investigative journalists have explored food and beverage industry relationships with governments, health professional associations, and the academy in several countries.

One recent example is the newspaper's investigation in Malaysia, a country in which nearly half the adult population is overweight or obese, and in which sales of processed foods have more than doubled in the last five years.[100] At the end of their investigation, the journalists concluded that the "ethos of corporate partnership" pervades health initiatives in Malaysia. The health ministry collaborated with representatives of several food companies to develop a food-labeling scheme that conferred a "healthier choice" label on SSBs and sugary cereals. Although several multinational food and beverage companies are involved in these relationships, investigators focused on one multinational in particular (Nestlé). One of its breakfast cereals (Stars) was labeled "Selected Healthier Choice Malaysia Ministry of Health," even though it is more than a quarter sugar by weight. Running alongside government-industry relationships, journalists also found relationships between the same corporation (among others) and both NGOs and the academy. In addition to funding studies—including one purporting to show that consuming its sugary breakfast drink (Milo) made children more active—the company sponsored the Nutrition Society and nutrition conferences. The Society produced an educational pamphlet touting the "wonders of whole grain" that also contained advertisements for two other brands of the company's cereal (Koko Krunch and Cookie Crisp) that bear the "whole grain" label but are also more than a quarter sugar by weight. The findings of this informal country study are consistent with other evidence of the webs of relations that this and many other multinational corporations have been weaving across the globe.

This kind of investigative journalism should also serve as an invitation for further academic inquiry. Comprehensive independent analyses of partnerships can and ideally would include interviews of the parties involved in and affected by the partnership. Interviews can provide researchers with the opportunity to gain a richer understanding than documents alone (including questionnaires) can provide. (Alas, this was an exercise that I did not have the resources to conduct for this book.) Although comprehensive analyses can be expensive, they often shed light on more subtle ethical dimensions that might otherwise be missed.[101] Systematic reviews and meta-analyses of existing partnerships can highlight the cumulative effects of partnerships and provide further evidence of the systemic concerns I articulate here—including framing effects, agenda distortion, and technological biases. Sometimes technology might provide the best solution for a global health challenge. But at other times, it will not. In some cases, technology may only be effective—and ethically defensible—as part of a broader package of solutions addressing social and environmental influences on health. As a former UN Special Rapporteur for the Right to Food noted, "[m]alnutrition in all its forms cannot be addressed only by a food sciences approach."[102]

A newly published casebook explores twelve partnerships with the food and beverage industry across the globe.[103] Notably, the casebook concludes that there is "a striking contrast between the broad political commitments to collaborate and the limited evidence base for the effectiveness of partnership approaches to improving nutrition."[104] Put another way, although policymakers tend to be enthusiastic about partnerships, there is little evidence that they achieve what policymakers hope and say they will achieve. On the contrary, the weight of evidence more broadly (especially the failure to procure any major success in global efforts to address obesity, diabetes, and other NCDs) suggests that these collaborative approaches have largely been ineffective. But, as I explain in the next two chapters, even when a proposed public-private partnership could help address a public health challenge, there may still be powerful ethical objections to such a collaboration.

6.5 CONCLUSION

It might be possible to redesign some of the partnerships described in this chapter. We could try to remove corporate logos and color schemes. We could try substituting a different company "partner"—one whose products are not contributing to the public health problem the partnership is trying to address. This would alleviate some of the most acute ethical challenges presented by individual collaborations. But it would not address chronic, cumulative, and systemic problems such as framing effects. Nor would it address the ways in which partnerships distort the agendas and priorities of government bodies.[105] The conspicuously problematic features identified here are similarly not the only threats to public trust in government bodies. Trust in public health agencies is imperiled by the broader strategies of their industry partners. When companies promote unhealthy products (including marketing them to children) while pursuing corporate philanthropy to enhance their corporate image, they not only "buy loyalty" and "stifle opposition,"[106] they also undermine trust in their public partners. Industry strategies of influence call for counter-strategies. In order to preserve their own independence, integrity, and credibility, public bodies need strategies to insulate themselves from industry influence. In the pages that follow, I provide the theoretical foundations for—and some practical guidance to promote—the development of such strategies.

7

In Praise of Separation

IMAGINE THAT THE White House decides to partner with the Supreme Court and congressional leaders to bring us the next generation of health care reform. Let's call the draft legislation "POTUScare." (You may also replace POTUS with the surname of any US president you like or, for that matter, don't like.) The implementation of POTUScare, the White House argues, would be speedier and smoother than the Affordable Care Act, also known as Obamacare. That law was plagued by costly litigation, as well as political challenges, for many years. But thanks to the proposed collaboration with the Supreme Court, lawmakers would know which draft provisions of POTUScare would be unlikely to withstand constitutional challenge, and they could revise or remove them. Millions of dollars in legal fees and years of doubt and delay might be avoided. In addition, the judiciary might develop a deeper understanding of the objectives of the White House, and vice versa.

This proposal might appear beneficial for all concerned—except perhaps appellate lawyers! But, as you might expect, there are fundamental reasons for objecting to it, whatever the potential benefits of the proposal and whoever the president may be. If the judiciary collaborates with the other branches of government, it undermines public trust and, more fundamentally, it erodes its ability to perform its core functions. Judges who collaborate in making the laws cannot determine the constitutionality of those laws. (A judge who adjudicated the constitutionality of a law that she helped draft would be violating the legal maxim *nemo iudex in sua causa*. The court would be attempting to act as a judge "in its own cause.") The US Supreme Court cannot hold the legislative and executive branches accountable if it collaborates with them. Such collaboration would undermine one of the central rationales for the court's existence.

The modest proposal I describe above is not as far-fetched as it might seem. Later in this chapter, I discuss a similar real-world proposal. Thankfully, the arguments for judicial collaboration did not prevail in that case, despite the potential benefits. In this chapter, I will argue that there are similarly sound reasons to resist the public-private partnership paradigm *despite* the alleged benefits of these relationships.[1] Collaboration with industry actors can imperil the core functions of governments and intergovernmental bodies; hamper their ability to promote the public good; undermine their integrity; and erode public trust.[2] In this chapter, I outline two analogous bodies of norms that can help us identify and address the problematic nature of public-private partnerships (PPPs). The first is separation of powers, which constrains interactions between branches of government (public-public interactions). The second is antitrust (known as competition law in Europe), which regulates interactions among corporate actors (private-private interactions). The implications of these norms for public-private interactions (including partnerships) have not yet been fully articulated.[3] I address this lacuna here by developing a framework that will help us create norms for this growing "third space."

7.1 PUBLIC-PUBLIC INTERACTIONS

7.1.1 Separation of Powers

Although the French jurist Baron de Montesquieu never employed the phrase "*la séparation des pouvoirs*," the concept is most often attributed to him. "All would be lost," Montesquieu wrote, "if the same man or the same body of principal men, either of nobles, or of the people, exercised these three powers: that of making laws, that of executing public resolutions, and that of judging the crimes or the disputes of individuals."[4] The framers of the US Constitution were undoubtedly influenced by Montesquieu. In his discussion of the judiciary in the *Federalist Papers*, Alexander Hamilton quotes the Baron directly and writes: "there is no liberty, if the power of judging be not separated from the legislative and executive powers."[5]

Hamilton was not only concerned with mere separation. Having observed that liberty would have "everything to fear" if there was a "union" of the judiciary with either of the other two branches of government, he emphasized that "all the effects of such a union must ensue from a dependence of the former on the latter, notwithstanding a nominal and apparent separation."[6] He worried too that the judiciary was "in continual jeopardy of being overpowered, awed, or influenced by its co-ordinate branches."[7] Concerns about influence also troubled James Madison. He wrote in the *Federalist Papers* that "none of [the three branches of government] ought to possess, directly or indirectly, an *overruling influence* over the others, in the administration of their respective powers" (emphasis added), and that the "most difficult task is to provide some practical security for each, against the invasion of the others."[8]

The importance of the separation of powers doctrine and the concern about influence have been reasserted many times since. In the first federal Congress of the United States, James Madison declared, "If there is a principle in our Constitution, indeed in any free Constitution, more sacred than another it is that which separates the legislative, executive and judicial powers."[9] Although the framers did not have the benefit of the ethnographic and behavioral science research on reciprocity and influence that I outline in chapter 4, they were clearly attuned to its themes and concerns.

More than half a century ago, the constitutional law scholar Edward Corwin described the US Constitution as "an invitation to struggle."[10] Contemporary scholars have similarly observed that the framers of the Constitution constructed a system of "[d]ivided powers competing with one another."[11] "The Framers were Newtonians," the legal scholar Lawrence Lessig has written. "They were building a machine that would be pulled by a clear balance of gravities. Allowing the wrong body to interfere with those intended gravities was, in their view, 'corruption.'"[12]

7.1.2 Structural Separation

It would be challenging to claim that the constitution in the United Kingdom was *designed* to adhere to the separation to powers[13]—a claim made all the more difficult given that the constitution is essentially unwritten. But, as some legal scholars have observed, the development of the constitution has been influenced by the perceived demands of the separation of powers doctrine.[14] This is evidenced by twenty-first century constitutional reforms related to the country's highest judicial office (the Lord Chancellor) and the court of final appeal (the Appellate Committee of the House of Lords). The very name of the court revealed the lack of formal or structural independence from the legislative chamber. As Walter Bagehot, the nineteenth-century essayist and author of the treatise, *The English Constitution*, observed, "the judicial function . . . is a function which no theorist would assign to a second chamber [of the legislature] in a new Constitution, and which is a matter of accident in ours."[15]

The most conspicuous exception to the separation of powers was the anomalous figure of the Lord High Chancellor of Great Britain (usually referred to more concisely as the Lord Chancellor). He participated in all three branches of the government: he was a member of the Cabinet (which contains the most senior officials in Her Majesty's Government), the presiding officer of the House of Lords (the second chamber in the bicameral legislature), and the head of the judiciary in England and Wales. These anomalies have since been addressed. The Constitutional Reform Act of 2005 separated the legislative, judicial, and executive functions embodied in the Lord Chancellor. They are now discharged by different officeholders. The Act also established the clear separation of the highest court and its judges from the legislative branch. In 2009, the Appellate Committee of the House of Lords was replaced by the UK Supreme Court, with the serving judges (the Lords of Appeal in Ordinary) transitioning to become justices of the new judicial body. For our purposes, the unsuccessful objections to the proposed reforms are just as important as the reforms themselves.

Before the reforms were passed, the Lord Chancellor and several other senior judges argued that the former's multiple roles "provided the natural conduit between the judiciary and the executive."[16] They expressed the view that the Lord Chancellor could "act as a safety valve avoiding undue tension between the judiciary and the government and possibly between the judiciary and Parliament as well,"[17] and that "judicial independence had generally been served well by having a defender at the heart of government."[18] Several judges—and an independent commission[19]—made similar arguments to defend the membership of the court of final appeal's judges in the second (upper) chamber of the legislature. They argued that the judges "contribute[d] to general debates and to the consideration of proposed legislation, giving the benefit of their extensive judicial experience;" that they "clarif[ied] legal points or help[ed] to identify issues which require decision"; that they "[brought] to bear their understanding of how law works in practice; that they [drew] on their commitment to the rule of law and due process to identify proposed legislation or other developments which could threaten either of those concepts."[20] They also argued that the benefits flowed the other way too: judges' membership of the legislative body enabled them to "derive a greater understanding of the problems of the legislator, of social trends, [and] of the proper limits of judicial innovation."[21]

One might doubt whether a somber debate from the red leather benches of the House of Lords would provide the most effective means of identifying "social trends." (Historically at least, its members were predominantly privileged elderly white men.) But even if one could substantiate the claims about the purported enhancements of legislative and judicial functions that come from judges straddling the judicial and legislative branches, serious objections still arise. Simply put, other considerations override these claims about the value of enhanced communication, shared information, experience, and expertise. First and foremost, judges' participation in the legislative process could have an adverse impact on their judicial function—either because it undermines the performance of that function, public trust in the discharge of the function, or both. Second, there are less problematic means of achieving similar benefits. Other members of the legislature have legal training, expertise, and experience derived from legal (but not judicial) practice. These lawyers can and do make similar contributions to legislative debate.[22] Similar arguments apply to judicial collaboration with, as well as membership of, the executive branch.

7.1.3 Interaction and Influence

Even when structural separation is in place, certain kinds of interactions create opportunities for influence. For this reason, concerns about judicial function are not limited to judges' dual or multiple roles. If the judiciary fails to maintain arm's length relations with other branches of government, it creates opportunities for influence by the other branches. In 2005, the Appellate Committee of the House of Lords held that the indefinite detention of *foreign* nationals (but not British citizens) on grounds of suspected international terrorism was discriminatory and incompatible with the European Convention on Human Rights.[23] Following this decision, the incoming Home Secretary Charles Clark began working on new antiterrorism legislation. He soon found himself wrestling with the following question: What kinds of provisions would most likely withstand an inevitable further round of legal challenges?

The minister thought he could answer that question expeditiously by adopting an approach similar to the one I posited in jest at the beginning of this chapter. Clarke suggested that senior judges meet with him to discuss human rights issues raised by the government's proposed counter-terrorism policy. He argued, "some proper discussion about what might or might not be legal would be a very helpful thing . . . because we have spent five years since 9/11 without getting to a system that works."[24] When his overtures were not positively received by the judiciary, he complained that he was "frustrated at the inability to have general conversations of principle with the law lords . . . because of their sense of propriety."[25] Clark dismissed concerns about judicial integrity,[26] and he described as "risible" the objection that judicial independence would be corrupted by the discussions he proposed.[27] He complained of "a constitutional tension [between the executive and judiciary] which is not properly resolved and which it would be beneficial to resolve."[28]

Several sitting and retired senior judges were quick to respond to the minister. One lamented that the secretary of state "apparently fails to understand that the Law Lords and Cabinet Ministers are not on the same side."[29] This judge added that the public interest and the separation of powers require an arm's length relationship and that a "cosy relationship" between ministers and senior judges would be "a worrying development." Another senior judge warned that judges "must be particularly careful not even to appear to be colluding with the executive when they are likely later to have to adjudicate on challenges of action taken by the executive."[30] Several judges pointed out that tensions between the judiciary and the executive are "inevitable," "healthy," and "entirely proper," and that these tensions are characteristic of the "checks and balances of modern constitutional life."[31]

The secretary of state lost the argument, and, in more than one sense, the judiciary prevailed. The Select Committee on the Constitution concluded that Clarke's request posed "an unacceptable breach of the principle of judicial independence" and emphasized that the court of last resort "should not even be perceived to have prejudged an issue as a result of communications with the executive."[32] The committee also pointed out that there were other "channels of communication" between the executive and judiciary, such as formal consultation processes. Such processes, it concluded, could and should be employed when the executive was proposing legislation likely to affect the judiciary or the administration of justice.[33]

These exchanges show how considerations of judicial independence and integrity, and concerns about both influence on and public trust in the judiciary, overrode arguments about the practical benefits of collaboration. I spent some time outlining the unsuccessful arguments in favor of judicial collaboration because there are strong parallels with arguments made in favor of PPPs and other forms of collaboration with industry actors.

Before turning my attention back to PPPs, I should acknowledge that, in order to make the point most clearly, I have focused on the hazards to judicial function resulting from violation of the separation of powers.[34] Other scholars have made persuasive arguments about the significance of separation between legislative and executive branches. Adopting an approach similar to mine, Jeremy Waldron, an eminent scholar of law and philosophy, also relies on notions of function and integrity. He argues that "[t]he importance of the Separation of Powers Principle is predicated on the vital distinction between various functions of governance—legislative, adjudicative, and executive—considered in and of themselves."[35] Waldron adds that "these respective tasks have, each of them, an integrity of their own" and that "contamination" occurs when executive considerations affect the legislative process or when tasks specific to the executive are "tangled up" with the tasks of lawmaking.[36] He argues for modes of governance "articulated" across the three branches and warns readers of the dangers of abandoning such an approach. Although I recognize the perils arising from judicial collaboration with the other branches of government are not exactly the same as the perils that arise when those branches collaborate with industry, there are potent similarities between the arguments proffered in favor of each kind of collaboration and the principles that inform the objections to both collaborations.

7.1.4 Broader Implications

The kinds of arguments that failed to prevail in the separation of powers context remain unreflectively influential in relation to partnerships and other collaborations with industry. These arguments might be characterized as *the communication rationale,* the *information rationale,* the *nonconflict rationale,* the *experiential rationale* and the *expertise rationale.* Although the meaning of these terms could be deduced from my discussion of separation of powers, I will explain the rationales more fully in the context of PPPs.[37]

The communication rationale asserts that collaborations between public and private sector open and sustain channels of communication. These channels of communication provide opportunities for each of the parties to share its goals and objectives, thereby enhancing the ways in which each understands the other. Collaborations, it is argued, also provide a mechanism for the exchange of information about topics in which both parties have an interest.[38] These two rationales, often offered independently, are strongly related to the nonconflict rationale. According to the nonconflict rationale, collaboration provides opportunities to avoid potential conflict and to defuse existing conflict. This rationale rests on the assumption that conflict is inherently problematic.[39] However, it is often necessary for a government to engage in conflict (for example, bringing legal proceedings against industry actors who are violating federal regulations) to protect and promote public health and the environment.

According to the experiential rationale, collaboration provides not only valuable information but also valuable experience. But whether that experience is beneficial depends on the nature and implications of the experience. When collaborative experiences with private sector entities promote asymmetric reciprocity, and create or exacerbate private sector influence, this is ethically problematic. The transfer of expertise may also be problematic. Corporate expertise is oriented toward making a profit, marketing, and building brand loyalty. This kind of expertise may lead to a bias toward the development of technological solutions to public health problems that may be readily commercialized. These solutions may not be the best solutions. Nor may they be the most enduring approaches in the face of long-term public health problems.

Proponents of these rationales tend not to address whether the underlying objectives could be realized in other less problematic ways[40]—in particular, through relations conducted at arm's length. Consider, for example, the communication rationale. The objectives of multinational corporations are usually articulated in mission statements, corporate prospectuses, and reports for shareholders. Although public officials' understanding of these documents can be enhanced by oral communication, this need not take place behind closed doors or through PPPs. If policymakers require industry feedback on the potential impact of proposed regulations on their business activities, corporate executives can be invited to submit written comments during formal notice and comment procedures and to provide testimony in congressional hearings.

One of the most common justifications for collaborations with industry is the provision of *resources*. These may be human resources such as seconding personnel or informational resources. But, for the greater part, resource justifications are financial. Public officials argue that industry partners provide government bodies with funds that enable these agencies to do more. However, these interactions can distort the mission of public sector bodies and undermine their integrity and public trust. The starting point for policymakers should *not* be whether the purported benefits might accrue from the proposed collaboration. Rather, given the inherently problematic nature of these interactions, public institutions should begin by exploring whether the potential benefits might be obtained in some other way.

Popular rationales for PPPs in public health are insufficient to justify the current status of these and similar collaborations with industry as the default paradigm. The importance of competition or struggle, central to the separation of powers, has been neglected in public-private interactions.[41] I recognize that the functions of policymakers and legislators are different from those of judges and that political judgment is not the same as legal judgment. But we need to protect the independence, integrity, and credibility of government agencies, all of which can be imperiled by industry influence.[42]

7.2 PRIVATE-PRIVATE INTERACTIONS

Antitrust law in the United States and competition law in Europe are both premised on the notion that the function of corporations is to compete with each other and that the public good is undermined when corporations collaborate rather than compete. Consumers are usually harmed when corporations agree to increase or set their prices (often called price-fixing) or when companies divide markets among themselves in order to avoid competing in the same market. The norms that have been embedded in the law in an effort to protect competition in the marketplace—norms regulating private-private interactions—can also help us think further about how to address public-private interactions. This is the case whether one looks at competition law in the European Union or antitrust law in the United States. Given my background in European law, I will say more about the former.[43] But legal provisions and case law on both sides of the Atlantic recognize that collaboration, consensus, and influence are of profound concern.

European law prohibits agreements and "concerted practices" that have "as their object or effect the prevention, restriction or distortion of competition within the internal market."[44] Concerted practices are not exhaustively defined. But they fall short of a formal agreement and include coordination that "knowingly substitute[s] practical cooperation . . . for the risks of competition."[45] As with separation of powers, *influence* is a central concern. Companies may violate the law by engaging in direct or indirect contact that has the object or effect of influencing the market behavior of an actual or potential competitor.[46] Corporations can legitimately try to anticipate and respond to the behavior of their competitors.[47] But they must determine their own "market policy." They are not supposed to disclose their market-conduct plans to their competitors. Sharing strategic information, such as plans for pricing or product quantities, can impede competition—even when it does not occur behind closed doors.[48] For this reason, public announcements may also violate the law.

Consensus is currently a buzzword in global health policy. But it is recognized as problematic in European competition law. Where there is evidence of some form of contact between corporate actors and of a *consensus* (or meeting of minds) to cooperate rather than compete, the courts may presume that these interactions had an effect on market behavior.[49] The burden then falls on the companies to show otherwise.

Competition law prohibits concerted practices involving multiple parties. (The term "hub and spoke" refers to concerted practices in which two or more suppliers collude with the help of a distributor, or two or more distributors collude with a supplier.[50]) An "integrated set of schemes" can also constitute a single infringement.[51] The concerns addressed here by competition law are analogous to my concerns about the private sector's webs of influence. In the former instance, the law's concern is the impact on the market policy of private sector bodies. In the latter, we should be concerned about impacts on the policies of governments and intergovernmental agencies.

Concerted practice is a "versatile concept" in European law.[52] Courts avoid defining it with precision because they are anxious not to "artificially restrict the breadth of the concept." Corporations respond to regulation with adaptive practices. The legal term must be sufficiently clear for corporations to know what kinds of behaviors are prohibited. But, if the definition is too narrow, corporations could easily circumvent the law. Similarly, we need a sufficiently versatile set of tools to address industry influence in public policy. Although conflict of interest rules and policies can play an important role addressing influence, prevailing approaches are—without more—not sufficiently versatile. (I return to this problem and offer some solutions at the end of the chapter.)

Competition and antitrust laws take violations very seriously. At the time of this writing, legislation in Britain provides for criminal prosecution of perpetrators with sentences of up to five years and fines as well.[53] In the United States, violation of the equivalent Sherman Act provisions is a felony punishable by up to ten years in prison in addition to fines.[54] The US Supreme Court has described *collusion* as "the supreme evil of antitrust."[55] Although I prefer to avoid Manichean language, this phrase makes clear the seriousness with which the law views collusion.

If we think of separation of powers as addressing the exercise of power by and relations among the branches of government, and antitrust as addressing the exercise of power by and relations among private sector entities, there is a third space we need to address: relations between the public and private sectors, and the exercise of power by the private sector over the public sector. There are some formal rules governing a number of public-private interactions: for example, rules that regulate (in some jurisdictions more than others) lobbying and campaign finance; public procurement rules establishing procedures government bodies are required to follow when contracting with the private sector; and codes of ethics for lawmakers and judges.[56] But we lack a thicker set of principles governing public-private interactions. The principle of institutional integrity that I developed in chapter 2 is one of the core principles that can help fill the gap.

7.3 THE THIRD SPACE: PUBLIC-PRIVATE INTERACTIONS

My review of separation of powers and the law of competition or antitrust can help us assess existing norms in the third space (public-private interactions) and determine how they might be enhanced.[57] Figure 7.1 illustrates the three spaces. In the public sphere are public-public interactions in which reciprocity and influence are regulated by separation of powers. In the private sphere are private-private interactions in which reciprocity and influence are regulated by competition or antitrust laws. Concerns about influence straddle both political and economic power, including market power. Although there are valid concerns about the adequacy of existing norms and enforcement in antitrust, these norms—taken together with the norms embedded in the doctrine of separation of powers—can help us recognize the profound need for new norms to address the private sector's exercise of power and influence in policy spheres. Figure 7.1 shows that where public and private overlap (public-private interactions), there are six animating principles that might help public officials better address the ethical hazards of reciprocity and influence arising from public-private interactions. Although I describe these as ethical principles, they can and should inform the development of laws and regulations in addition to institutional policies and ethics codes—as I will now explain.

7.3.1 *The Function and Taxonomy of Norms*

Norms may be embedded in laws, regulations, ethics codes, and institutional policies (among others).[58] They come in a variety of forms. *Bright-line* rules may prohibit

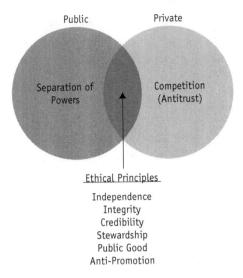

Public   Private

Separation of   Competition
Powers   (Antitrust)

Ethical Principles

Independence
Integrity
Credibility
Stewardship
Public Good
Anti-Promotion

FIGURE 7.1 The Third Space: Norms for Public-Private Interactions

certain forms of conduct. For example, an institutional policy might prohibit partnerships with or the receipt of financial or in-kind contributions from certain kinds of industry actors.[59] Rules may also mandate certain behaviors, requiring those to whom they are addressed to take positive action. *Safe harbors* provide that certain forms of conduct, *if* performed in certain ways, are permissible—or presumptively permissible. A government regulation could permit specific kinds of interactions between an agency and corporations provided those interactions occur within or follow specified procedures, such as open consultation or public procurement. While rules tend to specify that certain actions are within or out of bounds, *principles* will ordinarily be necessary to help public officials and administrators (among others) understand the purpose of those rules and to guide them as they navigate areas not clearly addressed by the rules.[60]

Principles can perform several distinct but related normative functions. The first function is *foundational*. Principles can provide a more coherent foundation for existing rules and procedures. The second function is *interpretive*. A principled foundation can facilitate and enrich the interpretation of existing rules and procedures. The third function is *interstitial*. Principles might promote the identification and filling of gaps in existing rules and procedures. The fourth function is *prudential*. Principles can promote the exercise of discretion permitted by existing rules or procedures in a manner that neither is nor appears arbitrary. They may also inform decision-making in the absence of formal rules or procedures. Principles have an *expressive* function too. They tell us something about the values of an institution, community, or society, and about the perceived threats to those values. In conjunction with other norms (such as bright-line rules and safe harbors), principles can be part of a broader framework that mandates, constrains, guides, and informs the conduct of institutions and individuals.

Violations of laws and policies can attract a variety of sanctions for both the relevant institution and the individuals involved in prohibited behaviors. These include civil liability, disciplinary penalties or, most seriously, criminal prosecution. Norms must be sufficiently flexible to capture problematic behaviors and interactions; but the more serious the consequences of any violation, the more clearly defined they must be. Bright lines and safe harbors can provide valuable clarity. But they can also create or exacerbate a culture of *compliance* rather than a culture that promotes ethical sensitivity and ethical decision-making. Rules may lead people to ask themselves certain kinds of questions, most commonly: "How can I get through these hoops and hurdles to do what I need or want to do?" This can lead to moral blindness, crowding out the important question: "What is the right thing to do?" Bright lines may unintentionally signal that certain forms of conduct are not problematic because they are not among those listed as strictly prohibited. For example, a rule prohibiting relationships with tobacco and firearms companies might appear to suggest that partnerships with other kinds of industry actors do not create ethical hazards.[61] Similarly, a policy focusing solely on individual conflicts of interest might lead to the neglect of institutional conflicts. And a policy addressing institutional conflicts of interest might signal that influence arising from other interactions not covered by the policy is unproblematic.

7.3.2 Toward a New Set of Norms

I have shown how industry actors understandably engage in various kinds of interactions as part of their strategies of influence. Governments (and, for that matter, universities and health-related NGOs) need their own strategies to address the many sources of industry influence. Conflicts of interest frameworks are one key part of any strategy. But they need not be, and should not be, the only tool. Industry interactions may influence public health agencies (and other entities) in ways that are ethically problematic even when they do not violate conflicts of interest policies.

There are a host of definitions of conflicts of interest. One of the most influential (but contested) approaches defines conflicts of interest as "circumstances that create a risk that professional judgments or actions regarding a primary interest will be unduly influenced by a second interest."[62] Although the concept can be applied to institutions and individuals, public sector bodies have generally been more effective at addressing their employees' conflicts than their own institutional conflicts.

As the case studies discussed in chapter 6 make clear, many public health agencies have developed close institutional relationships with industry. In some cases, they appear to have gone out of their way to create conflicts of interest! In other cases, where institutional conflicts have been recognized, they have been poorly managed, if at all, and rarely are they eliminated. One explanation for this is that the concept of conflict of interest is often misinterpreted or misapplied.[63] In one recent analysis of Scaling Up Nutrition (SUN), a global nutrition partnership, "primary interest" (for the purpose of identifying a potential conflict) was framed as the joint endeavor.[64] This places beyond consideration the ways in which the collaboration itself might create conflicts of interest.

Once policymakers recognize the range of ethical hazards presented by industry influence, they should have a better understanding of how to interpret and supplement conflict of interest rules and policies. These hazards can be highlighted by an appropriate body of principles. I offer here a working set of principles that should be periodically revisited and revised to ensure they serve this purpose: independence, integrity, credibility, stewardship, public good, and anti-promotion.

7.3.2.1 Independence

One of the main concerns about influence is its impact on the independence of the public institution. We often think about independence in the context of discrete judgments and decision-making. But evidence of the erosion of independence may be far subtler than an apparently isolated decision that clearly favors the commercial interests of an industry actor exercising influence. Close relationships with industry actors may lead government agencies to frame public health problems and their solutions in ways that are less threatening to the interests of industry actors. As we have seen, obesity becomes primarily a matter of personal responsibility, resulting from lack of exercise and "energy imbalance." And the solution that emerges is often a partnership with a soda company to promote physical activity. The principle of independence should be interpreted and applied broadly to address these kinds of concerns.

The absence of dependence is not the same as independence. Physicians do not "depend" on pharmaceutical companies to buy them pens. They can afford to purchase their own writing implements! But studies show that small gifts to doctors can influence their judgment and decision-making.[65] A small gift may similarly influence a public health agency. And multiple small-scale partnerships with a variety of industry sponsors may be as influential as a major partnership with one large multinational. Some proponents of PPPs argue for the inclusion of multiple private partners in collaborations to minimize the influence of any single industry actor. But this solution can exacerbate framing effects, particularly when the interests of these partners are aligned in relevant ways. Despite aggressive competition in the marketplace, corn refiners and cane sugar companies both share an interest in policymakers focusing attention on lack of physical activity. Both actors have strongly opposed food-labeling laws requiring the disclosure of added sugars. There may be other signs that the independence of public health agencies is being eroded. Webs of industry relations can distort the agendas of public health agencies, creating a bias toward initiatives that employ technological solutions with demonstrable effects in the short term. At the same, agencies may be neglecting the social dimensions of health problems and potential solutions that may be more effective in the longer term. For these reasons, the principle of independence should be interpreted in such a way to capture apparently small interactions that, either individually or cumulatively, might allow industry actors to exert influence over public health agencies.

7.3.2.2 Integrity

Influence imperils not only the independence of institutions, but also their integrity. I argued in chapter 2 that an essential component of integrity is consistency among what an institution does (its practices), what it says it does (its mission), and what it is obligated to do (its purpose). In chapter 4, I showed how reciprocity with industry actors can undermine the integrity of public bodies. Public health agencies should strenuously avoid reciprocal relations with, and the associated influence by, corporations whose mission, purpose, or practices are in tension with their own. The same applies to relationships with trade associations and other NGOs whose members or donors match that description. But public officials should also be on guard for more subtle threats to the integrity of their institution that may result from the reframing of public health challenges, and their solutions, or from the distortion of their agendas and priorities. Given the extended treatment of integrity in chapter 2 and the associated guidance for public health agencies in the next chapter (see the integrity matrix), I will not dwell on integrity here.

7.3.2.3 Credibility

The word credibility is often used in a manner that elides two distinct concerns: trust and trustworthiness. Like integrity, trustworthiness is an attribute (or property) of an institution. Trust, on the other hand, is an attitude toward an institution, usually based on perceptions of that institution. Although we can measure trust in surveys and polls, trustworthiness is not susceptible to empirical measurement. An institution that lacks integrity—because, for example, it does not do what it says it does, or what it has expressly committed itself to do—is also likely to lack trustworthiness. The distinction between trust and trustworthiness is particularly important. The leaders of institutions may be attentive to whether their institution garners the trust of the relevant publics. But they often neglect to address trustworthiness. It is ethically problematic to try to restore trust in an institution without also addressing the practices that undermine its integrity and trustworthiness. The former task is an exercise in what is now called "public relations" and usually involves the engagement of a firm specializing in such services. The latter is the work of institutional ethics (that admittedly draws on other fields, such as organizational psychology.)

The distinction between trust and trustworthiness is important for other reasons too. If an institution, such as a public health agency or NGO, fails to disclose its close relationship with an industry actor (particularly one involving a financial conflict of interest), trust in the institution will be imperiled—especially when the relationship is exposed by a third party, such as an investigative journalist. Whether disclosure of the relationship by the institution itself promotes or undermines trust in that institution among the relevant publics is, of course, an empirical question. But disclosure per se is insufficient to ensure the trustworthiness of the institution. If a public health agency is transparent about its close relationship with an industry actor but the relationship distorts the agency's public health mission or its ability to fulfill that mission, its trustworthiness (as well as its integrity) will be imperiled. (Recent evidence also suggests that the disclosure of financial conflicts of interest may license or exacerbate the very conduct that undermines integrity and trustworthiness.[66] For this reason, it is better to eliminate and avoid such relationships than to maintain, disclose, and manage them.)

To protect the independence, integrity, and credibility of public health agencies, public officials should recognize the limitations of conflicts of interest frameworks in capturing and addressing the problem of influence. They should also be aware that solutions designed to address conflicts of interest often do not eliminate influence more broadly. A good example is "money blinds"—a proposal that seeks to keep the identity of recipients, especially researchers, and corporate donors hidden from each other by employing an intermediary.[67] The intermediary would take the corporate sponsor's funds and choose the most appropriate team to conduct the research. But, even if each of the parties could not guess the other's identity (and they might well be able to do so), such arrangements still permit industry actors to influence and distort research agendas. A soda company that funds research on exercise and obesity is still framing the problem and setting the agenda in ways that are commercially advantageous, even if it cannot choose or exert pressure on the research team.

The principles of independence, integrity, and credibility are relevant to all institutions. Keeping all three in mind should help policymakers and institutional leaders interpret conflicts of interest rules and supplement those rules with other norms. I would add three more principles that are of particular importance for public institutions, especially public health agencies. Like the three principles already discussed, these three additional principles are related but distinct.

7.3.2.4 Stewardship

The concept of stewardship appears in both the public health and ethics literature.[68] Although the term has attracted definitional disputes and theoretical critique,[69] I propose it here as a principle to be developed and applied in order to complement integrity. The integrity principle emphasizes the ways in which partnerships and other close relationships may be harmful to the institutions interacting with industry. As we saw in chapter 4, stewardship directs attention to *others,* those whose interests and well-being institutions have a duty to promote and protect. When a public health department enters a partnership with a soda company, this creates several ethical hazards. The erosion of the department's integrity is an important one. But it is not the only one. If the close relationship promotes the consumption of products that are exacerbating obesity and diet-related NCDs, the arrangement may undermine the health and well-being of children and other vulnerable populations. The principle of stewardship can and should direct public officials' attention to individuals and communities that public health agencies have a legal or ethical obligation to protect. Officials should be especially attentive to obligations expressed or implied in their agency's founding or constitutive documents. Taking obligations of stewardship seriously can facilitate the recognition of industry influence as an ethical problem, and serve as a bulwark against such influence. Proponents of PPPs and MSIs often invoke stewardship in *support* of these arrangements.[70] But as I employ the concept here, stewardship provides a powerful rationale for refusing to enter (and for withdrawing from) close relationships with industry.

7.3.2.5 The Public Good

Public bodies, including public health agencies, should be oriented toward the *public good.*[71] Although the terms the *common good* and the *public good* can be and often are used interchangeably, there are two reasons to describe this principle using the latter rather than the former term. The first reason is that, as we saw in chapter 3, public officials often conflate the *common good* and *common ground.* There is, of course, some linguistic similarity: the terms have "common" in common; and while "good" and "ground" are not homonyms, they are not far apart either. Although the linguistic similarity is hardly the sole cause of the conflation, it may be exploited to promote that conflation. Second, the use of the word "public" can help policymakers keep in mind the distinction between "public" and "private." It may also remind them of the importance of the distinction and make them more attentive to when and why it is being blurred.

One might think of the public good principle as a kind of magnetic field: a force that can operate on an institution, pulling its policies toward the public good. The constitutive document of a public institution, such as a health department, will usually specify the ways in which that institution should be promoting the public good. But public officials focusing on individual objectives or initiatives may lose sight of this broader orientation. When a government body is interested in collaborating with a pharmaceutical company to develop a new prescription drug or vaccine, public officials may fail to consider that a patented prescription drug or vaccine is a private good, the sale of which may or may not promote the public good. The latter will depend on a variety of other factors—not least, whether the drug or vaccine is accessible (economically and geographically), how effective it is, and how serious are the side effects.

7.3.2.6 The Anti-Promotion Principle

Just as orientation toward the public good should exert an ineluctable force of attraction for public institutions, I would argue for a complementary force repelling the institution from policies and practices that promote private interests, especially commercial interests of industry actors inimical to the public interest. Some scholars frame concerns about the promotion of private interests in terms of corruption.[72] Zephyr Teachout argues that an "anti-corruption principle" animates and is embedded in the structure of the US Constitution, analogous to the separation of powers.[73] Its central concern, she concludes, is the promotion of private interest in the exercise of public power.[74] Whether or not one embraces Teachout's claim as a matter of constitutional interpretation, a principle addressing the promotion of private interests in the exercise of public power should have a central role in the work of public institutions—including intergovernmental organizations. One could call it the anti-corruption principle, as Teachout does. But many public officials are likely to misconstrue "anti-corruption" given its popular usage in domestic and international policy spheres (where it describes measures taken to address and prevent the abuse of public office for *personal* gain—most commonly, by means of bribery or other criminal conduct).[75] Although I have not found an ideal substitute, the "anti-promotion principle" is a workable alternative. This term has the advantage of capturing three different kinds of ethically problematic promotions. First, it calls on public institutions not to put (or promote) private interests, including the commercial interests of powerful industry actors, ahead of the public interest. Second, it attunes public institutions to the hazards of either intentionally or unwittingly burnishing the reputation of industry actors and increasing loyalty to their brands—and it reminds them to take measures to avoid this. Finally, it calls on public officials to take steps to ensure that industry actors are prohibited from exploiting any of their interactions with government bodies, especially public health agencies, to burnish their corporate reputation and to promote loyalty to their brands.

* * *

Principles have long been employed in biomedical ethics, public health ethics, and other fields of applied ethics to promote and facilitate ethical decision-making.[76] Principles may do this without any hierarchy or flow charts to resolve potential tensions. But they should be applied *reflectively* rather than mechanistically. (Reflection means thinking carefully about not only what the principles mean and how they might be applied, but whether there is also a compelling case for adding, removing, or substituting principles.) The six principles I have proposed here—both individually and cumulatively—support this book's claim that the default relationship between public and private sector bodies should be arm's length interactions. These principles can and should help public officials develop laws, codes, and policies regarding partnerships and, more broadly, devise strategies to address industry influence in all its forms.

7.4 CONCLUSION

Public-private partnerships, multistakeholder initiatives, and other close relations with industry are premised on a positive conception of consensus, compromise, and collaboration. But the "three C's" are not inherently good. On the contrary, tension between regulators and corporations is ordinarily necessary to protect public health. And achieving common ground with industry may put off the table measures that might promote public health. The default relation between industry and government should be arm's lengths relations involving institutional tension, "struggle," and direct conflict. This view may be controversial in the discourse about PPPs but it is consistent with the norms that have already developed in other contexts. Separation of powers and antitrust norms are *not* premised on the Manichean view that any of the relevant parties are malevolent. On the contrary, they rest on the idea that the public good will be best served when the relevant institutions remain at arm's length—when the judiciary maintains its distance from the legislative and executive branches, and when corporations compete rather than cooperate with each other. For analogous reasons, we need more rigorous norms to govern relations between the public and private sector. Although there are currently pockets of rules and policies governing public-private interactions, I have proposed a set of animating principles that can enrich our understanding of existing rules and policies, and help us fill the gaps in a manner that is both comprehensive and coherent. Application of these principles would promote greater separation between the public and private sectors and should pave the way for the exploration of alternative approaches in public health.

8

Toward Systemic Ethics

Public-private leads to private-private, and soon you have [the corporation] running most
or even all government services.

—DAVE EGGERS[1]

IN THE PREVIOUS chapter, I made the case for the development of a thicker set
of norms to govern public-private interactions, and for public health agencies to
move away from partnership as the paradigm for public health interventions. I recognize that such a shift cannot occur overnight. But I call on public health agencies
to develop a strategy that will promote a shift over time. In this chapter, I offer some
systemic ethical guidance for agencies that are not yet willing or able to break away
from the paradigm of industry collaboration. This guidance includes what I call the
"integrity matrix." The matrix can help public health agencies identify some of the
most acute perils arising from collaboration with industry actors. But it should not
be extracted from the broader guidance in this chapter regarding systemic influence. Nor should it detract from the exploration of alternative approaches to public
health that do not employ industry partnership or similar paradigms. While most
other guides are premised on broad support of partnerships and provide tools to
facilitate their development, the purpose of my approach here is to facilitate the progressive recognition of the systemic ethical perils of the public-private partnership
(PPP) paradigm and to promote the development of alternatives.

8.1 THE LANGUAGE OF PARTNERSHIP

The term "public-private partnership" has been used to describe a wide variety of
interactions—from information exchange to the joint delivery of products.[2] But

the term itself tells us little about the arrangement. It does not indicate, for example, what each actor contributes to the collaboration. Nor does it tell us what the anticipated outcome may be. A similar point may be made about other terms used as substitutes for "partnership," such as "alliance." The term "multistakeholder initiative" usually indicates multiple participants from government, industry, the academy, and civil society. But that term similarly tells us little more, if anything. The work of explaining what these relationships involve usually falls to taxonomies that categorize the arrangements according to one or more criteria, such as the nature of the contributions and outcomes.

There are good reasons to abandon the language of partnership (and, for that matter, other synonyms or related terms that tell us little about the nature of the arrangements). Focusing on the interactions inherent in the relationship can help identify the ethical implications of these interactions.[3] Some scholars have also expressed concern that the use of the term "partnership" tends to mask inherent inequalities of power and resources among the participants—for example, inequalities between multinational companies and public health agencies; between trade associations and public health NGOs; and, in the context of global partnerships, between representatives of North and South.[4]

Partnership is a term of art in law and business. More than a century ago, it was defined as "the relation which subsists between persons carrying on a business in common with a view of profit."[5] The *Oxford English Dictionary* currently defines partnership as "[a]n association of two or more people as partners for the running of a business, with *shared expenses, profit, and loss*" (emphasis added).[6] The concepts of "business" and "profit" are clearly problematic for government bodies. In addition, PPPs lack the shared features of partnership in the traditional sense.

From the public partner's perspective, the principal justification for the partnership is usually the financial resources or in-kind contributions that the private partners bring to the collaboration. Alas, PPP agreements often allow the private partners to withdraw from the arrangement at short notice. Sometimes companies pull funding after a downturn in business revenues eliminates the tax benefits that previously came from setting off charitable contributions to partnerships against profits from commercial activities. In such cases, public health agencies are left holding the metaphorical baby. To maintain the public health initiative, governments scramble to find alternative sources of funds.

Even when private partners "stay the course" and meet their financial commitments, public bodies may incur losses not shared by their industry collaborators. Public health agencies risk losing their integrity when a partnership undermines their mission or purpose. Corporate executives often express concern that their company's reputation will be tarnished by its participation in an "inefficient" partnership.[7] But this risk is different in kind from the integrity hazards faced by public bodies, and it is a risk exacerbated by the partnership paradigm itself. The paradigm reinforces the view that public health agencies are inefficient and unable to address global health challenges effectively on their own.[8] Trust and reputation hazards are often not shared either. A partnership may burnish the reputation of a private actor among consumers while at the same time undermining a local community's trust in the participating public body.

While sitting as the chief justice of the New York Supreme Court, Benjamin Cardozo famously observed, "Joint adventurers, like copartners, owe to one another, while the enterprise continues, the duty of the finest loyalty."[9] Public health agencies should, of course, not enter arrangements that create duties of loyalty to private sector bodies. Such duties would be inconsistent with the agencies' fundamental obligations to protect and promote the health and well-being of the relevant publics. It is not enough for public health agencies to demonstrate that, unlike partnerships in the traditional sense, their close relationships with industry actors do not create duties of loyalty as a matter of law. Even absent such duties, public health officials who label industry actors "partners" are likely to experience the tug of loyalty—with deleterious effects for the public whose health their agencies have an obligation to promote and protect. This is yet another reason why the language of partnership is problematic: it can exacerbate the perils of asymmetric reciprocity that I describe in chapter 4. If you are my apparently generous corporate "partner," I will be reluctant to undermine your commercial interests. I will also try to avoid actions that you might merely *perceive* as undermining your interests. From an industry partner's perspective, this is one of the principal benefits of these arrangements, especially partnerships with governments.

Ethically problematic reciprocity is not only the product of the language of partnership but also of the gifts for which partnerships are often vehicles. In Appendix B, "The Anatomy of the Gift," I provide an analysis of the various dimensions of gifts that can help public bodies identify the ethical implications and perils of corporate gifts. This is intended to complement the broader framework I set out in section 8.2 for assessing the systemic ethical implications of interactions with industry actors. Although designed primarily for government bodies and intergovernmental organizations, this framework (like my analysis of the gift) can also be applied by academic institutions and civil society organizations.

8.2 TOWARD SYSTEMIC ETHICAL ASSESSMENT OF INDUSTRY INTERACTIONS

Whatever labels are applied to interactions with industry actors, we should examine their ethical implications from a systemic perspective. The USDA partnership program, like many others also discussed in chapter 6, would have benefited from more rigorous analysis.[10] The agency's application form for potential "national strategic partners" requests that applicants—among them, fast food companies, snack food companies, trade associations, and industry public relations firms—explain "how [their] company's mission/health mandate is consistent with the Dietary Guidelines for Americans and the work that the Center for Nutrition Policy and Promotion (CNPP) does." The companies are not asked to address the potential inconsistencies or tensions. Not surprisingly, the agency received dozens of applications framed as sales pitches, emphasizing the purported synergies while ignoring inconsistencies, divergences, and tensions. Given Panglossian approaches of this kind, it is easy to see why partnerships are often characterized by industry participants and public officials alike as a "win–win–win."[11]

A number of organizations have developed guidelines for the ethical assessment of partnerships.[12] Notably, some of these guidelines are the result of work conducted by the International Life Sciences Institute (ILSI). The organization describes itself as a "public, nonprofit, scientific foundation that advances the understanding and application of science related to the nutritional quality and safety of the food supply."[13] However, the organization depends primarily on funding from the private sector, and it was recently described by the *New York Times* as "the food industry's premier research center."[14] Its past presidents include the then chief science and health officer at Coca-Cola. She helped "orchestrate a strategy of funding scientists who encouraged the public to focus on exercise and worry less about how calories contribute to obesity,"[15] and—at the same time—she also served as coauthor on a widely circulated ILSI-funded article setting out partnership guidelines.[16] In addition, ILSI's stated values include "collaboration . . . with industry, government, and academic scientists."[17] The drafting process for its partnership guidelines was itself a collaboration with industry. In light of all this, we should not be surprised that this process generated guidelines promoting collaboration with industry![18]

The *systemic* analysis I propose here is avowedly more demanding than the analysis ordinarily required by other tools and guides.[19] Unlike the guidelines developed by ILSI and many others, my approach does not rest on an assumption—often explicitly stated—that partnerships are inherently good. On the contrary, it is informed by my analysis of the ethical perils arising from close relationships with industry actors. The framework I outline in this chapter provides for an initial or ex ante review that is very demanding in its own right. But if the interaction proceeds, what is required thereafter will be equally demanding if not more so: ongoing monitoring and evaluation, and ex post analysis. If an institution finds the framework outlined here too onerous, this is a good reason for its leaders not only to reconsider the proposed relationship but also, more broadly, to reassess its reliance on partnerships with industry actors to achieve its goals.

Before proceeding any further, I want to anticipate one objection and provide a response that ties what follows to my analysis in the preceding chapter. You might argue that if I am critiquing partnerships or public health agencies for entering them, I have to show that there were alternatives—that a particular public health agency did not have to collaborate with this particular industry actor or any industry actor at all. Although I do discuss some alternative approaches in general terms, it is not the responsibility of commentators or critics to show there were alternatives to any particular industry collaboration. On the contrary, the burden of proof falls on public bodies to provide public justification for their relationships with industry. If public bodies wish to protect their integrity and credibility, *they* must be willing and able to discharge this burden. This task is as challenging as it is important. A recent analysis of scholarship on PPPs in health promotion concluded there is a "scarcity of evidence" to support the claim—made by proponents of partnerships—that they are effective either per se or in comparison with "compulsory approaches," such as increased regulation of industry.[20] (For this reason, the authors recommend a precautionary approach to PPPs.)

8.2.1 *A New Place to Start: Changing the Default*

Public health agencies should begin by asking themselves three questions. First, *what important public health challenges are not being addressed sufficiently or at all?* And second, *which challenges—and which methods of addressing them—might other entities have no (or insufficient) interest in pursuing?* (The relevant entities would include philanthropic foundations in addition to the private sector.) These two questions are more likely to direct policymakers' attention to serious but neglected long-term public health challenges and to the structural and environmental factors exacerbating them. Third, *how can we address these challenges without entering close relationships with industry actors?* This question will help public officials avoid the ethical perils these relationships entail.

When industry actors *solicit* relationships with the promise of potential benefits, public officials should consider whether there are other ways of obtaining those purported benefits *without* entering ethically problematic relations with industry. These alternative approaches may involve arm's length interactions with the same industry actors or closer relationships with public institutions—whether peer institutions or agencies at other levels of government. (I say more about these alternatives later.)

I am troubled by partnership guidelines that (a) begin by asking whether the private actor is able to provide resources and opportunities to help the public actor meet its goals, and (b) invite consideration of alternatives only if this question is answered in the negative.[21] Such approaches play into industry strategies of influence and permit the private sector to shape public health agendas and priorities. These ethical perils—and the related concerns discussed throughout this book—make a compelling case for changing the default employed by public health agencies. In short, there should be a strong presumption *against* (rather than in favor of) close relationships with industry in public health interventions. In order to rebut the presumption in exceptional and limited cases, a compelling justification should be required.

8.2.2 Rebutting the Presumption

Corporations or third parties engaged by them conduct "due diligence" to identify and address the legal and financial risks of merging with, acquiring, or entering close relationships with other corporations. But public bodies often fail to take analogous precautions when they approach—or are approached by—a potential collaborator from the private sector. In either case, public health agencies should ideally commission an independent analysis of the potential *ethical* perils of entering into close relationships with industry actors. If an agency cannot afford to commission a report from an independent third party, that itself may be a good reason to decline the relationship. But if employees are tasked with making an internal assessment, they should be insulated not only from implicit or explicit pressure to endorse the proposed relationship, but also from structural incentives to do so.

Public bodies trying to rebut a strong presumption against partnership should do more than merely show that, on balance, public health would be promoted by the partnership. Risk-benefit balancing is commonly the central feature of partnership analyses. But it is problematic for several reasons. First, while the word "risk" signals that the potential undesirable effects might not occur, the word "benefit" suggests certainty that the goals of the relationship will be achieved.[22] The probability that the stated goals will *not* be achieved is often neglected. Second, if the objective is framed broadly and ambitiously (for example, reducing childhood obesity by 20 percent over five years in some population), it may be difficult or impossible to point to any risk that appears substantial enough to outweigh such a potential benefit. Third, the actual or potential adverse effects are often far less tangible than the short-term goals. Contrast, for example, the visible impact of a new inner-city playground with the subtle distortion of an agency's strategic priorities or the erosion of its integrity. For these reasons, risk-benefit assessments tend to tip the scales in favor of collaboration with industry actors. Placing integrity in the foreground of any analysis can help address this problem.

8.2.3 *The Integrity Matrix*

I argued in chapter 2 that institutional integrity requires consistency among what an institution does (its practices), what it says it does (its mission), and what it is obligated to do (its purpose). To help public officials apply this concept to their own institutions and potential collaborations, I have developed what I call the "integrity matrix" in figure 8.1.[23] This matrix can help public officials apply the concept of integrity to their own institutions and assess the ethical implications of their relationships with other bodies, especially corporations. Academic institutions and civil society organizations—such as health professional associations and public health NGOs—can also use the matrix. Ideally, the assessment would be conducted or reviewed by an independent body or, failing that, by an internal group structurally insulated from influence by decision-makers and incentives to approve the collaboration.

The matrix requires an assessment of the potential collaborator's mission, purpose, and practices. In the case of a corporation, the practices may be broken down

	What You Do (e.g. public health interventions, education and communication, regulatory activities)	What You Say You Do (e.g. your institution's mission statement, policies, and statements in internal and external communications)	What You Are Obligated To Do (e.g. obligations in founding documents, and other obligations acquired by your institution)
What They Do (e.g. their goods, services, marketing, and other business practices)			
What They Say They Do (e.g. their mission statement, values statements, and internal policies if obtained)			
What They Are Obligated To Do (e.g. under articles of incorporation, contractual obligations)			

FIGURE 8.1 The Integrity Matrix

into several components—including the sale of goods or services, and marketing practices. The most thorough analysis of a corporation will involve consideration of materials that may not be in the public domain. It should be relatively easy to determine the kinds of goods and services provided by the company and the contents of its mission statement. But its internal policies and practices may not be readily available. It may also be difficult for a public institution to determine some ingredients of a company's products particularly when the manufacturer claims that this is proprietary information. (Companies have gone to great lengths to conceal the recipes for a wide range of products that have an impact on public health—from soda to "fracking" fluid.[24]) Public bodies—or independent evaluators—can require potential collaborators to complete questionnaires. But they may not be in a position to determine the veracity or completeness of the responses.

Evaluators could, of course, request internal policies and other documents that might assist with verification. Relevant documents might include information about current or pending litigation (civil or criminal) and regulatory action in which the company is involved. If such requests seem invasive, they are no more so than the kind of questions that might be asked of an applicant by a life or health insurance company. And while the purpose of the required disclosure to insurance companies is to protect their financial interests, the case for disclosure prior to government collaboration with industry is even more compelling—to protect the integrity of the government body and the health and well-being of those the public body has an obligation to protect. Although there is no guarantee that the materials provided would be complete, the relevant public body could also require that the chief legal and information officers of the company sign an affidavit verifying they are complete. A company's reluctance to provide materials could, in itself, be a potential red flag.

Inconsistencies between one's own institution and a potential collaborating institution (in any pairwise comparison) are likely to create serious ethical problems for one's own institution. In some cases, these problems may include not only loss of integrity, but also violation of the institution's obligations, and harm to others whom the institution is supposed to protect. An especially acute inconsistency occurs when a public health agency with a mission to reduce obesity wishes to collaborate with a corporation whose leading brands and associated marketing practices are exacerbating obesity and diet-related NCDs. In such a case, the agency should not be able to rebut the presumption against collaboration. Sometimes divergences or tensions will be much subtler and require closer scrutiny.

Even when a public health agency wishes to collaborate with a corporate actor whose business practices appear to promote health (such as the manufacture and sale of an antibiotic, a vaccine, or an effective pain medication), there will still be divergences and tensions. One kind of divergence or tension is chronic, and the other more acute. But they are related. The chronic form arises from the fact that the primary obligation of a public health agency is to serve as guardian (or steward) of public health. Corporations, on the other hand, depend for their continued existence on the generation of profits. Even in the case of "for benefit" corporations discussed in chapter 3, their mission and purpose is not to promote health at any cost; their survival depends on the generation of profits by selling goods or services. (A company's success may depend more on whether its consumers *believe* the company's products promote health than on whether they actually do so.) This kind of divergence could be characterized as a second-order divergence. Even if there appears to be a first-order convergence (the development of a pharmaceutical product to address a public health challenge), there will be a fundamental second-order divergence between profit generation and serving as a guardian of public health. (These are not only the responsibilities of corporations and public health agencies respectively, but the very objectives on the basis of which each entity justifies its existence.) This form of divergence is inevitable and should not be ignored or downplayed. It also leads to a potentially serious acute divergence. Should the company's products prove harmful (even though they may be designed to improve health), the public health agency will have an obligation to protect the public from those products. But the corporation will have a powerful incentive to downplay the health risks or harms and to try to prolong sales for as long as possible to protect revenue streams and profits (especially when potential legal exposure is limited or dwarfed by those profits). When public health agencies "partner" with a corporation in the development of a product that is intended to promote or improve public health, they undoubtedly court these hazards.

Although the integrity matrix is designed primarily to address collaborations with corporations, it can be adapted for any potential collaborator. When applying the matrix, public officials should also take into account other institutions with whom the potential *collaborator* also has close relationships. The relationships that one's partner has with other partners (particularly those whose practices, mission, or purpose are at odds with one's own) may also undermine the integrity of and trust in one's own institution—especially when these relationships are viewed as part of the same web. This is why it is important for public bodies considering a potential collaboration to request information about the potential collaborator's close relationships or interactions with other entities.

Public health agencies wishing to develop close relationships with academic institutions and civil society organizations should take into account those bodies' relationships with industry actors. The mission, purpose, and practices of a global health NGO that has *no* close relationships with industry are more likely to be aligned with those of the WHO. However, a national public health agency will be well advised to avoid collaborating with an NGO that has close relations with industry, given the opportunities for indirect corporate influence in such a case. Looking at the current collaborators of a potential collaborator is, however, just the beginning of a systemic analysis. In order for a public health agency to fully appreciate its potential place in the relevant webs of influence, additional inquiries and analysis are also required.

8.2.4 From Model Partnerships and Single-Interaction Analyses to Systemic Analyses

The perennial quest for a model partnership might seem logical at first glance.[25] (I have been asked many times: "Show us a partnership that isn't problematic, and we'll copy that!") But the quest for a model raises serious ethical concerns—as does the isolated analysis of a single partnership. The main hazard is that this approach bypasses and ignores the cumulative effects of multiple relationships. A thorough assessment of systemic effects should explore whether the relationship is part of a complex web of relations—including other public-private interactions and multistakeholder initiatives—that cumulatively create or exacerbate the adverse effects (such as framing effects and agenda distortion) that I describe in chapter 5 and illustrate in chapter 6. Some partnership guides advocate multiple small partnerships or multiple private partners in a larger partnership to reduce the influence of any single corporation. However, both these approaches can exacerbate framing effects. For example, different industry actors in the same sector (food and beverages) are likely to share an interest in emphasizing individual responsibility for and technological solutions to obesity—especially solutions that may be readily commercialized. Framing effects are arguably the most intractable problem resulting from webs of collaboration with industry actors.

Although the systemic analysis of close relationships with industry is somewhat demanding, we recognize that this kind of analysis is vital in other contexts. Before prescribing a drug, R_n, to treat her patient's new disease or condition, D_n, the physician should know what other diseases or conditions the patient has (D_1, D_2, D_3, etc.), and should review any other drugs the patient has been prescribed (R_1, R_2, R_3, etc.) whether by her or by another physician. This information will allow the physician to determine potential interactions among the drugs the patient has been prescribed and to identify the ways in which the additional drug, R_n, might exacerbate some other condition (D_1, D_2, D_3, etc.).

When a public health agency is contemplating closer interactions with a private sector institution, it should also review the other bodies with whom the agency, its potential collaborator, and their respective peers interact. How might these interactions work cumulatively to distort the agency's agenda and priorities? How might they also serve to frame public health issues and their potential solutions in ways that are least threatening to their industry collaborators? And how might this exacerbate certain public health challenges? For example, might it lead to the neglect of longer term problems that cannot be resolved by readily commercialized technological solutions that industry actors tend to employ?

A second analogy may also help emphasize the importance of systemic analysis. In the previous chapter, I reviewed the prohibition of "concerted practices" in European competition law. This body of law is sensitive to systemic concerns and regulates integrated schemes and arrangements involving multiple corporations. Even if one interaction might appear relatively innocuous when viewed in isolation, it may be problematic when viewed as part of a larger set of practices or system of relationships. Similarly, seemingly innocuous public-private interactions may cumulatively undermine the public good.

8.2.5 Beyond the Integrity Matrix: Additional Justificatory Requirements

An interaction should not proceed, whatever the purported benefits, when it threatens to undermine the integrity of the public body or harm third parties that the public body has an obligation to protect. In such cases, the presumption against entering a close relationship with the industry actor should not be rebutted. While the integrity matrix can help identify some of the most pressing ethical concerns, it is not intended to be exhaustive. Frameworks in public health ethics can help public health agencies identify and apply additional requirements that they should meet to justify any close interaction. These requirements include the following: the proposed interaction responds to a pressing unmet public health need; it has a legitimate public health objective; there is evidence demonstrating the interaction will achieve its objective; the interaction is proportionate with that objective; the interaction involves a relationship no closer than is necessary to achieve that objective; and the interaction has been stripped of its most ethically problematic features.[26] It will be difficult for public health agencies to meet these requirements, especially given the lack of evidence regarding the efficacy of partnerships and other close relationships with industry.[27] Chapter 6 is replete with real case studies that could not satisfy these criteria. Many have been shown to have had little or no effect, among them, the Public Health Responsibility Deal Networks in Britain. (The same chapter also highlights numerous problematic features, such as a corporation's use of its relationship with a public health agency in promotional materials to burnish its reputation and increase brand loyalty.[28])

8.2.6 Conditions and Counterbalancing

Even if a public health agency can make a highly compelling case for entering a closer relationship with industry, that relationship is likely to prioritize a goal favorable to industry over another that is not. For example, a relationship may distort the research agenda of the public body by prioritizing research that would promote the interests of the industry actor at the expense of research that would not. In such a case, if a public health agency decides to proceed with the relationship, it should consider imposing a condition that matching funds be found elsewhere to support related research that might be inimical to (or, at least, not consonant with) the interests of the industry collaborator. The proposed industry collaboration would then proceed only when the required funds are made available to support additional research that would further the public body's mission and purpose but would otherwise be neglected. Counterbalancing is essential in any effort to address the *systemic* effects of industry interactions.

8.2.7 Ongoing Monitoring and Assessment, and Ex Post Evaluation

In the event that a public body decides to proceed with a close collaboration, it should require the industry actor to enter a binding legal obligation to disclose any material change in circumstances. This would include the company becoming defendant in litigation regarding the company's products or entering a close relationship with another public body. In addition, an independent third party should monitor and assess not only the collaboration itself but also the broader impacts and ethical implications of the collaboration. When the relationship concludes, the third party should also conduct an ex post evaluation. Attention to cumulative effects of industry interactions should inform the ongoing monitoring and ex post evaluation of all interactions,[29] as well as ex ante analysis.

Evaluators should explore whether the collaboration either in isolation or in conjunction with other relationships burnished the reputation of the relevant corporate actors and increased brand loyalty for its unhealthy products. Although more difficult to determine, evaluators should also consider whether the collaboration alone or in conjunction with others diverted researchers' attention from the potential adverse effects of consuming a corporate collaborator's products and whether the collaboration might have caused policymakers to neglect other longer term public health challenges.

Notably, three evaluations of the ParkLives initiative, a collaboration between Coca-Cola and local authorities in Britain to promote physical activity (discussed in chapter 6), have not explored whether the initiative promotes the consumption of the company's products—especially SSBs. This would exacerbate the very problems that the local governments are trying to address: obesity and diet-related NCDs. Where there is a plausible concern that the interaction might have such an effect, public bodies have an obligation to explore and address it. The plausibility of the concern in this case is highlighted by the evaluators' finding that the initiative is enhancing the soda company's reputation—a conclusion that the evaluators appear (unreflectively) to consider positive.

8.2.8 Disintegration and Withdrawal

Some proponents of close relationships between government and industry actors advocate "integrative partnership."[30] But the integrity matrix should remind public officials that, when collaborating with private sector bodies, *integration imperils integrity.* The subtle influence and asymmetric reciprocity resulting from such relationships can pull public bodies further away from their mission and purpose. In such a case, *disintegration* of the close relationships may be the only way to preserve or restore the integrity of one's own institution. The matrix highlights integrity because it is important for its own sake. But it also focuses attention on the institution's obligations and potential impact on others. A public health agency should not enter a relationship that violates its legal or ethical obligations to others, especially vulnerable populations whose health and well-being it has an obligation to protect. If an existing relationship is having such an effect, the public health agency should seek to withdraw from the relationship in a way that best protects those populations.[31] If public officials take systemic analysis seriously, they should recognize that other developments may also provide compelling reasons to withdraw. (These developments might include the collaborator becoming a defendant in litigation or entering a close relationship with another entity.) Ideally, in any collaboration, the public health agency would have the foresight to reserve its right to withdraw and to require financial payment from the collaborator when the latter's conduct provides grounds for withdrawal.

8.2.9 Applying this Framework to the Case Studies in the Introduction

In the introduction to this book, I provided a couple of case studies involving industry collaborations—one a proposed partnership with local government (figure 1.1 on page 7), the other an academic collaboration (figure 1.2 on page 8). These are hypothetical case studies based on real-world examples. (If you do not recall them, feel free to return to chapter 1 and reread them. But I do not comprehensively analyze them here. Instead, I say a few words about how they should be addressed.) When analyzing ethics case studies, it is important to figure out, among other things, what the case study tells us, and what it does not; what we know, and what we do not know. Each of the case studies in chapter 1 gives us enough information to raise serious concerns. If the local public health department in figure 1.1 takes money from a fast food company to build a kids' playground, this may burnish the reputation of the company, add a health halo to the company's products, and promote the consumption of those products—thereby exacerbating obesity and diet-related NCDs, the very problems the local authority is trying to address. So: we know enough to say that public health, the integrity of the public health department, and public trust in that department may all be imperiled by the proposed arrangement. In my view, these concerns provide sufficient reasons not to proceed with the partnership. But if you disagree and think that the proposed relationship merits further exploration, you should now recognize there are many things we do not know about the case that would be essential for a comprehensive systemic analysis. For example, the case study does not reveal the webs of relations the fast food company has with other public bodies. Nor does it describe the other food and beverage companies with whom the health department also has close relations. Similarly, the academic collaboration case study (figure 1.2) does not tell us enough to appreciate fully the ways in which the collaboration might influence the work of the department and of the field more broadly. Are there other corporate actors that support the work of the department or its faculty? How many other universities do research in the same or similar areas? Are their food and nutrition departments also funded or supported by the same industry actor that wishes to fund this department (or by other industry actors in the same sector)? It may be challenging to answer these questions. But it is dangerous to ignore them.

8.3 THE PERILS OF INCLUSION: MULTISTAKEHOLDER INITIATIVES

Industry actors play increasingly large roles in policymaking processes—not least, in the context of policies related to obesity and public health more broadly. The participation of industry is often justified using the language of "inclusion" and "stakeholders."[32] The term "stakeholder" was originally employed to refer to parties (other than shareholders) who might be affected by the practices of a corporation. These include—among others—employees, consumers, and residents whose air or water is being polluted by a company's factory or power plant. Now the term has been repurposed or, some might say, turned on its head. Corporations argue they are "stakeholders" in policy processes because they may be adversely affected by the policies under development.[33] Put simply, the language of "stakeholders" was initially employed to introduce public interest considerations to the private sphere (corporate activities). Now it is being used to "smuggle" private interests into the public sphere, especially in public health policy.

Corporations' new status as stakeholders is not simply used to justify representations by them regarding proposed policies. Because companies may be potentially adversely affected, so the argument goes, they are entitled to participate as decision-makers. I take issue with this increasingly pervasive use of the language and practice of "stakeholder inclusion." Policymakers should consider which parties— including companies and their employees—may be affected by their policymaking and how. But it does not follow from this that every party affected by a policy has the same right to participate in the policymaking process—and especially not the right to participate qua decision-maker. The inclusion of corporations and trade associations as stakeholders in policy decisions has become an institutional reflex in public health. But this practice clearly creates avenues for industry influence, and more critical reflection is warranted.

Imagine that a local authority is trying to decide how to respond to the drug crisis. Its policy would have an impact on various people, among them, adult drug users, schoolchildren who have access to drugs, their parents, community members affected by drug-related violence, health professionals, law enforcement officers—and, of course, the head of the criminal drug trafficking organization supplying the community with heroin and fentanyl. They all have a "stake" in the authority's decision, and we would certainly want many of them to have an opportunity to make representations. But few would argue that the head of the heroin ring should be a decision-maker in the policy process. His commercial interests will undoubtedly be affected by some potential responses, such as an increase in the number of drug enforcement officials in the area. But the city council does not have a legal or ethical obligation to protect the commercial interests of the leader of a heroin ring. Quite the contrary! If we move from illicit drugs to prescription drugs, the answer is similarly clear, even though policymakers may often fail to see it.

The current opioid crisis in the United States appears due in substantial part to the actions of a few corporate actors, in particular: pharmaceutical companies that have been promoting opioids, such as oxycodone, for use in nonterminal patients while downplaying the risk of addiction; and commercial distributors that have profited substantially from the delivery of conspicuously large quantities of these pharmaceuticals (often to very small communities). While these corporations were making billions of dollars from the sale and distribution of prescription opioids, they were sowing the seeds of the opioid crisis—and more. As discussed in chapter 3, in 2017, an estimated 72,000 people died in the United States alone from drug overdoses, and the total societal costs of the opioid crisis are estimated to be in excess of half a trillion dollars per year. Bringing on board pharmaceutical companies as partners in the development of policy responses—as the National Institutes of Health (NIH) in the United States appears to be doing—is not only ethically problematic because some of these actors caused or contributed to the problem.[34] It is also problematic because pharmaceutical companies have vested commercial interests in the outcome of the federal government's response to the crisis. Those commercial interests might not be advanced by increased regulation of prescription opioids. On the other hand, they might be well served by an initiative to promote the development of new pharmacological agents. The determination of whether either or both of these policy responses is appropriate should be made by the government, not the pharmaceutical companies. The latter can make representations. But they should not be brought on board as decision-makers—whether described as "stakeholders" in an MSI, "partners" in a PPP, or in some other way.

Consider another example raised by the case studies outlined in chapter 6: the role of the food and beverage industry in the development and implementation of obesity policy. Americans spend more than 40 percent of their food budget on foods prepared outside the home—a substantial increase on the 25 percent spent in 1970.[35] There is evidence that eating foods outside the home significantly increases calorie intake, and that this effect may be exacerbated in those who are already obese.[36] As part of a suite of efforts to reduce obesity, a public health agency might consider developing a potential public information campaign that draws on this recent research and encourages people to eat more meals that they cook themselves at home. Food industry actors could be invited to make representations to the government about the potential impact of such a campaign on their business. But these actors should not be decision-makers in the development of that policy. They have a commercial interest in the outcome of the policy process. Their interests would be best served if the public health agency did not develop such a campaign or if the campaign is implemented in a way that makes it relatively ineffective.

In public health policy, open consultation has been eclipsed by joint decision-making or, worse still, by industry actors taking the lead not only in developing but also drafting policy. Britain's Public Health Responsibility Deal Networks (RDNs) are a case in point. Voluntary pledges were reportedly drafted by an invited group of *industry* representatives across a variety of sectors including snack food, soft drinks, and alcoholic beverages.[37] (Other companies were then invited to sign on to the pledges as partners.) Industry appears to have taken the lead in both the development and implementation of the RDNs which might explain why, as discussed in chapter 6, they were shown to be of minimal effect.

To be clear, not all stakeholders are the same. Nor need they be accorded the same treatment by policymakers. Public health agencies have an obligation to protect the health and well-being of communities within their jurisdiction; they do not have an obligation to protect the commercial interests of corporations marketing their products to those communities. Thinking about the purpose of one's institution and, in turn, the obligations of the institution can help public officials distinguish among entities claiming to be stakeholders. The greater the inconsistencies, divergences, and tensions between the mission, purpose, and practices of the policymaker, and those of any so-called joint or consensus decision-maker, the greater the hazards to the integrity of, and public trust in, the policymaker, the policymaking process, and the resulting policies. When a public health agency is developing a policy to promote the health of a community, it might understandably wish to include an organization representing members of that community as a decision-maker in a policymaking process. But the policymaker should scrutinize any relationships that the community organization has with industry actors—especially entities with a commercial interest in the policy outcomes.[38] Otherwise, the policymaker may unwittingly expose his agency to indirect influence.

Before leaving this discussion, I wish to address one final point. The participation of industry actors in open consultation procedures need not be problematic per se. But policymakers should still be sensitive to the issues that such consultation processes raise. Corporations participating in open consultations often have far greater resources than public interest groups or individuals affected by the proposed policies. (While the combined advertising expenditures of Coke and Pepsi exceed the program budget of the WHO,[39] the disparity between the resources of these corporations and the budgets of public health NGOs is even more stark.) Corporations and trade associations can produce substantial glossy reports that make detailed arguments in support of their position and marshal a considerable body of research—including studies they funded for this purpose. There may well be very good reasons for members of the public to support or oppose a particular policy. But individuals do not have the time and resources to generate this kind of material. Brief submissions from a million members of the public may be given less weight by a policymaker than a glossy report from a major industry group.[40] A public radio reporter recently posed the question: "[Who are the] folks who do comment with the detail, data and analysis that can change minds [about a proposed policy]?" After reading the scholarly literature on rule-making processes,[41] and interviewing experts in the field, she concluded: "Deep-pocketed industries."[42] Policymakers should bear in mind this disparity and take steps to rectify it. For example, their agencies might commission public interest research to redress the imbalance or establish a fund supporting the pursuit of such research.

Another concern is that representations made by industry groups in open consultations may be given undue weight because close relationships between industry and government (including relations in unrelated areas) have created or exacerbated subtle reciprocity and influence. If an industry actor has "brought money to the table" to support another public policy initiative—or there is a real prospect that it will do so—policymakers may be less responsive to comments from members of the public that are inimical to the commercial interests of that industry actor (or its commercial sector). For these reasons, public interest groups frequently express exasperation about their limited influence in policymaking processes and about what they understandably perceive as disproportionate industry influence.[43]

Public health agencies should be responsive to public health concerns, not the commercial interests of industry. Companies will often argue that the promotion of their commercial interests will, in turn, promote public health. But public officials should interrogate industry claims of direct or indirect benefits to public health. As I explained in chapter 3, they should not assume that the promotion of corporate interests will inevitably promote the public good.

8.3.1 A Note on Close Versus Arm's Length Interactions

In short, what I have argued here is that the default interaction between government agencies and the private sector should be arm's length, rather than partnership or other close relationships. The danger of trying to create an exhaustive list of interactions that are "close" and those that are at "arm's length" is that it may serve as an invitation for industry actors to try to exert influence through interactions that public officials assume to be safe because they are labeled arm's length. Clearly, there are a variety of potential interactions between industry actors and other groups; some are closer, others are more distant. Rather than attempting to define exhaustively what is close and what is arm's length, it may be simpler to say that the kinds of interactions that should be considered close are those that may (a) give rise to subtle reciprocity or influence, and/or (b) undermine an institution's independence, integrity, and credibility. We may then denote as arm's length's interactions that do not create such risks.[44] This rough working guide could be supplemented with provisional lists of interactions. But any list should be frequently revisited, scrutinized, and revised. We might say with some confidence that the oral testimony by the CEO of a corporation before a congressional committee is per se an arm's length interaction. (This kind of interaction might be described as a safe harbor.)[45] We may also broadly agree that the case studies in chapter 6 are examples of close relationships (although some appear to be closer than others). There will obviously be some interactions that may not be easily classified as either close or arm's length.[46] In light of the ethical perils arising from the cumulative effects of a variety of interactions with industry, I would advise public health agencies to treat such interactions as close until proven otherwise.

8.4 CONCLUSION

This chapter offers a framework for analyzing the systemic ethical implications of industry interactions. It is intended for public officials, but it should also be of value to academic administrators and staff at CSOs. This guidance should help those who use it better navigate the status quo. But the project of the book is more ambitious. Industry strategies of influence call for a new paradigm in public health and the re-examination of older paradigms. Public health agencies should consider alternative forms of arm's length interaction with the private sector, such as basic contracts for delivery of goods and services. They should also explore closer relationships with other bodies that do not create the kinds of ethical problems highlighted here. In particular, public health agencies should consider more "public-public partnerships"—an approach endorsed by the UN Sustainable Development Goals (SDG 2015, Target 17.17). These may be vertical (e.g., federal and state health agencies in the United States collaborating with the WHO); horizontal (e.g., local health agencies collaborating with each other); or a combination of both horizontal and vertical. Public-public interactions might involve information exchange about public health challenges and how to address them. They might also involve more intensive collaboration on interventions to address health, such as coordinated legal action against corporations whose products and marketing practices undermine public health.[47]

9

Conclusion

Give me a place to stand, and I will move the world.
—ARCHIMEDES

WHEN I WAS in primary school, there was a poster on the wall of my math class-room that showed an old man standing on a rocky outcrop nestled in the clouds. The man gripped one end of a giant wooden beam with both hands. Planet Earth was resting precariously on the other end. Above the man, surrounded by glinting stars, were the words I quote in the epigraph. This expression of the lever principle is commonly attributed to Archimedes of Syracuse, the ancient Greek mathematician, astronomer, and inventor. Archimedes meant it literally: if he could find somewhere to stand, and the lever were long enough, he could move an object substantially larger and heavier than himself—even one the size of our planet. But the lever might also serve as a metaphor to help us think about the problem I address in this book.[1] Governments argue that close relationships with industry give them "leverage" over companies. But Archimedes teaches us that to exert leverage we require *distance* from the object we are trying to move. This is a lesson that public officials and policymakers would do well to keep in mind.

Collaboration plays into industry strategies of influence with serious implications for public health and for public bodies.[2] Public health agencies that enter partnerships, multistakeholder initiatives, and other close relations with industry are more likely to frame public health problems and their solutions in ways that are least threatening to their industry partners. Collaborations also distort policy agendas when agencies prioritize interventions for which they can procure industry support over forms of intervention for which they cannot. When governments partner with industry to tackle problems that can be demonstrably reduced in the short term—often using readily commercialized technological solutions—they are likely to neglect longer term problems that require social or structural solutions. More problematic still, these relationships create powerful incentives for public health officials to avoid exercising their regulatory and tax powers to directly address the ways in which industry actors exacerbate public health crises. In such cases, the integrity of and public trust in public health agencies and their policies can be seriously imperiled, and in ways that may not be easily remedied.

In this book, I have focused on close relationships with industry actors from the food and beverage sector. But there are many examples from other sectors. As I write this conclusion, the opioid epidemic (which I could only touch on in this book) is drawing considerable attention. The epidemic demonstrates the ways in which corporations whose products—prescription opioids—are ostensibly designed to promote individual and public health (through better management of pain) may instead create or exacerbate a public health crisis. It is estimated that 72,000 American lives were lost to drug overdoses in 2017, and that the societal costs of the opioid crisis exceed half a trillion dollars per year.[3] This cost is borne primarily by families, communities, and government bodies. Although many local, county, and state governments are suing pharmaceutical companies to recover their losses, the US federal government has launched a public-private initiative to address the epidemic.[4] Initial participants include the largest manufacturer of prescription opioids—a company that played a major role in fueling the epidemic by downplaying the risk of addiction while using financial relationships with patient advocacy groups and health professional associations to promote their leading opioid brand.[5]

Unsurprisingly, the federal government's announcement of the public-private opioid initiative made no mention of the ways in which industry actors have contributed to the epidemic.[6] The National Institutes of Health (NIH) were clearly trying to avoid antagonizing their corporate partners. The resulting emphasis on the development of pharmacological solutions (purportedly less addictive opioids) rather than on the increased exercise of regulatory powers over the pharmaceutical industry might well be in the interests of the pharmaceutical companies participating in the initiative. But partnering with industry plays into the latter's strategies of influence and undermines the government's ability to explore all potential measures that might help reduce the epidemic and restore public health.

Government bodies need *counter-strategies* to address industry influence in all sectors, and these strategies should be continually revised to address adaptive practices of industry. Academic institutions and civil society groups need similar strategies. In addition to partnerships and MSIs, there are other sources of industry influence that I do not address here. These include lobbying, campaign finance (including the creation of PACs and super PACs in the United States), and revolving doors through which individuals move back and forth between government positions and lucrative industry jobs. I have focused on partnerships and analogous collaborations because, unlike other forms of influence, their ethically problematic nature is less well appreciated. (They are far more often lauded than critiqued by policymakers.) But, to be clear, public institutions need comprehensive counterstrategies that address the individual and cumulative effects of all current and potential sources of influence.

The path of least resistance—taking money from and working with industry—creates systemic ethical challenges. We have been on this path for decades, and it may take some time to change direction. But change is possible. As social scientists studying institutional reform have pointed out, profound change need not always occur by means of a sudden single "exogenous shift or shock."[7] It can sometimes be accomplished through the accumulation of smaller adjustments that bring about more fundamental change over time. These adjustments are more likely to have this effect when they are part of a mid-to long-term strategy. Public officials are in a position to initiate systemic change more readily than they may be inclined to recognize—not least, by developing and articulating a strategy to wean their agencies off industry funding. The leaders of public institutions often blame the system. But we can and should hold officials responsible for their role in an ethically problematic system if they do not make efforts to criticize and change it.[8]

A public health agency may not be able to withdraw from all close relationships with industry actors tomorrow—particularly when this might interrupt a major public health program or expose the agency to potential legal liability. But the agency can change its default to avoiding, rather than seeking out, industry partnerships. It could also develop a strategy that includes the goal of being free from all industry partnerships within, say, five years and a commitment to instead exploring collaborations with other *public* institutions, especially those with a similar public health mission. Public health agencies can and should speak out collectively about the ethical and pragmatic challenges of the status quo and about the need for public funding to achieve their public health missions. Several current and former public health officials could write a joint letter to the *New York Times* (among other national and international newspapers of record) calling attention to the critical lack of public funds and describing the impact of this on their ability to tackle the most intractable public health problems.

We need public health agencies—as well as research universities—to tackle some of the world's most pressing problems and their public health sequelae including obesity, opioid addiction, cancer, and climate change. If these institutions depend on industry funding to address our most challenging problems, they will only develop solutions that promote the interests of industry. If we are truly serious about solving these problems, however, we must be willing and able to explore all potential solutions, including those that threaten industry interests. We need not demonize industry to protect public health. But we need not—and should not—insist on common ground with industry to promote public health. On the contrary, we imperil public health, as well as the integrity of public health agencies, when we confound the common good and common ground.

It is time to explore new paradigms in public health and perhaps revisit and revise some old ones.[9] But we cannot and will not do any of this until we recognize that the current state of affairs is profoundly ethically problematic. To return to the metaphor with which I began: we must first acknowledge that something is wrong with the water.

Appendix A

SELECTED INTERNATIONAL POLICIES

A.1 THE WORLD HEALTH ORGANIZATION

Article 71 of the WHO's Constitution (1946) provides that the organization may consult and cooperate with international NGOs and, with the consent of the government concerned, with national NGOs. However, for many years, the WHO's Principles Governing Relations with NGOs provided that the WHO should not establish formal relations with an NGO unless the organization is "free from concerns which are primarily of a commercial or profit-making nature."[1] While that policy was in force, the WHO entered into formal relations with roughly 200 organizations. The list includes international professional associations (such as the World Medical Association), charities and organizations providing humanitarian relief (such as Médecins Sans Frontières), and patient advocacy organizations (for conditions such as thalassaemia).[2] Despite the requirement just quoted, the WHO also admitted several NGOs that represented the interests of industry, had corporate members, and/or were dependent on industry support for their funding.[3] In 2000, the WHO also developed guidelines for partnering with private sector bodies.[4] However, both policies have recently been replaced.

In May 2016, after years of debate—particularly regarding the relationship between the private sector and the WHO—the World Health Assembly adopted the Framework of Engagement with Non-State Actors (FENSA).[5] The framework requires that any engagement with a nonstate actor must demonstrate a clear benefit to public health; conform with the WHO's Constitution, mandate, and program of work; respect the intergovernmental nature of the WHO and the decision-making authority of member states; support and enhance the scientific and evidence-based approach of the WHO's work, and be conducted with transparency, openness, inclusiveness, accountability, integrity, and "mutual respect." The framework anticipates some concerns about influence. It provides that engagement with nonstate actors should protect the WHO from undue influence, especially when developing and applying policies, norms, and standards; should not compromise the WHO's integrity, independence, credibility, and reputation; and should be effectively managed "where possible avoiding conflict of interest and other forms of risks to WHO" (para 5). FENSA recognizes some risks of engagement: "being primarily used to serve the interests of the non-State actor concerned with limited or no benefits for WHO and public health"; "conferring an endorsement of the non-State actor's name, brand, product, views or activity"; "whitewashing of a non-State actor's image through an engagement with WHO"; and "competitive advantage for a non-State actor."[6] Although FENSA applies to all kinds of nonstate actors, these risks mainly arise when the WHO engages with industry actors.

The document—like earlier drafts—has attracted some criticism, especially from public health NGOs. They have expressed concern that the framework "lumps together" public interest NGOs and business interest NGOs under the term nonstate actors; that it permits the latter to participate in the governance of and the development of policy at the WHO; that it employs a problematic definition of conflicts of interest; and that it is not accompanied by a detailed policy to address conflicts of interest resulting from increased engagement with the private sector.[7] (I argue in this book that conflicts of interest policies are necessary but not sufficient. The WHO needs a broader strategy to address all forms of influence by corporations and industry groups.) Although we may need to wait and see how FENSA is interpreted and applied by the WHO, the organization's pilot database of nonstate actors should provide some significant clues.[8]

A.2 THE FOOD AND AGRICULTURE ORGANIZATION (FAO)

The FAO is the UN body with responsibilities for, among other things, setting standards in food safety, food quality, and nutrition. In 2000, the FAO adopted principles for cooperation with the private sector that prohibit partnering with "organizations or enterprises whose products, programmes or methods of operation are . . . unethical or otherwise antithetical to its mandate."[9] The policy also states that the FAO will not enter partnerships that might undermine its credibility "as a steward of public trust and funds." Although the FAO's principles emphasize that partnerships "do not imply any right to . . . special access to the [FAO's] decision-making machinery ... or to influence its policies or its position on scientific and technical issues," the policy does not provide any mechanisms or guidance for FAO staff that might help them address the subtle reciprocity and influence arising from close relationships with industry.

More recently, the FAO has developed a general partnership strategy,[10] and a strategy for industry partnerships.[11] Both are expressly "living documents" to be refined in the light of experience. The new industry "strategy" (which will be the basis for the future revision of the 2000 policy) recognizes "the potential risks" to the FAO's "intergovernmental character"; its independence and impartiality; and its "neutrality/scientific credibility."[12] The strategy also acknowledges the risk of undue influence on FAO standard setting. But, at the same time, it encourages private sector bodies to partner with the FAO and touts as potential benefits "increased opportunity to be heard in international policy development and standard setting processes for food and agriculture."[13] (Other benefits include "enhanced dialogue with governments and an opportunity to contribute to the development of national planning frameworks.") There is a patently unresolved tension between FAO's articulation of the risks of collaboration and the language it uses to encourage private sector bodies to engage in collaboration. Like other UN agencies, the FAO needs a strategy to address industry influence in all its forms, including partnership.

A.3 JOINT APPROACHES OF THE WHO AND FAO

The first nutrition conference, jointly hosted by the WHO and the FAO in 1992, encouraged "active cooperation among governments, multilateral, bilateral and non-governmental organizations, the private sector, communities and individuals" to eliminate all forms of malnutrition.[14] Although the resulting action plan called for claims in food labeling and advertising to be "carefully controlled" and for prohibitions on false and misleading advertising, it otherwise promoted a collaborative approach with industry.[15] The plan called on governments to "[e]ncourage the private sector . . . to promote nutritional wellbeing by considering the impact of its activities on nutritional status." In the key paragraph on "promoting appropriate diets and healthy lifestyles," only one provision addressed the role of industry. It called on governments to "[e]ncourage institutionalized food services and the catering sector to provide and promote healthy diets."

The second conference in 2014 similarly adopted a declaration that "collective action is instrumental to improve nutrition, requiring collaboration between governments, the private sector, civil society, and communities."[16] The declaration expressed a commitment to "strengthen and facilitate contributions and action by all stakeholders." The reader has to go to the much longer report of the meeting for recognition of the threat to policy processes arising from "conflicts of interest introduced by inappropriate relationships with powerful economic actors, including transnational corporations."[17] The report calls on member states and UN agencies "to design and implement effective rules and regulations on conflict of interest, and review and potentially terminate or re-design . . . all Public-Private Partnerships (PPP) and multi-stakeholder arrangements." There is a tension between this paragraph, cautioning member states and UN agencies about private sector influence in policy processes and the FAO's website (discussed in the FAO section earlier). The site encourages private sector entities to partner with the FAO to obtain "increased voice in the international sphere and enhanced dialogue with governments, creating the opportunity to contribute to international policy development, standard setting processes for food and agriculture, and national planning frameworks."[18]

A.4 UNITED NATIONS: POLICIES AND APPROACHES

Not surprisingly, the policies of the WHO and FAO, both specialized agencies of the UN, broadly reflect the approach of the UN. The Political Declaration on Non-Communicable Diseases adopted by the General Assembly in September 2011 declared that effective NCD prevention and control called for "health in all policies and whole-of-government approaches" across many sectors including health, agriculture, environment, labor, trade, and economic development.[19] In short, the declaration calls on governments to focus on the health implications of their policies, whatever the sphere of policymaking. Although the declaration highlights "the fundamental conflict of interest between the tobacco industry and public health,"[20] it does not take off the table relationships with other industry sectors. The declaration provides that member states should engage "non-health actors and key stakeholders, *where appropriate, including the private sector* and civil society, in collaborative partnerships to promote health" (emphasis added).[21] But it gives no guidance as to when it may not be appropriate for member states to "engage" with nontobacco private sector entities (such as food and soda companies).

The 2014 Outcome Document on NCDs reiterates that the "primary role and responsibility" of governments is to "generate effective responses for the prevention and control of non-communicable diseases at the global, national and local levels." Although the outcome document provides that states may engage with private sector bodies (among other actors),[22] it acknowledges the importance of "protecting public health policies . . . from undue influence by any form of real, perceived or potential conflict of interest."[23] But, like the 2011 Declaration, the 2014 Outcome Document offers no guidance for states wishing to address influence.

In September 2015, the UN General Assembly adopted the 2030 Agenda for Sustainable Development, together with a set of 17 Sustainable Development Goals (SDGs) and 169 associated targets. Many of the SDGs are related to nutrition and health. They include ending hunger, achieving food security, improving nutrition, and promoting sustainable agriculture (SDG2); ensuring healthy lives and promoting well-being for all at all ages (SDG3); ensuring availability and sustainable management of water and sanitation for all (SDG6); ensuring sustainable consumption and production patterns (SDG12); and conserving and sustainably using the oceans, seas, and marine resources for sustainable development (SDG14). SDG17 endorses "effective public, public-private and civil society partnerships, building on the experience and resourcing strategies of partnerships."[24] But it provides no guidance addressing the ethical perils of public-private partnerships, nor any recommendations regarding when collaborations should be established with other public bodies and with CSOs rather than industry actors.

A.5 THE ROAD AHEAD . . .

The director general of the WHO recently presented a document to the Executive Board that provides guidance to member states on conflicts of interest.[25] The approach taken in this report differs in a number of ways from the approach I take in chapter 7. The difference that may be most obvious to readers is that the discussion of integrity is folded into "balancing of risks and benefits" in the middle of the WHO's analytic framework; in my approach, integrity is placed in the foreground.[26] The WHO approach also differs from mine in that it does not address the broader systemic effects of collaborating with industry, including the cumulative effects of engagement with a variety of industry actors. There is a further limitation: the director general confined the scope of the report to conflicts of interest.[27] As I argue in chapter 7, conflicts of interest policies are necessary but not sufficient to address the myriad sources of industry influence in policy processes. The document describes itself both as a "draft approach," to be piloted and tested, and as a "living document that may be revised according to Member States' needs and the evolution of engagement with external actors." So, there should be further opportunities to provide critical feedback on the draft guidance.[28]

Between the completion of the manuscript and the publication of this book, there has been a flurry of activity—much of it in preparation for the UN High-Level Meeting on NCDs in New York at the end of September 2018. This activity demonstrates the urgency of the concerns articulated here. First, the UN and the WHO have conducted several global assessments of both action taken and progress toward the reduction of NCDs—including the target of reducing premature mortality from NCDs by one-third by 2030 (SDG 3.4). The most recent assessments repeatedly use terms such as "inadequate," "insufficient," and "disappointing."[29] Second, multiple reports by the UN and the WHO acknowledge that the influence of and "interference" by industry, especially multinational corporations, has impeded health policies and public health interventions (including regulation and taxation) that could help reduce NCDs.[30] Despite this, the reports emphasize the need to achieve common ground with the private sector.[31] They also continue to call for public-private partnerships, "coalitions and alliances," and other forms of "engagement" with the private sector.[32] The prevailing view is that, with the exception of the tobacco industry, the ensuing conflicts of interest can be managed.[33] This book raises concerns with such approaches. In short, the search for common ground with industry can undermine rather than promote public health (see chapter 3). The partnership paradigm also imperils the integrity of public health agencies (see chapters 7 and 8). These agencies need not only conflicts of interest policies but also comprehensive counter-strategies to insulate themselves from corporate influence. And, as I argue in the conclusion, public health needs another paradigm!

Appendix B

THE ANATOMY OF THE GIFT

Early anatomists obviously lacked imaging technologies. In order to look inside the human body, they had to dissect it. The sixteenth-century drawings of Andreas Vesalius record his efforts to tease apart—and render in ink—sinew, nerves, and vessels. To address the ethical implications of gifts, we should similarly tease apart their various dimensions. In this part of my analysis, I make allusions to blood and organ donation because there are interesting parallels between what we might call "the gift of anatomy" and "the anatomy of the gift."[1] I also draw on the discussion of reciprocity in chapter 4.

The *parties* to the gift are important. In addition to *donors* and *recipients,* other parties may also be involved. Gifts channeled through *intermediaries* may or may not be ethically problematic, depending on how and why they are being channeled. Sometimes the intermediary is a truly independent organization.[2] The purpose of such an intermediary might be to reduce influence by the donor. But the presence of an independent intermediary does not prevent *agenda distortion*—a systemic problem I describe in chapter 5—if the donor requires the gift to be applied for a particular purpose. At other times, an intermediary is created or employed to co-ordinate a gift from several donors.[3] A donor may use an intermediary to conceal the origin of the gift from the public. When the source of the gift is known to the recipient but not the public, this may eliminate or minimize the *appearance* of influence without addressing the influence itself. Such an approach is, of course, ethically problematic.[4] The intermediary may have a name that suggests it is a public interest NGO or consumer organization, even when it was created to promote—or primarily serves to promote—industry interests.[5]

Two further points about the nature and identity of the parties to the gift merit attention. Although a gift from an individual philanthropist could enhance the reputation of a company when that company is named after the donor or a member of the donor's family, a gift from the corporation itself is far more likely to burnish the company's reputation and increase brand loyalty. *Beneficiaries* of the gift need not be parties over whom influence is sought. As we learned from the analysis of reciprocity and influence in chapters 4 and 5, public officials (like the rest of us) can be influenced by gratitude for benefits received by others, whether or not they asked the donor to confer these benefits.

An assessment of any gift should consider two key dimensions: *compatibility* and *externality*. When physicians are deciding whether to transplant a kidney, they conduct a number of tests to determine whether donor and recipient are compatible. (They look at the blood types of the donor and recipient, and also the tissue types.[6]) The purpose is to find the best match between donor and recipient. In the case of an institutional gift, the compatibility of donor and recipient is also important. When an industry actor proposes a gift to a public institution, an assessment of compatibility requires a comparison of the donor and recipient institutions: what they do (practices), what they say they do (mission), and what they are obligated to do (purpose). (The integrity matrix in chapter 8 can assist with this comparison.) It also requires an analysis of the interests and obligations of the donor and recipient. There is a fundamental incompatibility when the donor company's products or practices have adverse effects on others, and the recipient public health agency has an obligation to protect the affected parties.

Economists often speak of "negative externalities"—by which they mean the costs that fall on "third parties." (I critique the latter term in chapter 4 but, for simplicity, I follow common usage in this appendix.) Ethical analysis of gifts should consider all the ways in which third parties might be adversely affected. Promotional materials, including companies' CSR reports, often tout potential benefits of corporate gifts for the intended beneficiaries. But potential adverse effects on other parties are usually neglected or downplayed. Potential recipients of gifts should be particularly sensitive to divergences between who might benefit and who might bear the burdens arising from the gift (and the relationships that the gift promotes.)[7] The burdens or harms arising from a gift may be subtle. When a public health agency is the recipient of a donation, this may change the agency's agenda or priorities. For example, the gift may exacerbate a bias toward short-term public health challenges—to the detriment of individuals or communities who would benefit from the agency's work on longer-term goals and solutions.

The *conditions of the gift* encompass what is given, and the terms on which it is given. The gift may be a "one-off" financial donation that can be spent in full. (Such a gift may nonetheless have long-term effects, and it may also be considered the basis of a partnership.)[8] Alternatively, a gift can take the form of an endowment permitting the recipient only to spend earned interest annually. Gifts may take effect immediately, at a specified date, on the occurrence of a particular event. But gifts need not be financial. They may also take the form of goods or services (gifts "in kind.") When a company voluntarily agrees to print a government agency icon on its packaging (as is the case with the MyPlate icon discussed in chapter 6), it is providing a service to the government—increased distribution of a government communication. No funds exchange hands, but the government considers the service valuable (even though it may be of greater value to the company, conferring a health halo on and promoting sales of its products.) Providing a valued service to a government agency may be as influential as a financial gift.

Donors may impose conditions specifying how, for what purpose, and for whose benefit funds may be disbursed. For example, the donor may require that the gift be used to address obesity among children from inner cities. Conditions can also be tacit or implied. (The phrase *quid pro quo* is sometimes used to capture conditions that are tacit or implied, as well as those that are expressed.) But, as the discussion of reciprocity in chapter 4 illustrates, "unrestricted grants" and other gifts without conditions can still be very influential and, in turn, ethically problematic. If there is good reason to believe that further gifts may be forthcoming, the recipient is unlikely to do anything that might jeopardize those future gifts. This is what I call "the tyranny of the next gift,"[9] an effect that may be exacerbated when potential future gifts could be even more substantial than the present one.

The conditions of the gift include mechanisms for *monitoring and enforcement.* A deed of gift may provide for the return of the gift or the termination of the relationship. Conditions are not the sole province of donors. Recipients may impose conditions too. Scandals involving high-profile donors are far from uncommon.[10] For this reason, academic institutions would be well advised to include a provision permitting them to remove the name of the donor (or other individual(s) after whom a building or university chair is named) if subsequent revelations about that person's conduct threaten to undermine the reputation of the recipient institution.

The *relational* dimensions of gifts are especially important. A first gift is often exploratory, a "testing" gift to determine if the recipient is responsive to the donor's directions, interests, suggestions, or concerns. Recipients may similarly use that first gift to assess whether the donor will try to interfere with its activities. As our exploration of reciprocity in chapter 4 made clear, a gift can be highly influential without direct interference from the donor. Recipients who are only vigilant about external pressure may fail to recognize the hazards of self-censorship. Gifts are rarely, if ever, stipulated as final—with the *finality* expressly in the deed of gift. But the main advantage of such a gift is that it would help avoid the tyranny of the next gift. To eliminate or reduce anticipatory reciprocity and the influence arising from a potential further gift, the recipient could make a public commitment that it will not solicit or accept any further donations from this particular donor. Such a commitment could even take the form of a legal obligation owed to a third party with a penalty or other incentive to comply.

The relational dimension of a gift has at least three components: what I call, respectively, *external relations, fiscal relations, and object relations.* The gift may have an impact on the relationships between the donor and third parties—for example, enhancing brand loyalty among consumers. It may also affect relations between the recipient and third parties—for example, undermining a community's trust in a public health agency. The relative size of a donation compared to other gifts and funding streams available to the recipient (fiscal relations) is also significant. There is reason to believe that the larger the gift relative to other sources of income, the more dependent the recipient will be on the donor, and the more potent the obligation to provide reciprocal returns. But there is no magic threshold beneath which gifts pose no ethical hazards. We cannot say, for example, that as long as an entity receives less than half its income from industry (whether a single actor or industry actors collectively) that there will be no concerns about independence, integrity, or credibility. Small gifts can be influential, and institutions can lose their independence without being or becoming financially dependent.[11] The relationship between the gift and the recipient's mission and purpose (object relations) are important too. But like fiscal relations, object relations are not reducible to a simple rubric. The more central a gift to the objectives articulated in the institution's founding documents and mission statement, the greater the recipient's dependence on and gratitude toward the donor. But gifts peripheral to these objectives present another ethical hazard. They may distort the institution's agenda and priorities.

It is important to distinguish *publicity,* in the sense of public disclosure, and the *promotion* of the gift. Publicity addresses which aspects of the gift, if any, are disclosed to the recipient, affected third parties, and the relevant publics. Promotion addresses how the parties—especially donors—promote the gift to policymakers, regulators, and consumers (among others). A corporation may heavily promote the existence of a gift on its website, in glossy brochures, or television advertisements. But the corporation may simultaneously keep many conditions of the gift secret and impose an obligation on the recipient also to keep those conditions confidential. Communication of the terms of the gift to the recipient but not to the beneficiaries, third parties, or the relevant publics is analogous to what some scholars call "acoustic separation."[12] But the targeting of communications in this way brings its own ethical perils—particularly if subsequent disclosure of the conditions of the gift undermines public trust in the recipient.

To be clear, promotion goes beyond mere disclosure or notification. Corporate donors may be required by applicable laws and regulations to report charitable gifts in their tax returns and annual reports. Recipient organizations may similarly be required to disclose receipt of those gifts. But the promotion of the gift to current or potential consumers (among others) goes beyond what is formally required and serves another purpose. Corporations promote their philanthropy to burnish their reputation and defuse concerns about their commercial activities. The policies of some institutions, such as the WHO, expressly prohibit donors using their gifts for "commercial, promotional, marketing, or advertising purposes."[13] But when corporations are *not* prohibited from using gifts to enhance their status and burnish their reputation, we should expect them to do so.

Promotion of a gift made to a public health agency is most problematic when it confers a health halo on and increases brand loyalty for a donor's unhealthy products. In such a case, it undermines public health and the agency's public health mission and purpose. Targeted communication—for example, informing other prospective funders or policymakers of the identity of the corporate donor but not broadcasting its name widely—might appear to mitigate this problem. But such an approach may inadvertently create another ethical problem. Beneficiaries or third parties may find themselves unwittingly participating in a project that the company is using to burnish its reputation among policymakers. That said, broadly speaking, when industry actors make gifts to government bodies (and, similarly, universities and CSOs), the ethical arguments tend to weigh strongly *in favor of disclosure* and *against promotion* of those gifts.

When independent third parties monitor and assess the effects of gifts, this may be analogous to physicians monitoring patients after their transplants. In addition to assessing the efficacy of the transplant and the toxicity of immuno-suppressants in the individual patient, doctors may also collect data to determine the long-term survival rates of both grafts and patients. (In the case of kidney transplants, this helps transplant units determine the extent to which greater compatibility between donor and recipient increases the likelihood of a successful transplant.) In the case of gifts from industry, ex post assessment conducted by an independent body might reveal recurring patterns of behavior and the systemic effects of webs of relations created or promoted by gifts, as well as the consequences of any single gift or relationship.

Medical students are often taught mnemonic devices to help them remember human anatomy. These devices tend to be conspicuously contrived but once learned they usually prove difficult to forget. A similar approach might help with what I call here "the anatomy of the gift." If we take the first letter of each of these dimensions of the gift (omitting repetitions), this gives us the acronym PRICE (figure B.1). The old adage "every gift comes at a price" might now serve as a reminder to consider the essential dimensions of any gift—whether or not it is framed as collaboration.

P	Publicity of Gift and Terms	What is disclosed and to whom. Same or different communications to different parties ("acoustic separation").
	Promotion of the Gift	Whether, how, and to whom promoted (e.g. use of gift as marketing tool).
R	Relational Dimensions	Impact of gift on relationship between parties; relationship of gift to mission and purpose of recipient (Object Relations); relationship of gift to other funding sources (Fiscal relations); impact of gift on relationships with "third parties" (External Relations).
I	Identity of the Parties	Donor, recipient, intermediaries, beneficiaries, and others affected.
C	Compatibility	Compatibility of institutions (see also the Integrity Matrix, Fig. 8.1) and of gift (see also Object Relations, in R above).
	Conditions of the Gift	Terms and conditions of gift; monitoring and enforcement.
E	Externalities	Potential benefits or harms to "third parties," especially those whom recipient has obligation to protect.
	Ex post assessment	Review of relationship ex post (as well as during and ex ante)—ideally, independent assessment that includes systemic analysis of webs of relations.

FIGURE B.1 The PRICE Mnemonic

NOTES

PREFACE

1. Italo Calvino, *The Road to San Giovanni*, trans. Tim Parks (New York: Vintage, 1994).

2. Case T-326/99 Nancy Fern Olivieri v. Commission of the European Communities and European Agency for the Evaluation of Medicines (EMEA) [2003] ECR-II 6057, http://tinyurl.com/Olivieri-v-Commission-2003.

3. Thompson et al., *The Olivieri Report* (2001).

CHAPTER 1

1. Wallace, *This Is Water* (2009).

2. Kraak et al., "A Q Methodology Study," (2014); Hernandez-Aguado and Zaragoza, "Support of Public-Private Partnerships," (2016).

3. FAO, "FAO Strategy for Partnerships with the Private Sector," (2013a).

4. UN, "United Nations Sustainable Development Goals," (2015).

5. Salter, "Short-Termism at Its Worst," (2013).

6. Sinclair, *I, Candidate for Governor* (1994).

7. Bazerman and Tenbrunsel, *Blind Spots* (2010).

8. Carlat, "Dr Drug Rep," (2007). See also Lo et al., *Conflicts of Interest* (2009).

9. Marks, "Toward a Systemic Ethics," (2014a), and Marks, "Caveat Partner," (2017).

10. Hirschman, *Crossing Boundaries* (1998).

11. FAO, "The Contribution of the Private Sector and Civil Society to Improve Nutrition," (2013b).

12. For a "web of influence" involving twenty-nine sugar industry actors, see Gornall, "Sugar: Spinning a Web of Influence," (2015). Although I focus on institutional rather than individual relationships. Gornall's diagram (adapted with permission here) shows that, webs of influence often include individuals, notably academic experts who serve on advisory bodies.

13. I use the terms "public" and "private" in this book to capture the distinction between different kinds of institutions. But I acknowledge that these terms may also refer to two other dichotomies: (1) the distinction between the domestic sphere on the one hand, and political or economic spheres on the other hand (a topic addressed by feminist ethics scholars); and (2) the distinction (that has become so important in our era of big data) between what we keep to ourselves and what is shared with others (whether or not we freely choose to share it).

14. U.S. Code, Titles 40–44.

15. See, e.g., Cladis, *Private Vision* (2006).

16. Kappeler and Nemoz, "Public and Private Partnerships in Europe," (2010).

17. For the Oxfam report in which this figure appears, see Beth Hoffmann, *Behind the Brands* (2013). This diagram, from Beth Hoffman, "Behind the Brands," (2013), is reproduced with the permission of Oxfam, Oxfam House, John Smith Drive, Cowley, Oxford OX4 2JY, UK, www.oxfam.org.uk. Oxfam does not necessarily endorse any text or activities that accompany the materials.

18. See, e.g., Nestle, *Soda Politics* (2015), 5–6, 11.

19. I discuss this further in chapter 3. Many well-known organic brands are also owned or have been acquired by multinational food companies. See, e.g., Cornucopia Institute, "Who Owns Organic Now?" February 13, 2014, https://www.cornucopia.org/wp-content/uploads/2014/02/Organic-chart-feb-2014.jpg.

20. Marks, "On Regularity and Regulation," (2011).

21. WHO, "Public-Private Partnerships for Health," (2013).

22. Some scholars define PPPs to include public procurement and contracting out public services. For a discussion of definitions, see Richter, *Public-Private Partnerships and International Health Policy-Making* (2004b).

23. UN Standing Committee on Nutrition (SCN), "Private Sector Engagement Policy," (2006).

24. Personal communication (e-mail) from the UN SCN Secretariat, January 8, 2018.

25. The SCN's 2006 policy permitted direct funds and in-kind contributions from nonfood-related PSOs that have "satisfactory assessment ratings with regard to their performance on human rights, labour rights, environment and good governance criteria."

26. Kraak et al., "Balancing the Benefits," (2012), citing Austin, "Strategic Collaboration," (2000).

27. See, e.g., Richter, "Public-Private Partnerships," (2004a).

CHAPTER 2

1. Lessig, "Institutional Corruption, Defined," (2013).

2. Thompson, "Two Concepts of Corruption," (2013).

3. Thompson, *Restoring Responsibility* (2004), 4.

4. See, e.g., Scott, *Institutions and Organizations* (2013), 56.

5. See, e.g., Wolfgang Streeck and Kathleen Thelen, "Introduction," in Streeck and Thelen, *Beyond Continiuity* (2005), 9–13. For a list of twenty-one definitions of "institution" from a variety of disciplines, see Heclo, *On Thinking Institutionally* (2008), 48–50. See also MacIntyre, *After Virtue* (2007), 194.

6. "Institution," OED Online, 7th ed. June 2017. http://www.oed.com.

7. I do not focus on the ethics of corporations—even corporations that acquire for-benefit status on the grounds that their purpose includes the promotion of public health. However, in chapter 3, where I discuss the common good, I consider for-benefit corporations in order to address the ethical implications of government bodies "partnering" or having close relationships with them.

8. Aristotle, *Nicomachean Ethics* (2012), bk. 1, chap.7. These ends may evolve over time. For example, we would now consider the ends of medicine to include the palliation of suffering and define health broadly to include (among other things) psychological well-being.

9. See, e.g., Pursey et al., "The Ethics of the Node Versus the Ethics of the Dyad?," (2006).

10. Taylor, "Institutional Corruption," (2014), esp. 17–18.

11. WHO, *Basic Documents*, 48th ed. (2014), 1.

12. Cf. Taylor, "Institutional Corruption," (2014), 17–18. Taylor argues that an "institution's telos is not a primordial feature of the social world simply awaiting discovery by intrepid social analysts," but is "politically constructed, which means that we have built it, and that we can demolish and reconstruct it, and, most importantly, that we might fight over how to do these things."

13. For a narrower view, see Newhouse, "Institutional Corruption," (2014).

14. Marbury v. Madison, 5 U.S. 137 (1803).

15. See, e.g., Gostin, "FDA Regulation of Tobacco," (2009) on the role of the Supreme Court in determining the scope of authority of the FDA.

16. Cf. Thompson, "Two Concepts of Corruption," (2013), 5, arguing that "the purposes of government (and many other public institutions) are multiple and contestable, and therefore cannot be fully specified and endorsed independently of a collective decision-making process." However, an institution's constitutive documents can establish the contours of—and mechanisms for resolving disputes about—an institution's purposes.

17. WHO Constitution (1946), Art. 1.

18. WHO Constitution (1946), Art. 2.

19. WHO Constitution (1946), Art. 75, giving the International Court of Justice (ICJ) authority to settle disputes regarding the interpretation or application of the WHO Constitution in cases where the dispute is not settled by negotiation, by the World Health Assembly, or by another mode of settlement agreed by the parties.

20. WHO Constitution (1946), Art. 73.

21. IRS, "Exemption Requirements—501(c)(3) Organizations," (requiring that the institution's "organizing document" limits the organization's purposes to the specified "exempt" purposes, and does not empower it to engage in activities that do not further those purposes except as an "insubstantial" part of its activities).

22. See, e.g., Barak-Erez, "The Doctrine of Legitimate Expectations," (2005) arguing that, despite the name, the doctrine of "legitimate expectation" does not protect pure expectation. On the contrary, Barak-Erez contends that administrative law primarily protects reliance—whether such reliance is based on regular practice by a government agency or an express promise made on its behalf.

23. See, e.g., Buchanan and DeCamp, "Responsibility for Global Health," (2006) discussing the responsibilities of organizations whose actions are inconsistent with their public commitments to global health.

24. To be clear—I am not arguing here that consistency between mission and practices is everything from an ethical perspective. The mafia may do exactly what it says it does. But we still think the organization is profoundly ethically problematic. My discussion both in this chapter and the one following highlights other important considerations.

25. See also Taylor, "Institutional Corruption," (2014), 19, arguing that focusing on an institution's "explicitly avowed social purposes" is a somewhat limited exercise that leads to "getting institutions back to their pre-established courses." Taylor also argues that "[f]unctionalism reminds us that social institutions are provisional settlements of ongoing processes of negotiation and contestation," and that "worries about corruption are sometimes demands that the terms of a settlement be rethought."

26. "Integrity," OED Online. June 2017, http://www.oed.com, accessed July 1, 2017.

27. Schafer, "Biomedical Conflicts of Interest," (2004). Cf. Lewis et al., "Dancing with the Porcupine," (2001), 784, describing intellectual integrity somewhat infelicitously as the university's most precious "commodity."

28. See, e.g., AAMC, *Scientific Basis* (2007).

29. AAUP, *Recommended Principles* (2014).

30. AAUP, *Recommended Principles*, loc. 3844. See also CAUT, *Open for Business,* (2013), 3, 59, 191.

31. AAUP, *Recommended Principles,* loc. 842. Cf. CAUT, *Open for Business,* (2013), 1, emphasizing "the right, without restriction by prescribed doctrine, institutional censorship, or limits to their civil liberties, to have freedom in their teaching, research and scholarship, service to the institution and service to the community and the public at large," and proposes that "the integrity of the university is measured by the extent to which it protects this necessary context for scholarly work."

32. See, e.g., World Bank, "Integrity Vice-Presidency," (2016), and MIGA, "Institutional Integrity," (2016). I discuss the narrow definition of corruption employed by the World Bank and other international organizations (emphasizing abuse of public office *for private gain*) later in this chapter.

33. Marks, "Toward a Systemic Ethics," (2014a); and Marks, "Caveat Partner," (2017).

34. See, e.g., Carter, *Integrity* (1996), 7.

35. Carter, *Integrity,* 1996, 7.

36. See Margaret Cohen, "A Psychoanalytic View of the Notion of Integrity," in Montefiore and Vines, *Integrity* (1999), 85–103. Cf. Amelie Rorty, "Integrity: Political, Not Psychological," in Montefiore and Vines, *Integrity* (1999), 104–116 (responding to the chapter by Margaret Cohen.)

37. Michel de Montaigne, "On the Inconstancy of Our Actions," in Montaigne, *The Essays: A Selection*, trans. M. A. Screech (New York: Penguin, 1994), bk. 2, ess. 1.

38. Montaigne, *Essays* (1994).

39. Blaise Pascal, *Pensees*, trans. W. F. Trotter (New York: E. P. Dutton, 1958), frag. 434.

40. Andrew Stark, "Public Integrity," (2001), reviewing Dobel, *Public Integrity* (1999).

41. Stark, "Public Integrity," (2001), arguing that "inconsistencies in personal history do not jeopardize integrity to the extent that they are internally generated, through character, reflection, or self-consciousness, rather than externally imposed, through interests, pressures,

or influences." But it may not always be easy to distinguish the former and the latter, especially when external factors subtly influence reflection. Cf. Halfon, *Integrity* (1989), 87, arguing that persons of integrity are "committed to doing what is best," and they "will not compromise their moral commitments but may revise a moral principle or reassess a moral idea without thereby undermining the commitment to do what is best." See also Dobel, *Public Integrity* (1999) for a dynamic account of integrity.

42. Although I focus on Deborah Rhode's work in this paragraph, see also Carter, *Integrity* (1996), 7, requiring consistency between speech and action. Carter argues that individual integrity has three components: "*discerning* what is right and what is wrong" (moral reflection); "*acting* on what you have discerned even at personal cost" (steadfastness); and "*saying openly* that you are acting on your understanding of right from wrong" even when others disagree.

43. Rhode, "If Integrity Is the Answer, What Is the Question?," (2003).

44. Rhode, "Integrity," (2003), 335, requiring adherence to "values that reflect some reasoned deliberation, based on a logical assessment of relevant evidence and competing views.") Rhode also draws on philosophical accounts of integrity including McFall, "Integrity," (1987).

45. Rhode, "Integrity," (2003), 336.

46. Rhode, "Integrity," (2003), 343.

47. Rhode, "Integrity," (2003), 343.

48. David Luban, "Integrity—Its Causes and Cures," in Luban, *Legal Ethics and Human Dignity* (2007), 291.

49. For a selection of essays on integrity in a variety of contexts (including academic integrity, integrity in fund-raising, and integrity in public service, see Montefiore and Vines, *Integrity* (1999); Dobel, *Public Integrity* (1999); and Wolfgang Amann and Agata Stachowicz-Stanusch, eds., *Integrity in Organizations* (2012).

50. Alan Montefiore, "A Philosopher's Introduction," in Montefiore and Vines, *Integrity* (1999), arguing that institutional integrity "depends on an adequate degree of consistency or self-integration over time."

51. Taylor, "Institutional Corruption," (2014), esp. 5-7. Conflicting purpose is one of four problems Taylor discusses: confused, conflicting, confounding, and changed purpose.

52. See USDA, "Mission Areas," https://www.usda.gov/our-agency/about-usda/mission-areas and USDA, "USDA Strategic Goals," https://www.usda.gov/our-agency/about-usda/strategic-goals.

53. I discuss this example further in Marks, "Toward a Systemic Ethics," (2014a), and in chapter 6 here.

54. Moss, "While Warning About Fat," (2010).

55. If one part of the mission cannot be removed, it could be given lower priority than the other. This could reduce inconsistencies and tensions, but not eliminate them entirely.

56. Carter, *Integrity* (1996), 13.

57. Marks, "Toward a Systemic Ethics," (2014a).

58. In chapter 6, I discuss UN Habitat's Support My School, an initiative that arguably promotes public health in the short term by improving sanitation while undermining it in the longer term by promoting consumption of SSBs.

59. Streeck and Thelen, "Introduction," (2005), 18–31.

60. Jacob Hacker, "Privatizing Risk," (2004), and revised in Streeck and Thelen, *Beyond Continuity* (2005), and Jacob Hacker et al., "Drift and Conversion: Hidden Faces of Institutional Change," (2015).

61. See Marks, "On Regularity and Regulation," (2011).

62. See, e.g., the *Journal of Functional Foods in Health and Disease*. According to its website, the journal "discusses various aspects of functional foods, bioactive compounds, and chronic diseases [and] develops research to better understand the mechanisms of disease and support the development of functional foods." It is premised on the view that functional foods are "essential to prevention and management of numerous diseases and health conditions." http://www.ffhdj.com/index.php/ffhd.

63. Shuchman, "Commercializing Clinical Trials," (2007). See also Lemmens and Freedman, "Ethics Review for Sale," (2000).

64. Shuchman, "Commercializing Clinical Trials," (2007).

65. The WHO's program budget for 2016-17 was $4.38 billion. See WHO, *Programme Budget 2016–2017* (Geneva: WHO, 2015), http://www.who.int/about/finances-accountability/budget/PB201617_en.pdf. This is dwarfed by federal, state, and local budgets in the United States. The CDC's budget request for 2017 was $6.98 billion. See CDC, "Budget Request Overview," https://www.cdc.gov/budget/documents/fy2017/cdc-overview-factsheet.pdf. The budget for New York City in 2017 was $82.1 billion. See NYC Office of Management and Budget, http://www1.nyc.gov/site/omb/index.page.

66. See Investopedia, "A Look at Coca-Cola's Advertising Expenses," August 13, 2015, http://www.investopedia.com/articles/markets/081315/look-cocacolas-advertising-expenses.asp. The 2014 advertising budget for Coca-Cola was $3.5 billion. The budget for PepsiCo was smaller but still substantial: $2.3 billion.

67. The Gates Foundation gave almost $3.9 billion in grants in 2014. See BMGF, *Annual Report 2014,* http://www.gatesfoundation.org/Who-We-Are/Resources-and-Media/Annual-Reports/Annual-Report-2014. Although the foundation characterizes only $1.1 billion as attributable to global health, some of its other expenditures (e.g., global development) also address global health issues.

68. Fear of displacement by philanthropic foundations may also have fueled the WHO's creation of the Global Coordinating Mechanism on NCDs, in which business and philanthropic organizations also participate. See www.who.int/ncds/gcm/en/.

69. Austin, "Strategic Collaboration," (2000).

70. For a different view of the "ideal," see Brinkerhoff and Brinkerhoff, "Public–Private Partnerships," (2011), 4, arguing that the "ideal type of [public-private partnership] would maximize organization identity and mutuality." They define "organization identity" as "the extent to which an organization remains consistent and committed to its mission, core values, and constituencies."

71. I discuss this further in chapter 6. Several analyses suggest partnerships have not been very effective at inducing corporations to develop and market healthier products.

72. I discuss the ethical implications of asymmetric reciprocity in chapter 4.

73. In its review of twelve industry collaborations, CAUT found that only two were "for the most part, structured in a way so as to preserve academic integrity, protect academic

freedom, and encourage the unfettered practice of teaching and learning." With regard to the other ten collaborations, the CAUT's report encouraged universities to "renegotiate offending portions of existing agreements." See CAUT, *Open for Business* (2013), 183. Withdrawal should also be on the table especially when the relationship is inherently problematic.

74. In this discussion of institutional corruption, I draw on Marks, "What's the Big Deal?" (2013).

75. Lessig, "Institutional Corruption Defined," (2013a). See also Lessig, "Institutional Corruptions," (2013) and Lessig, *Republic, Lost* (2011).

76. Lessig, "Institutional Corruption Defined," (2013a), 533, drawing on the metaphor of a magnet causing a compass to deviate from magnetic north.

77. See, most notably, Thompson, "Two Concepts of Corruption," (2013). In her interpretation of Dennis Thompson's work, Marie Newhouse (Newhouse, "Institutional Corruption," 2014) offers a narrow interpretation of institutional corruption, arguing that, when "properly understood," the term applies only to breaches of fiduciary duty. For a thoughtful critique of that position, see Taylor, "Institutional Corruption," (2014).

78. Lessig, "Institutional Corruption Defined," (2013a), and Lessig, *Republic, Lost* (2011).

79. For empirical research exploring the impact of these policies, which were also intended to address concerns about trust and confidence in health professionals and in medical research, see, e.g., Fugh-Berman et al., "Closing the door on pharma?," (2011).

80. Teachout, "The Anti-Corruption Principle," (2009), 347, 374, arguing, "[t]he integrity of the object of corruption is threatened by internal decay," and that "corruption—writ large—is the rotting of positive ideals of civic virtue and political integrity." In the latter passage, she employs a narrower definition of corruption ("political virtue is pursuing the public good in public life, political corruption is using public life for private gain") than appears in her later work (pursuing private interests in public office at the expense of the public good). Cf. Teachout, *Corruption in America* (2014).

81. Euben, "Corruption," (1998). See also Teachout, "Anti-Corruption," 373, fn. 157 (see also fn. 53).

82. See World Bank, "Helping Countries Combat Corruption," (2016).

83. See Transparency International, "What Is Corruption?," (2016).

84. For a philosophical overview of trust, see Carolyn McLeod, "Trust," (2006), discussing the work of Russell Hardin, Annette Baier, and others. For an overview of trust written for policymakers, see Vickerstaff et al., "Trust and Confidence in Pensions," (2012). Some scholars take the view that the language of trust should be used only in the context of interpersonal relations. See Luhmann, "Familiarity, Confidence, Trust," (1988). I have more sympathy with the view that the concepts of trust and trustworthiness can be applied to relations between individuals and institutions but their meaning and application in this context are not identical. See Ben-Ner and Putterman, "Trusting and Trustworthiness Symposium," (2001).

85. See McLeod, "Trust," (2006) characterizing trust as an attitude and trustworthiness as a property; and Ben Ner and Putterman, "Trusting and Trustworthiness," (2001) describing trustworthiness as "an objective attribute."

86. See Hardin, *Trust* (2006), 1, noting that "we do not simply want to increase trust per se, because we should not trust the untrustworthy." See also Rose, "Patient Advocacy Organizations," (2013).

87. Cf. Vickerstaff et al., "Trust and Confidence," (2012) arguing integrity is a component of trustworthiness; and Six and Huberts, "Judging a Public Official's Integrity," in Huberts, Maesschalk, and Jurkiewicz (2008), arguing integrity requires and presupposes trustworthiness.

88. For the Russell Sage Foundation series on trust, see www.russellsage.org/research/trust/books.

89. See, e.g., Hardin, *Trust and Trustworthiness* (2002). Other kinds of trust in the schema include *care* (you put the interests of others ahead of your own) and *sincerity* (you mean what you say, and say what you mean; and what you say is backed up by evidence.)

90. Kraak et al., "A Q Methodology Study," (2014).

91. See, e.g., Buse and Tanaka, "Global Public-Private Health Partnerships," (2011).

92. See CDC, "Mission, Role, and Pledge," http://www.cdc.gov/about/organization/mission.htm.

93. See, e.g., Hardin, *Trust* (2002).

94. On integrity as an ideal, see, e.g., Marie-Helene Parizeau, "Scientific Integrity," in Montefiore and Vines, *Integrity* (1999), 164, arguing that integrity presupposes an "ideal of coherence" regarding what is said and what is done.

95. Cf. Alan Hamlin, "Promoting Integrity and Virtue: The Institutional Dimension," in Montefiore and Vines, *Integrity* (1999), arguing that "virtue is the disposition to act in the public interest" (270); that "a virtuous disposition is a necessary condition for the realization of integrity, thereby ruling out the possibility of an interested agent of integrity"; and that the virtuous disposition to act in the public interest provides the "moral component" that integrity requires above and beyond consistency (271).

CHAPTER 3

1. *Hastings Center Report*, 11(1): 19–27 (1981); emphasis added.

2. See, e.g., Kempshall, *The Common Good in Late Medieval Political Thought* (1999).

3. For a discussion of Catholic approaches to the common good, for example, see Daniel Sulmasy, "Four Basic Notions of the Common Good," (2001).

4. See, e.g., Riordan, *A Grammer of the Common Good* (2008), 7. For a recent treatise for a general audience, see Reich, *The Common Good* (2018).

5. Rawls, *A Theory of Justice* (1971), 233.

6. Rawls, *A Theory of Justice* (1971), 246.

7. Gutmann and Thompson, "Valuing Compromise," (2013) 185.

8. Preamble to the US Constitution, http://www.law.cornell.edu/constitution/preamble. See also Galston, "The Common Good," (2013). The Universal Declaration of Human Rights (1948) also ties human rights to the promotion of the common good. The preamble declares that "the inherent dignity and of the equal and inalienable rights of all members of the human family is the foundation of freedom, justice and peace in the world." See Universal Declaration of Human Rights, G.A. res. 217A (III), U.N. Doc A/810 (1948), 71.

(The same text appears in the preambles to both the International Covenant on Civil and Political Rights and the International Covenant on Economic, Social and Cultural Rights.)

9. Cf. Bernardo Zacka, "Are Bureaucracies a Public Good?," in *The President's House Is Empty: Losing and Gaining Public Goods*, ed. Joshua Cohen (Boston: Boston Review, 2017).

10. Galston, "The Common Good," (2013). See also Reich, *Supercapitalism* (2008), 4, describing democracy as "a system for . . . determining the rules...whose outcomes express the common good." Cf. Thompson, *Political Ethics and Public Office* (1987), 107, arguing that the public interest is not the aggregation of subjective preferences, and must be created in the legislative process.

11. See also Simm, "The Concepts of the Common Good and Public Interest," (2011), 561, on the need for normative and procedural dimensions of the common good.

12. Gutmann and Thompson, "Valuing Compromise," (2013).

13. Galston, "The Common Good," (2013).

14. Although the commentary to the Model Code states that senators "may properly give precedence to the public interest and common good of the people of the United States," the authors recognize that responsibility to the people of the United States "cannot be divorced from the broader objective of promoting justice, peace, and human well-being throughout the world." The commentary further states that senators should "strive to respect and protect the human rights of all persons independent of their national affiliations." See U.S. Model Code (1981).

15. The Patient Protection and Affordable Care Act 2010 (PL 111-148) does not permit the undocumented to use their own funds to purchase insurance from health exchanges. See Marks, "The Undocumented Unwell," (2013).

16. Gardner, "Reestablishing the Commons for the Common Good," 2013.

17. For book-length treatments of the concepts discussed in this chapter, see, e.g., Held, *The Public Interest and Individual Interests* (1970), Gunn, *Politics and the Public Interest* (1969), and Kempshall, *The Common Good in Late Medieval Political Thought* (1999).

18. See, e.g., Solomon and Lo, *The Common Good: Chinese and American Perspectives* (2014).

19. Cf. Clarke E. Cochran, "The Common Good," (1978), arguing that a policy, decision, or social relationship can be considered "a means to" or "a requirement of" the common good, but cannot itself constitute "the common good."

20. See Kempshall, *The Common Good* (1999). The distinction between thinking about the common good more broadly, rather than in purely utilitarian terms may be reflected in the distinction between the Latin terms: *bonum communis* and *utilitas communis*.

21. Ackerman and Heinzerling, *Priceless* (2005).

22. We see this in policy discussions about hydraulic fracturing and other activities related to the production, storage, and transportation of "natural gas." See Marks, "Silencing Marcellus," (2014b).

23. Smith, *Wealth of Nations,* esp., bk. 5, chap. 1, pt. 3.

24. A drug company may have little or no incentive to develop an orphan drug for a small group of patients in a developing country when they and their government do not have the resources to pay for it. On incentives in the pharmaceutical sector, see Stiglitz and Jayadev, "Medicine for Tomorrow," (2010).

25. Smith, *Wealth of Nations*, bk. 5, chap. 1, pt. 3.

26. Reynolds, *Before Eminent Domain* (2010).

27. See, e.g., Kelo v. City of New London, 545 U.S. 469 (2005), a landmark Supreme Court decision on the exercise of eminent domain for the construction of a pharmaceutical facility. The case was recently dramatized in the movie *Little Pink House* (2017, dir. Courtney Moorehead). See also Susan Philips, "Invoking Power of Eminent Domain, Gas Industry Runs Roughshod over Private Property," (May 10, 2016), *NPR*, https://stateimpact.npr.org/pennsylvania/2016/05/10/39687/.

28. Some political philosophers have been more sensitive to this concern. See, e.g., Gutmann and Thompson, "Valuing Compromise," (2013), 185–198.

29. See, e.g., FAO, "The Contribution of the Private Sector and Civil Society to Improve Nutrition," (2013), stating: "Private companies, civil society, knowledge institutions and government . . . need to agree upon finding effective and efficient policies, sustainable practices and food solutions to reach the underserved consumer."

30. On Latin precursors, *publica utilitas, communis utilitas,* and *commune bonum,* see Reynolds, *Before Eminent Domain,* 92. See also Etzioni, "Common Good," (2015). Cf. Alasdair MacIntyre, "Common Goods, Frequent Evils," (2017), https://www.youtube.com/watch?v=9nxoKvb5Uo4.

31. Calhoun, "The Public Good as a Social and Cultural Project," (1998), 30.

32. Mansbridge, "On the Contested Nature of the Public Good," (1998).

33. Mansbridge, "On the Contested Nature of the Public Good," (1998), 12, 18.

34. Joseph Stiglitz, "Knowledge as a Global Public Good," in Kaul, Greenberg, and Stern *Global Public Goods* (1999), 308–325, drawing on Samuelson, "The Pure Theory of Public Expenditure," (1954).

35. Stiglitz, "Knowledge," (1999) provides an economic justification for the nonrivalrous dimension of public goods. In contrast, my focus in this book is on the ethical implications of the related concepts of the common good, public good, and public interest.

36. Glenna, et al., "University Administrators," (2007), 145.

37. See Bruce Jennings, Daniel Callahan, and Susan Wolf, "The Professions," (1987), and J. A. W. Gunn, "Public Interest," in *Political Innovation and Conceptual Change*, ed. Terence Ball et al. (1989).

38. Jennings, Callahan, and Wolf, "The Professions," (1987). On the disagreement between Rousseau, who rejected an aggregative approach to the common good, and Bentham, who is ordinarily taken to embrace it, see Gunn, "Public Interest," (1989). See also Karen Getman and Pamela Karlan, "Pluralists and Republicans, Rules and Standards," in *Conflict of Interest and Public Life: Cross-National Perspectives*, ed. Alison Gash and Christine Trost (2008), 58–59, on civic republicans' rejection of aggregation.

39. See, e.g., Etzioni, "Common Good," (2015).

40. The Model Code for the US Senate (quoted at the head of this chapter) invokes both concepts. Cf. the ethical principles drafted by the UK Committee on Standards in Public Life (the Nolan Committee), "The 7 Principles of Public Life," (1995), calling on the holders of public office to "act solely in terms of the public interest." https://www.gov.uk/government/publications/the-7-principles-of-public-life.

41. Gunn, "Public Interest," (1989), 196.

42. Governments may seek to defend such interventions on the grounds that the preferences of the relevant publics are inherently unstable or are premised on misinformation. Whether such claims are legitimate, of course, will depend on the circumstances.

43. See, e.g., the English case in the Court of Appeal, X v Y [1988] 2 All E R 648.

44. See, e.g., Public Interest Disclosure Act 1998 c.23 (U.K.), defining protected disclosures to include those regarding environmental damage, and hazards to human health and safety.

45. UN Economic and Social Council, Siracusa Principles on the Limitation and Derogation Provisions in the International Covenant on Civil and Political Rights, U.N. Doc. E/CN.4/1985/4, Annex (1985). See also Marks, "Toward a Unified Theory," (2012), 215.

46. See, e.g., the Preamble to the Universal Declaration of Human Rights (1948).

47. International Covenant on Civil and Political Rights, G.A. res. 2200A (XXI), 21 U.N. GAOR Supp. (No. 16) at 52, U.N. Doc. A/6316 (1966), 999 U.N.T.S. 171, *entered into force* Mar. 23, 1976 (Art. 12).

48. Siracusa Principles (1985).

49. Childress et al., "Public Health Ethics," (2002).

50. See, e.g., Cole, "The Three Leakers," (2014).

51. See the discussion of the Support My School partnership between the UN Habitats Program, Coca-Cola, and New Dehli Television (among others) in chapter 6.

52. See Simm, "The Concepts of the Common Good and Public Interest," (2011), 557, "public interest tends to be associated with specific practices and policies, whereas the common good is reserved for debates encompassing more general, long-term, and fundamental aspects of social life."

53. US Senate Model Code of Ethics (1981).

54. US Senate Model Code of Ethics (1981). See also Cochran, "The Common Good," (1978), and Teachout, *Corruption in America* (2014), 9, emphasizing the importance of "public orientation" and public good, even though the associated definitions and distinctions can be "difficult ones to parse."

55. Gunn, "Public Interest," (1989).

56. Ralph Gomory and Richard Sylla, "The American Corporation," (2013). See also Yang, "Maximizing Shareholder Value," (2013).

57. The company dates the origin of the credo to a board meeting in 1943. See "Minutes of a Meeting of the Board of Directors," Johnson & Johnson, December 13, 1943, cited at http://www.kilmerhouse.com/2013/12/the-writing-of-our-credo/.

58. Justin Hyde, "GM's 'Engine Charlie,'" (2008).

59. Hyde, "GM's 'Engine Charlie,'" (2008).

60. The Business Roundtable, "Statement on Corporate Responsibility," (October 1981) cited in Gomory and Sylla, "The American Corporation," (2013).

61. Milton Friedman, "The Social Responsibility of Business is to Increase Its Profits," (1970). See also Milton Friedman, *Capitalism & Freedom* (1962).

62. R. Edward Freeman, "A Stakeholder Theory of the Modern Corporation: Kantian Capitalism," in *Ethical Theory and Business*, ed. Tom Beauchamp and Norman Bowie (1988), and Freeman, *Strategic Management* (1984).

63. Business Roundtable, "Statement on Corporate Governance," (September 1997) cited in Gomora and Sylla, "The American Corporation," (2013).

64. At the same time, remuneration packages for corporate executives increased exponentially—often justified on grounds that those packages were necessary to recruit and retain executives who would ensure increased profitability and share value.

65. Gomory and Sylla, "The American Corporation," (2013).

66. A similar story is told by Robert Reich, former secretary of labor under President Clinton. He has argued that since the mid-1970s, under "supercapitalism," corporations have been driven toward the relentless pursuit of profits; power has shifted away from communities and employees to consumers and investors; and companies lobby aggressively to ensure that the "rules of the game"—including laws for the protection of the environment and public health—are as favorable as possible to their commercial interests. See Reich, *Supercapitalism* (2007), 50.

67. Gomory and Sylla, "The American Corporation," (2013).

68. Patrick Radden Keefe, "The Family That Built an Empire of Pain," (2017). See also US Senate Homeland and Governmental Affairs Committee, Minority Staff Report, "Fueling an Epidemic: Exposing the Ties Between Opioid Manufacturers and Third Party Advocacy Groups," (2018).

69. National Institute on Drug Abuse, "Overdose Deaths," August 2018, https://www.drugabuse.gov/related-topics/trends-statistics/overdose-death-rates; White House Council of Economic Advisers, "The Underestimated Cost of the Opioid Crisis," November 2017, https://www.whitehouse.gov/sites/whitehouse.gov/files/images/The%20Underestimated%20Cost%20of%20the%20Opioid%20Crisis.pdf.

70. Ormiston and Wong, "License to Ill," (2013); Matthew Kotchen and J.J. Moon, "Corporate Social Responsibility for Irresponsibility," (2012).

71. Reich, *Supercapitalism* (2007), 204. "Companies donate money to the extent—and only to the extent—it has public relations value, and thereby helps the bottom line. Shareholders do not entrust their money to corporate executives to give it away unless the return is greater."

72. Reich, *Supercapitalism* (2007), 206. See also 205, arguing that executives violate their fiduciary duties when they make donations from corporate funds without believing that it would enhance the firm's bottom line.

73. Reich, *Supercapitalism* (2007). Citing Alan Murray, "The Profit Motive Has a Limit: Tragedy," (2005).

74. The US Chamber of Commerce has created a foundation for charitable donations. Its website lists many corporations and their donations, https://www.uschamberfoundation.org/aid-event/hurricane-harvey.

75. Mudd, "How to Force Ethics on the Food Industry," (2013).

76. See Friedman, "Social Responsibility," (1970). Friedman also described social responsibility as "hypocritical window-dressing."

77. Marks, "Toward a Systemic Ethics," (2014a).

78. This can be especially problematic when public sector institutions have come to depend on corporate philanthropy to meet overhead costs and/or to complete a particular project.

79. Nestle, *Soda Politics* (2015), 111–112, arguing the "object lesson" for soda companies was "[y]ou can promote health as much as you like if, and only if sales grow by percentages that satisfy investors." See also Freudenberg, *Lethal but Legal* (2014), 234. As I made clear in chapter 1, we should not take at face value claims by a food company that their products are "good for you." We should also retain a healthy skepticism about the framing of low-nutrient energy-dense products as "fun for you"!

80. Salter, "Short-Termism at Its Worst, "(2013).

81. Murray, "Social Enterprise," (2013). See also Plerhoples, "Representing Social Enterprise," (2013), describing four "models of social enterprise" institutions (which are not mutually exclusive): (i) the stakeholder governance model, (ii) the pluralist ownership model (similar to so-called democratic workplaces), (iii) the corporate philanthropy model, and (iv) the beneficial product or services model.

82. Version 4-10-13 of the Model Benefit Corporation Legislation is available from the B Lab website, http://benefitcorp.net/storage/documents/Model_Benefit_Corporation_Legislation. pdf (B Lab is a nonprofit, tax-exempt under section 501(3)(c) of the US Inland Revenue Code.)

83. Model Law (2013), sections 102 and 201.

84. Cf. Murray, "Social Enterprise Innovation," (2013), 354–355 fn. 60, breaking this provision down into thirteen stakeholders.

85. Model Law (2013), section 301(a)(1). The corporation need not give priority to any particular interest unless it has specified a priority in its articles of incorporation. See section 301(a)(3).

86. Model Law (2013), section 401.

87. Model Law (2013), section 305(a).

88. Model Law (2013), section 305(c).

89. See http://www.benefitcorp.net/.

90. Del. Code Ann. Title 8, sections 361 368, http://delcode.delaware.gov/title8/c001/sc15.

91. For comparison tables, see Murray, "Social Enterprise Innovation," (2013), 371 and Alicia Plerhoples, "Delaware Public Benefit Corporations," (2014), 254–255.

92. Del. Code Ann. Title 8, section 366(c)(3).

93. Del. Code Ann. Title 8, section 366(b).

94. Del. Code Ann. Title 8, sec. 366(c)(2).

95. Del. Code Ann. Title 8, section 362(a)(1). These include (but are not limited to) artistic, charitable, cultural, economic, environmental, literary, medical, religious, scientific or technological benefits. See section 362(b).

96. Plerhoples, "Delaware Public Benefit," (2014), 271.

97. Del. Code Ann. Title 8, sections 362(a), 365(a). Cf. Freeman, "Stakeholder Theory," (1988) arguing that "management must keep the relationships among stakeholders in balance."

98. Del. Code Ann. Title 8, section 367. But see also sec. 365(b), providing that directors have no duty to any person "on account of any interest of such a person in the public benefit or public benefits . . . or on account of any interest materially affected by the corporation's conduct."

99. Murray, "Social Enterprise Innovation," (2013), 363.

100. Plerhoples, "Delaware Public Benefit," (2014), 259.

101. Plerhoples, "Delaware Public Benefit," (2014), 267.

102. Plerhoples, "Delaware Public Benefit," (2014), 263.

103. Elaine Watson, "Plum Organics Sales Surge 44% in 2015," December 16, 2015, https://www.foodnavigator-usa.com/Article/2015/12/16/Plum-Organics-baby-food-sales-surge-44-in-2015.

104. Fast Company, "Campbell's Soup," http://www.fastcoexist.com/company/campbells-soup. Companies in the food and agriculture sector accounted for 5 percent of the companies reviewed in Plerhoples, "Delaware Public Benefit," (2014).

105. Stephanie Strom, "Has 'Organic' Been Oversized?," (2012), discussing the acquisition of independent organic food companies by multinationals, and the resulting influence of the latter on what foods may be labeled organic. For a diagram showing multinational ownership or acquisition of organic brands, see Cornucopia Institute, "Who Owns Organic Now?," February 13, 2014, https://www.cornucopia.org/wp-content/uploads/2014/02/Organic-chart-feb-2014.jpg.

106. Murray, "Social Enterprise Innovation," (2013), 360.

107. Freeman, "Stakeholder Theory," (1988).

108. Samuel Taylor Coleridge, *Biographia Literaria* (London: Rest Fenner, 1817), vol. 2, chap. 14, 2.

109. I explore framing effects in more detail in chapter 6.

110. See also Brown, *Undoing the Demos* (2015), critiquing the concept of "governance."

111. I say more about agenda distortion in chapter 6.

112. Birn, "Philanthrocapitalism, Past and Present," (2014).

113. I discuss reciprocity and influence more fully in chapters 4 and 5.

114. These relations may result in the importing of commercial values and concerns into public institutions. See, e.g., UN Secretary-General, "Enhanced Cooperation between the United Nations and All Relevant Partners, in Particular the Private Sector," A/68/326 (2013) (promoting the UN's interactions with the private sector, but cautioning about the need to safeguard the UN's "brand.")

115. Cf. Reich, *Supercapitalism* (2007): "[C]ompanies exist only to serve consumers and thereby make money for investors. *This* is how they serve the public" (207).

116. See, e.g., AAUP, *Statement of Principles on Academic Freedom and Tenure*, 1940, (contending that "institutions of higher education are conducted for the common good," which "depends upon the free search for truth and its free exposition.") I discuss the systemic ethical implications of industry-academy relations in chapter 5.

117. See, e.g., CAUT, *Open for Business* (2013), 186–192. See also Freudenberg, *Lethal but Legal* (2014), 252, citing Jennifer Washburn's work but arguably understating the systemic ethical perils of such partnerships.

118. On the ways in which the prevailing account of the public good has been shaped by industry, see, e.g., Brown, *Undoing the Demos* (2015). See also Teachout, *Corruption in America* (2014), 260, critiquing the view that "the public good is served by efficiency."

119. Teachout, *Corruption in America* (2014), 260–261.

CHAPTER 4

1. Marcus Tullius Cicero, *On Friendship*, trans. F. O. Copley (Ann Arbor: University of Michigan Press, 1967) (*Nihil est enim remuneratione benevolentiae, nihil vicissitudine studiorum officiorumque iucundius.*)

2. On CSR initiatives involving soda companies, see Nestle, *Soda Politics* (2015), esp. chapters 17–19. See also Brownell and Warner, "The Perils of Ignoring History," (2009).

3. Global accountancy firms prepare tax guides for corporations wishing to deduct the cost of corporate social responsibility activities from their tax liability. See, e.g., Deloitte, Corporate Social Responsibility (2015), https://www2.deloitte.com/content/dam/Deloitte/in/Documents/tax/in-tax-csr-flyer-noexp.pdf, and Ernst & Young (EY), Corporate Social Responsibility (n.d.), http://www.ey.com/publication/vwluassets/ey-advisory-csr-opportunities-and-challenges-tax-perspective/$file/ey-csr-opportunities-and-challenges-tax-perspective.pdf.

4. Industry donors also feature and promote these gifts on websites and social media. See, e.g., http://www.coca-colacompany.com/topics/sustainability/ (Coca-Cola) and www.chevron.com/corporateresponsibility/ (Chevron).

5. Cialdini, *Influence* (2009) has sold over 3 million copies since it was first published in 1984.

6. Suchak and Waal, "Monkeys Benefit from Reciprocity," (2012); Brosnan and Waal, "A Proximate Perspective on Reciprocal Altruism," (2002), 131; and Waal, "Attitudinal Reciprocity," (2000).

7. Trivers, "Evolution," (1971).

8. Atwood, *Payback* (2008).

9. Jean Piaget, *The Moral Judgment of the Child*, trans. Marjorie Gabain (New York: Macmillan, 1965), and Lawrence Kohlberg, *Essays on Moral Development* (San Francisco: Harper & Row, 1981).

10. See, e.g., Jonathan Haidt and Jesse Graham, "When Morality Opposes Justice," (2007). See also Jonathan Haidt, *The Righteous Mind* (2013)

11. Becker, *Reciprocity* (1986), 1.

12. Becker, *Reciprocity* (1986), 1.

13. Becker, *Reciprocity* (1986), 4.

14. Gouldner, "The Norm of Reciprocity," (1960), 171, arguing that the "norm of reciprocity" in its "universal form" makes "two interrelated, minimal demands: (1) people should help those who have helped them, and (2) people should not injure those who have helped them."

15. Cf. Ruth A. Putnam, "Reciprocity and Virtue Ethics," (1988) at 389, arguing more generally "when our reciprocating action would produce or perpetuate injustice, it is prohibited by overriding considerations of justice." See also Gutmann and Thompson, *Why Deliberative Democracy?* (2004), 133–134, 141–142; Christie Hartley, "Two Conceptions of Justice as Reciprocity," (2014) (on reciprocity in the work of John Rawls).

16. Schafer, "Biomedical Conflicts of Interest," (2004), 21.

17. AAMC, *Scientific Basis* (2007), 7.

18. AAMC, *Scientific Basis* (2007), 7.

19. Schafer, "Biomedical Conflicts," (2004).

20. I draw loosely here on de Waal, "Attitudinal Reciprocity," (2000), and Brosnan and de Waal, "Reciprocal Altruism," (2002).

21. Brosnan and de Waal, "Reciprocal Altruism," (2002), 148.

22. Becker, *Reciprocity* (1986), 42, 137. See also Epstein, "Public-Private Contracting," (2014), 36.

23. Becker, *Reciprocity* (1986), 138.

24. Sah and Fugh-Berman, "Physicians Under the Influence," (2013).

25. Cf. Kolm, "Reciprocity," (2006), in Kolm and Ythier, *Handbook of Giving* (2006), 479, arguing that we tend to "prefer reciprocal trust to general diffidence, convivial reciprocity to contractual relations, and contractual obligation to hierarchical command."

26. Mauss, *The Gift* (1990).

27. Mary Douglas, "No Free Gifts," preface to Mauss, *The Gift* (1990), ix.

28. Mauss, *The Gift* (1990), 39–41. Cf. Gregory, *Savage Money* (1997), 77, rejecting Mauss's mystical notion of the "spirit" in the gift but acknowledging an "indissoluble bond" between giver and gift." For a more fundamental disagreement, cf. Derrida, *Given Time* (1992), 12, arguing that "[f]or there to be a gift, there must be no reciprocity, return, exchange, countergift, or debt."

29. Mauss, *The Gift* (1990), 65.

30. See, e.g., Brown and Milgram, *Economics and Morality* (2009).

31. Kolm, "Economics of Giving," (2006), in Kolm and Ythier, *Handbook of Giving* (2006), 80–90.

32. See Kolm, "Reciprocity," (2006), 423, arguing that this is one of three "polar motives" for reciprocity.

33. See, e.g., Mudd, "How to Force Ethics on the Food Industry," (2013).

34. Titmuss, *The Gift Relationship* (1971), 74–75, citing Schwartz, "Social Psychology of the Gift," (1967). Titmuss argues although there is no gratitude imperative in the case of a blood donation from an unnamed stranger, the recipient may subsequently become a donor to "pay it forward." (88).

35. Wright, *The Moral Animal* (1994), 204–205.

36. Kolm, "Reciprocity," (2006), 432, suggesting the mechanism for this is "a classical kind of 'halo effect.'"

37. Cardy and Dobbins, "Affect and Appraisal Accuracy," (1986).

38. Sah and Fugh-Berman, "Physicians Under the Influence," (2013).

39. On dependence, see Gouldner "The Norm of Reciprocity," (1960), 169, citing Malinowski, *Crime and Custom* (1926), and Godelier, *The Enigma of the Gift* (1999), 42–43. See also Kolm, "Reciprocity," (2006), 449, arguing that gifts put the giver in the position of "moral creditor," eliciting sentiments of pride, superiority, domination, and power.

40. See, e.g., Schwartz, "Social Psychology," (1967), 2, on the impact of the unreciprocated gift on the recipient's status.

41. Gudeman, *Anthropology of Economy* (2001), 89–90. See also Godelier, *The Enigma of the Gift* (1999), 33, arguing "it is in the process of the production and reproduction of hierarchies among individuals, groups, and even societies, that the strategies of giving and keeping play distinct and complementary roles."

42. Malinowksi, *Argonauts of the Western Pacific* (1922), 352, referring, in particular, to the opening and closing gifts of the exchange.

43. Douglas, "No Free Gifts," preface to Mauss, *The Gift* (1990), xiv.

44. Marcel Henaff, *The Price of Truth: Gift, Money, and Philosophy* (2012), 115 (with the heading: "Ceremonial Gift-Giving Is Not a Moral Gesture.")

45. James Andreoni, "Philanthropy," in Kolm and Ythier, *Handbook of Giving*, vol. 2 (2006), 1201–1259.

46. Henaff, *The Price of Truth* (2012), 114.

47. Henaff, *The Price of Truth* (2012), 115. Henaff focuses on individual rather than corporate donors in these passages but discusses CSR elsewhere in the volume.

48. See, e.g., images from the Support My School initiative (discussed in chapter 5): http://bit.ly/2lnapq6 (enlarged check); http://bit.ly/2zIp4BD (child in school uniform beside the logo for the initiative and the soda company), and http://bit.ly/2ldNaj7.

49. Dinah Rajak, "I Am the Conscience of the Company: Responsibility and the Gift in a Transnational Mining Company," in Brown and Milgram, *Economics and Morality* (2009).

50. Jonathan Parry, "On the Moral Perils of Exchange," in Parry and Bloch, *Money and the Morality of Exchange* (1989). See also Raheja, *The Poison in the Gift* (1988).

51. Parry, "On the Moral Perils," (1989), 68. Cf. Gregory, *Savage Money* (1997), 69, using the term "bads" to describe the "transfer of impurities, inauspiciousness, sin, and the like."

52. Parry, "On the Moral Perils," (1989), 76–77.

53. For example, the Center for Nutrition Policy and Promotion in the USDA encourages food companies (among others) to become "national strategic partners" for these reasons. See Marks, "Toward a Systemic Ethics," (2014a).

54. Parry, "On the Moral Perils," (1989), 71.

55. Fox and Swazey, *Spare Parts* (1992), 40 (also invoking Mauss).

56. Fox and Swazey, *Spare Parts* (1992), 40.

57. Thompson et al., *The Olivieri Report* (2001).

58. Lévi-Strauss, *Elementary Structures of Kinship* (1969), 84. But cf. Schwartz, "Social Psychology," (1967), 11, arguing that "gift exchange influences group boundaries by clarifying them."

59. Gudeman, *The Anthropology of Economy* (2001), 80–93 (reviewing the contributions of Marcel Mauss, Claude Lévi-Strauss, Karl Polanyi, and Marshall Sahlins to the anthropological discourse on gifts and reciprocity).

60. See, e.g., Austin, "Strategic Collaboration," (2000).

61. Anthropologists have long recognized the relationship between gifts and power. See, e.g., Sahlins, *Tribesmen* (1968) at 91, drawing on Malinowski's term "fund of power."

62. Rajak, "Conscience of the Company," (2009).

63. Rajak, "Conscience of the Company," (2009), 218.

64. See, e.g., Chevron, "In the Community," accessed January 1, 2017, http://www.chevron.com/countries/usa/inthecommunity/.

65. Rajak, "Conscience of the Company," (2009).

66. Rajak, "Conscience of the Company," (2009), 222.

67. Sahlins, *Stone Age Economics* (1972), 191–196.

68. Sahlins, *Stone Age Economics* (1972), 196.

69. Young, "Asymmetrical Reciprocity," (1997), 356.

70. Titmuss, *The Gift Relationship* (1971), 74.

71. Thompson et al., *The Olivieri Report* (2001). See also Rose, "Patient Advocacy Organizations," (2013).

72. Cf. Gregory, *Savage Money* (1997), 65–67, arguing "[r]eciprocal recognition presupposes agreement as to the meaning of a transaction," but also recognizing that "[r]ival cognitions create contradictions: the transaction is now a gift, now a commodity according to the play of reciprocal and asymmetrical recognition."

73. Cf. Epstein, "Public-Private Contracting," (2014), characterizing this as "consummate" rather than "perfunctory" performance.

74. See UN, Outcome Document of the High-Level Meeting on Non-Communicable Diseases (2014), finding that "limited progress" had been made in response to its call for industry to curtail marketing of unhealthy foods to children, reformulate products to provide healthier options that are affordable and accessible, and follow labeling standards. See also Kraak et al., "Industry Progress," (2011).

75. Trivers, "Evolution," (1971) using the term "subtle cheating" to include cheating behaviors that are unintentional.

76. Trivers, "Evolution," (1971), 50.

77. Trivers, "Evolution," (1971), 46–47. Cf. Wright, *The Moral Animal* (1994), 208, arguing that reciprocal altruism is a misnomer and that "with reciprocal altruism the goal is that the organism be left under the impression that we've helped; the impression alone is enough to bring the reciprocation"; and observing "the general tendency of people to burnish their moral reputations . . . [a]nd hence hypocrisy."

78. See AAMC, *Scientific Basis* (2007). The study discussed in this report was later published as Ann H. Harvey et al., "Monetary Favors and Their Influence," (2010).

79. For a brief review, see Dana and Loewenstein, "A Social Science Perspective on Gifts to Physicians From Industry," (2003).

80. Sah and Fugh-Berman, "Physicians Under the Influence," (2013).

81. Mudd, "How to Force Ethics on the Food Industry," (2013).

82. I discuss institutional integrity in detail in chapter 2. See also Marks, "Toward a Systemic Ethics," (2014a).

83. See, e.g., Kolm, "Reciprocity," (2006).

84. Kolm, "Reciprocity," (2006), 413.

85. Kolm, "Reciprocity," (2006), 415. See also Kolm's discussion of intergenerational reciprocities—e.g., elderly parents being cared for by their children who (if they reach old age) are, in turn, cared for by their own children (395).

86. Jeff Shields, "Big Beverage Gives $10 million to CHOP," (2011) (now incorrectly dated October 17, 2013.)

87. Compare the limited acknowledgment of third party effects in Gouldner, "The Norm of Reciprocity," (1960), 163, and Godelier, *The Enigma of the Gift* (1999), 42.

88. Malmendier and Schmidt, "You Owe Me," (2012) (noting a limited exception, studies on bribery.)

89. Malmendier and Schmidt, "You Owe Me," (2012), arguing that experiments show small gifts can have a large impact, even if they are given "unconditionally in a one-shot relationship" and observing that disclosure does not reduce these effects.

90. Cf. Taylor, "Institutional Corruption," (2014), providing a thoughtful response to the narrow focus on fiduciary duties in Newhouse, "Institutional Corruption," (2014).

91. For a broad view of vulnerability, see Goodin, *Protecting the Vulnerable* (1986), 118: "If A's interests are vulnerable to B's actions and choices, B has a special responsibility to protect A's interests; the strength of this responsibility depends strictly upon the degree to which B can affect A's interests." Disparities in knowledge as well as power may exacerbate vulnerability. Cf. Levine et al., "The Limitations of "Vulnerability," " (2004).

92. Lowenstein, "For Good, For Country, or For Me," (1986), reviewing John T. Noonan, *Bribes* (New York: Macmillan, 1984), 1482–1483.

93. Proponents of PPPs often invoke the idea of stewardship in *support* of partnerships. See, e.g., Travis et al., "Towards Better Stewardship," (2002). But as I employ the concept here, stewardship provides a powerful rationale for refusing to enter (or withdrawing from) partnerships.

94. WHO, "FENSA," (2016), which provides that "WHO does not engage with the tobacco industry or non-State actors that work to further the interests of the tobacco industry" and "also does not engage with the arms industry." (para. 44). For other industries, FENSA merely provides that the WHO shall exercise "particular caution . . . when engaging with private sector entities and other non-State actors whose policies or activities are negatively affecting human health and are not in line with WHO's policies, norms and standards" (para. 45). A similar approach was taken in the document FENSA replaced: WHO, "Guidelines on Interaction with Commercial Enterprises to Achieve Health Outcomes," (2000), EB107/20 (para. 9).

95. See also Heugens et al., "The Ethics of the Node versus the Ethics of the Dyad? (2006), arguing "purpose" is the institutional equivalent of *telos*, when applying virtue ethics in institutional contexts, and noting "audacity becomes the merchant but not the banker, creativity the designer but not the accountant, and impartiality the mediator but not the attorney.") See also Beadle and Moore, "MacIntyre on Virtue and Organization," (2006), and Geoff Moore and Ron Beadle, "In Search of Organizational Virtue in Business: Agents, Goods, Practices, Institutions and Environments," *Organization Studies*, 27(3): 369–389 (2006), drawing on Alasdair MacIntyre, *After Virtue* (1981) among others.

CHAPTER 5

1. Lewis et al., "Dancing with the Porcupine," (2001), 785.

2. For a more detailed discussion of these examples, see chapter 6.

3. See, e.g., AAUP, *Recommended Principles* (2014), and CAUT, *Open for Business* (2013), accessed January 1, 2017.

4. See, e.g., Watson-Capps and Cech, "Companies on Campus," (2014) for a qualified endorsement of this approach.

5. Henry Etzkowitz, "From Conflict to Confluence of Interest: The Co-Evolution of Academic Entrepreneurship and Intellectual Property Rights," in Murray and Johnston, *Trust and Integrity in Biomedical Research* (2010), 74. See also Etzkowitz, *The Triple Helix* (2008).

6. Etzkowitz, "From Conflict to Confluence," (2010), 76.

7. Etzkowitz, "From Conflict to Confluence," (2010), 76.

8. Etzkowitz, "From Conflict to Confluence," (2010), 99.

9. See, e.g., Bok, *Universities in the Marketplace* (2004), and Washburn, *University Inc.* (2006).

10. See, e.g., Lewis et al., "Dancing with the Porcupine," (2001), and Schafer, "Biomedical Conflicts of Interest," (2004).

11. Lewis et al., "Dancing with the Porcupine," (2001).

12. Campbell et al., "Ties That Bind: Relationships Among Academia, Industry, and Government in Life Sciences Research," in Murray and Johnston, *Trust and Integrity* (2010). See also Campbell et al., *The Triple Helix* (2004).

13. AAUP, *Statement of Principles on Academic Freedom and Tenure*, 1940, (emphasis added).

14. CAUT, *Open for Business* (2013), 192.

15. CAUT, *Open for Business* (2013), 3, 59, 191.

16. CAUT, *Open for Business* (2013), 183.

17. "university," in the *Oxford English Dictionary*, www.oed.com

18. CAUT, "Guiding Principles for University Collaborations," (2012), also published as Appendix A in CAUT, *Open for Business* (2013), 189. See also AAUP, *Recommended Principles to Guide Academy-Industry Relationships* (2014).

19. See also Anthony Kronman, *Education's End* (2008).

20. See, e.g., PSU News, "Penn State's New Natural Gas Center Keeps PA at the Forefront of Industry," March 6, 2013, http://news.psu.edu/story/267496/2013/03/06/impact/penn-states-new-natural-gas-center-keep-pa-forefront-industry.

21. See, e.g., Rose et al., "Patient Advocacy Organizations," (2017); Aaron and Siegel, "Sponsorship of National Health Organizations," (2017).

22. FAO, "The Contribution of the Private Sector and Civil Society to Improve Nutrition," (2013b). This is technically a misnomer since the word "quadrant" usually refers to *each* of four parts, not to all four together.

23. See Penders and Nelis, "Credibility Engineering in the Food Industry," (2011).

24. Penders and Nelis, "Credibility Engineering in the Food Industry," (2011).

25. Michele Simon, *Are America's Nutrition Professionals in the Pocket of Big Food?* (2013).

26. Neuman, "Save the Children Breaks with Soda Tax Effort," (2010).

27. Save the Children, "Our Vision, Mission, and Values," https://www.savethechildren.net/about-us/our-vision-mission-and-values.

28. Freedhoff and Hebert, "Partnerships," (2011).

29. Rose, "Patient Advocacy Organizations," (2013).

30. For a more comprehensive analysis of potential responses to industry influence, see chapters 7 and 8.

31. See, e.g., Freedhoff and Hebert, "Partnerships," (2011).

32. Chandon and Wansink, "Biasing Health Halos," (2007), and Wansink and Chandon, "Can 'Low Fat' Nutrition Labels Lead to Obesity?" (2006).

33. I discuss this example further in chapter 6.

34. Shi Tang et al., "Taste Moral, Taste Good: The Effects of Fairtrade Logo," (2017).

35. AAMC, *Scientific Basis* (2007).

36. W. Hofman et al., "Evaluative Conditioning," (2010).

37. Sah and Fugh-Berman, "Physicians Under the Influence," (2013).

38. Bekelman, Li, and Gross, "Scope and Impact," (2003).

39. Lo and Field, *Conflict of Interest* (2009), 104–108.

40. Lesser et al., "Relationship Between Funding Source and Conclusion," (2007), and Vartanian et al., "Effects of Soft Drink Consumption," (2007).

41. Yank, Rennie, and Bero, "Financial Ties," (2007).

42. Yank, Rennie, and Bero, "Financial Ties," (2007), 1204.

43. Cf. Michael Pinto-Duschinsky, "Fund-raising and the Holocaust: The Case of Dr Gert-Rudolf Flick's Contribution to Oxford University," in Montefiore and Vines *Integrity* (1999), 237–238, on the need to guard against "the distorting . . . effects of fund-raising on academic standards [and] the direction of teaching and research."

44. Thomas and Earl, *Opportunities in the Nutrition and Food Sciences* (1994), 109.

45. See, e.g., studies sponsored by the International Tree Nut Council Nutrition Research and Education Foundation (http://www.nuthealth.org/nutrition-research/).

46. See Marks, "On Regularity and Regulation," (2011).

47. Thursby and Thursby, "University Licensing," (2003), a study of six institutions purporting to show that the proportion of basic to applied research did not alter in the 1980s and 90s; and Eric Campbell et al., "Ties That Bind: Relationships Among Academia, Industry, and Government in Life Sciences Research," in Murray and Johnston, *Trust and Integrity* (2010), 115–116, arguing that the ratio of basic to applied research funded by NSF was stable as of 2004. But cf. Sterckx, "Patenting and Licensing of University Research?" (2011), arguing that the Thursbys' data do not support their claim. See also Bok, *Universities* (2003).

48. N. P. Cox, C. Heaney, and R. Cook-Deegan, "Conflicts Between Commercial and Scientific Roles in Academic Research," in Murray and Johnston, *Trust and Integrity* (2010), 62.

49. In 2014, companies marketing a satiety supplement paid $26.5 million to settle FTC charges that they had deceived consumers with unfounded weight-loss claims and misleading endorsements. See http://www.ftc.gov/system/files/documents/cases/140107sensastip.pdf.

50. CAUT, *Open for Business* (2013), 188, argues that integrity can be compromised by "indirect *distortion* of the core academic relationships and functions of universities and their faculty."

51. CAUT, *Open for Business* (2013), 188

52. See, e.g., the 1998 agreement between Novartis and the University of California at Berkeley (in which the drug company agreed to provide $25 million over 5 years). This was described by the UNESCO Courier as being the first time (but not the last!) that "the work of an entire university department . . . was . . . underwritten by a multinational company, with interests in health care, agribusiness and nutrition." http://unesdoc.unesco.org/images/0012/001242/124272e.pdf.

53. See the Olivieri case discussed in the Preface, and Marks, "Expedited Industry-Sponsored Translational Research," (2008).

54. Birn, "Philanthrocapitalism," (2014), 5. See Birn and Richter, "U.S. Philanthro-capitalism," (2017).

55. Birn, "Philanthrocapitalism," (2014), 7.

56. Birn and Richter, "US Philanthrocapitalism," (2017)

57. Gates Foundation, "How We Work," http://www.gatesfoundation.org/How-We-Work.

58. Stuckler, Basu, and McKee, "Global Health Philanthropy," (2011); Birn, "Philanthrocapitalism," (2014); and Jaeah Lee and Alex Park, "The Gates Foundation's Hypocritical Investments," (2013). Other criticisms have been directed at the leadership of BMGF, noting that several of them were formerly pharmaceutical industry executives. There are also concerns about the Foundation's lack of "real-time transparency" and accountability. See Birn, "Philanthrocapitalism," (2014), 10, 14.

59. See Center for Health Science and Law (Canada), "Open Letter to the Executive Board of the WHO," (January 2017), http://healthscienceandlaw.ca/wp-content/uploads/2017/01/Public-Interest-Position.WHO_.FENSAGates.Jan2017.pdf.

60. Birn, "Philanthrocapitalism," (2014), 17.

61. See the Global Fund to Fight AIDS, Tuberculosis, and Malaria, "Constituencies," accessed January 1, 2017, http://www.theglobalfund.org/en/board/constituencies/.

62. Kuypers, *Bush's War* (2006), 8. For a broader analysis, see Kuypers, *Rhetorical Criticism* (2009), noting "[f]rames are often found within a narrative account of an issue or event, and are generally the central organizing idea." Framing analysis is generally attributed to Erving Goffman in *Frame Analysis: An Essay on the Organization of Experience* (1974/1986).

63. Entman, "Framing," (1993).

64. See Christakis and Fowler, *Connected* (2009). Cf. Marmot, "Fair Society, Health Lives," (2013).

65. Koplan and Brownell, "Response of the Food and Beverage Industry to the Obesity Threat," (2010). See also Freedhoff and Hebert, "Partnerships," (2011), noting that the food industry emphasizes inactivity as the prime cause of obesity in (inter alia) partnership activities.

66. See, e.g., Porter, "David Cameron," (2008), and Hughes, "More Spent on Treating Obesity-Related Conditions," (2016).

67. Snow, et al. "Frame Alignment Processes." (1986).

68. See also Marks, "Toward a Systemic Ethics," (2014a), and Marks, "Caveat Partner," (2017), my response to Tjidde Tempels et al., "Big Food's Ambivalence: Seeking Profit and Responsibility for Health," (2017).

69. For a discussion of framing effects in interventional studies, see Lewis et al., "Dancing with the Porcupine," (2001), 784.

70. See Wikler, "Personal and Social Responsibility," (2002), observing that the "appeal of the notion of personal responsibility masks an ideological vulnerability that is ripe for exploitation—a fact that the tobacco industry has already demonstrated."

71. Some academics have recently begun using the term "commercial determinants of health" as a framing counter-strategy. See Kickbusch, Allen, and Franz, "Commercial Determinants of Health," (2016). But the origins of the term go back at least four decades: see Wikler, "Persuasion and Coercion," (1978).

72. Kearns et al., "Sugar Industry and Coronary Heart Disease Research," (2016).

73. Brownell and Warner, "The Perils of Ignoring History," (2009), 266–267.

74. Robbins and Nestle, "Obesity as Collateral Damage," (2011).

75. Christakis and Fowler, *Connected* (2009).

76. Thompson, "Are Your Friends Making You Fat?" (2009).

77. See, e.g., *Fair Society, Healthy Lives: The Marmot Review* (2010), concluding that policies to need to address the social determinants of health.

78. Freedhoff and Hebert, "Partnerships," (2011). See also Koplan and Brownell, "Response of the Food and Beverage Industry to the Obesity Threat," (2010), critiquing food industry emphasis on physical activity.

79. Thaler and Sunstein, *Nudge* (2009), describing nudging as a form of "libertarian paternalism" that employs "choice architecture" to influence individuals to make decisions that better reflect their values and interests (including health).

80. See, e.g., the Behavioral Insights Team in Britain—also known as the "Nudge Unit." It was originally described as "the first government institution dedicated to the application of behavioral sciences." It is now described as a "partnership," in the form of a "social purpose company" that is "independent of the UK government," but "partly owned by the Cabinet Office." https://www.gov.uk/government/organisations/behavioural-insights-team. President Obama subsequently established the Social and Behavioral Sciences Team in the United States, a subcommittee of the National Science and Technology Council, with representatives from several federal agencies: https://sbst.gov, accessed January 20, 2017.

81. Geof Rayner and Tim Lang, "Is Nudge an Effective Public Health Strategy to Tackle Obesity? No," (2011).

CHAPTER 6

1. Mudd, "How to Force Ethics on the Food Industry," (2013).

2. UN Office of the High Commissioner of Human Rights, Press Release, May 19, 2014, http://www.ohchr.org/EN/NewsEvents/Pages/DisplayNews.aspx?NewsID=14617.

3. Some examples analyzed here are drawn from Marks, "Toward a Systemic Ethics," (2014a).

4. FAO/WHO, "International Conference on Nutrition: Final Report of the Conference," (1992), (paras. 13, 18).

5. Ng et al., "Global Burden of Disease," (2014).

6. FAO/WHO, Rome Declaration on Nutrition (ICN2, 2014). The Declaration also states, "dietary risk factors, together with inadequate physical activity, account for almost 10% of the global burden of disease and disability."

7. Jessica Todd and Lisa Mancino, "Eating Out Increases Daily Calorie Intake," (2010); and Jessica Todd, Lisa Mancino, and Biing-Hwan Lin, "The Impact of Food Away from Home on Adult Diet Quality," (2010).

8. Basu et al., "Soft Drink Consumption," (2013).

9. Stuckler, Basu, and McKee, "Manufacturing Epidemics," (2012).

10. Jacobs and Richtel, "How Big Business Got Brazil Hooked on Junk Food," (2017).

11. Soares, "Putting Taxes into the Diet Equation," (2016).

12. Stuckler, Basu, and McKee, "Manufacturing Epidemics," (2012), 2; Trefis Team, "How Coca-Cola Plans to Make India Its Third Largest Market," *Forbes*, September 7, 2017, https://www.forbes.com/sites/greatspeculations/2017/09/07/how-coca-cola-plans-to-make-india-its-third-largest-market/#32c27a622e84.

13. Institute of Medicine (IoM), *Food Marketing to Children and Youth* (2005).

14. Kraak et al., "Industry Progress," (2011), also finding that several of the limited or moderate changes made by companies appeared to reflect an industry strategy of responding primarily to negative publicity.

15. FTC, "A Review of Mood Marketing to Children and Adolescents: Follow Up Report," (2012).

16. FTC, "Follow Up Report," (2012), ES-6; 45.

17. FTC, "Follow Up Report," (2012), ES-5.

18. FTC, "Follow Up Report," (2012), ES-5.

19. UN Political Declaration on Non-Communicable Diseases (2011), paras 43(f), (g), and (h).

20. UN, "Outcome Document," (2014).

21. UN, "Outcome Document," (2014). Although the document acknowledged that "an increased number of private sector entities has started to produce and promote food products consistent with a healthy diet," it noted that "such products are not always broadly affordable, accessible and available in all communities and countries."

22. For analogous recommendations at the national level, see e.g., IoM, *Food Marketing* (2005), especially recommendation 6, encouraging the government to partner with the private sector to create a social marketing program promoting healthful diets for children and youth. The IoM has since been renamed the National Academy of Medicine (NAM).

23. Austin, "Strategic Collaboration," (2000).

24. Jeff Fields, "Big Beverage Gives $10 Million to CHOP," (2011).

25. The ABA reportedly spent $28,760,000 on lobbying in 2009-2010 alone. Data extracted from the database, www.opensecrets.org.

26. The ABA has at least two websites, www.ameribev.org and www.deliveringchoices.org (the latter aimed at consumers). Its foundation, called the Foundation for a Healthy America, launched its own website, http://www.beveragefoundation.org.

27. According to documents filed with the IRS, contributions to the foundation in 2011 exceeded $4.1 million from Coca-Cola, $3.8 million from PepsiCo, and $1.9 from the Dr. Pepper/Snapple Group. The ABA also contributed $461,335. (This information appears on the foundation's tax form, IRS 990, www.guidestar.org.)

28. Josh Goldstein, "Philadelphia Soft-Drink Tax Proposed," (2010). See also Kass, et al., "Ethics and Obesity Prevention," (2014).

29. Tricia Nadolny, "Soda Tax Passes; Philadelphia Is First Big City," (2016).

30. Children's Hospital of Philadelphia, "Our Mission," http://www.chop.edu/about-us/our-mission#.V8wlqmVgfOw.

31. Cf. Falbe et al., "Impact of the Berkeley Excise Tax," (2016).

32. Brownell, "Thinking Forward," (2012).

33. Cf. William Neuman, "Save the Children Breaks with Soda Tax Effort," (2010), (charity receiving money from soda companies changes position on soda taxes.) See also Jacobson and Brownell, "Small Taxes on Soft Drinks," (2000).

34. Bob Warner, "City Turns Down Beverage-Industry," (2011).

35. John Byrne, "Chicago Soda Tax Fizzles," (2015). See also Gostin, "Big Food is Making America Sick," (2016).

36. Anahad O'Connor and Margot Sanger-Katz, "As Soda Taxes Gain Wider Acceptance," (2016).

37. See https://www.parklives.com.

38. McCartney, "Is Coca-Cola's Antiobesity Scheme the Real Thing?" (2014).

39. Yoni Freedhoff and Hebert, "Partnerships," (2011).

40. UK Active Research Institute, "ParkLives Year 3 Evaluation Report," September 2017, http://researchinstitute.ukactive.com/downloads/managed/CocaColaParkLives_Year3EvaluationReport_Final.pdf.

41. UK Active Research Institute, "ParkLives Year 1 Evaluation Report," 2015, 19, http://researchinstitute.ukactive.com/downloads/managed/ukactive_Parklives_Yr_1_Evaluation_Report-v2.pdf. The report also employs concepts that I critique in this book, among them, the use of "risk to benefit ratio" to "overcome internal objection" to the partnership, and the purported "aligning of priorities and focus" of the soda company and local authorities.

42. UK Active Research Institute, "ParkLives Year 2 Evaluation Report," July 2016, 27, http://researchinstitute.ukactive.com/downloads/managed/CocaColaParkLives_Year2EvaluationReport_Final.pdf.

43. See USDA, "Mission Areas," https://www.usda.gov/our-agency/about-usda/mission-areas and USDA, "USDA Strategic Goals," https://www.usda.gov/our-agency/about-usda/strategic-goals.

44. Moss, "While Warning About Fat," (2010).

45. Historical guidelines (including the relevant 2005 version) are available at http://health.gov.

46. For broader critiques of transparency, beyond the scope of this paper, see Fung, Graham, and Weil, *Full Disclosure* (2007); and Lessig, "Against Transparency," (2009). See also Cosgrove and Whitaker, "Finding Solutions to Institutional Corruption," (2013).

47. Datz, "Harvard Serves Up Its Own 'Plate'," (2011).

48. Datz, "Harvard Serves Up," (2011).

49. Both documents from the program are available at http://www.choosemyplate.gov/partnering-program/national-partners/become-partner.html.

50. A list of national strategic partners is available at http://www.choosemyplate.gov/partnering-program/national-partners/partner-list.html.

51. Notably, the mission refers to "consumers" rather than citizens, residents, or the public.

52. See Ludwig and Nestle, "Can the Food Industry Play a Constructive Role in the Obesity Epidemic?" (2008), arguing "[a]dvice to eat less often, eat foods in smaller portions, and avoid high-calorie foods of low nutritional quality undermines the fundamental business model of many companies."

53. Marks, "On Regularity and Regulation," (2011). See also Pomeranz et al., "Innovative Legal Approaches to Address Obesity," (2009).

54. USDA Center for Nutrition Policy and Promotion, "Everyone Has a Place at the Table!" (2011), http://www.choosemyplate.gov/partnerships/downloads/NutritionComm-icatorsNetwork/PartnershipProgramPromotion.pdf.

55. See IoM, *Food Marketing* (2005); Kraak et al., "Industry Progress," (2011); and UN, "Outcome Document," (2014).

56. Jackie Haven, deputy director and acting executive director of the CNPP, from the notes of a telephone interview on August 1, 2014 with investigative journalist, Brooke Williams. I am extremely grateful to Brooke Williams for sharing her interview notes.

57. See PHA's website, http://ahealthieramerica.org.

58. The White House, "First Lady Michelle Obama Launches Let's Move: America's Move to Raise a Healthier Generation of Kids," February 9, 2010, https://obamawhitehouse.archives.gov/the-press-office/first-lady-michelle-obama-launches-lets-move-americas-move-raise-a-healthier-genera.

59. Simon, Kocot, and Dietz., "Partnership for a Healthier America," (2017).

60. On September 7, 2016, I sent an email request to PHA for further information about what happens when companies do not comply with their commitments. However, my request failed to elicit a response.

61. Simon et al., "Partnership for a Healthier America," (2017).

62. Leon and Ken, "Food Fraud," (2017).

63. Mozaffarian, "The Health Weight Commitment Foundation," (2014).

64. See PHA 2016 Progress Report for Subway, https://www.ahealthieramerica.org/progress-reports/2016/partners/subway.

65. See, e.g., Statista, "Subway Ad Spending in USA," accessed December 1, 2017, http://www.statista.com/statistics/306676/ad-spend-subway-usa/.

66. See Chandon and Wansink, "Biasing Health Halos," (2007), discussed in chapter 5.

67. Leon and Ken, "Food Fraud," (2017), 407.

68. Leon and Ken, "Food Fraud," (2017), 405.

69. See Felicity Lawrence, "McDonald's and PepsiCo to Help Write UK Health Policy," (2010); and Felicity Lawrence, "Who Is the Government's Health Deal with Big Business Really Good For?," (2010).

70. Panjwani and Caraher, "Public Health Responsibility Deal," (2014), and Gilmore, Savell, and Collin, "Public Health," (2011).

71. Knai et al., "Has a Public-Private Partnership Resulted in Action on Healthier Diets in England?," (2015), concluding that the "most effective strategies to improve diet, such as food pricing strategies, restrictions on marketing, and reducing sugar intake, are not reflected in the RD food pledges". See also Knai et al., "Has a Public-Private Partnership Brought About Action on Alcohol Reduction?," (2015), and Knai et al., "Making the Workplace Healthier?," (2016).

72. M. A. Durand et al., "An Evaluation of the Public Health Responsibility Deal," (2015), concluding that effective voluntary approaches require (inter alia) incentives, sanctions, monitoring and scrutiny. Cf. Panjwani and Caraher, "Voluntary Agreements and the Power

of the Food Industry" in Modi Motswami, ed., *Public Health and the Food and Drinks Industry* (2018), 110–120.

73. See Article 101 of the Treaty on the Functioning of the EU (formerly, Art. 81, EC Treaty).

74. See, e.g., Backholer et al., "The Impact of a Tax on Sugar-Sweetened Beverages," (2016).

75. Backholer, Blake, and Vandevijvere, "Have We Reached the Tipping Point?," (2016), and Backholer and Vandevijvere, "Sugar-Sweetened Beverage Taxation," (2017).

76. UN Habitat, "UN Habitat at a Glance," http://unhabitat.org/about-us/un-habitat-at-a-glance/, accessed July 1, 2014.

77. New Delhi Television, "Support My School: About the Campaign," http://www.ndtv.com/micro/supportmyschool/aboutthecampaign.aspx, accessed July 1, 2014.

78. Trevor Williams, "The Power of Toilets," February 9, 2012, GlobalAtlanta.com, http://www.globalatlanta.com/article-photo/25342/1870/.

79. Coca Cola (India), "What's New: Happiness Telethon," http://www.coca-colaindia.com/presscenter/whats-new-HAPPINESS-TELETHON.html, accessed July 1, 2014.

80. Sabita Mahapatra et al., "Support My School," *IOSR Journal of Business and Management*, 2278-487X: 1–12 (2015).

81. I am not aware of any published studies exploring these potential effects. The soda company has a commercial interest in monitoring these effects, but not in publicizing them widely.

82. See also Nestle, *Soda Politics* (2015).

83. Keast, Nicklas, and O'Neil, "Snacking," (2010).

84. Candice Choi, "How Candy Makers Shape Nutrition Science," (2016). The US trade association for candy manufacturers is called the National Confectioners Association.

85. Robert Sansone et al., "The Flaviola Health Study," (2015).

86. Nestle, "Corporate Funding of Food and Nutrition Research," (2016).

87. Bes-Rastrollo et al., "Financial Conflicts of Interest," (2013).

88. O'Connor, "Coca-Cola Funds Scientists," (2015).

89. O'Connor, "University Returns $1 Million Grant to Coca-Cola," (2015).

90. Benjamin Rosenthal, Michael Jacobson, and Mary Bohm, "Professors on the Take," (1976), 42–47 (a historical critique of nutrition professors' ties to the food industry); Anna Gilmore and Simon Capewell, "Should We Welcome Food Industry Funding?," (2016).

91. O'Connor, "How the Sugar Industry Shifted Blame to Fat," (2016).

92. Kearns et al., "Sugar Industry and Coronary Heart Disease Research," (2016).

93. O'Connor, "Coca-Cola Funds Scientists," (2015). See also Nestle, "Food Industry Funding," (2016), arguing that food company sponsorship, "whether or not intentionally manipulative, undermines public trust in nutrition science, contributes to public confusion about what to eat, and compromises Dietary Guidelines."

94. See, e.g. Choi, "How Candy Makers," (2016).

95. See, e.g., Michaels, *Doubt Is Their Product* (2008); Naomi Oreskes and Erik Conway, *Merchants of Doubt* (New York: Bloomsbury, 2010); and White and Bero, "Corporate Manipulation of Research," (2010).

96. White and Bero, "Corporate Manipulation," (2010).

97. Michaels, *Doubt Is Our Product* (2010).

98. For a review of the relationships between two soda companies and nearly one hundred public health NGOs, see Aaron and Siegel, "Sponsorship of National Health Organizations," (2017).

99. For a "web of influence" involving twenty-nine sugar industry actors, see Gornall, "Sugar: Spinning a Web of Influence," *BMJ* (2015).

100. Thomas Fuller et al., "Nutritionists Take Money from Food Giants," (2017).

101. See, e.g., O. C. Ezizika et al., "Building Effective Partnerships: The Role of Trust in the Virus Resistant Cassava for Africa Project," *Agriculture and Food Security*, 1 (Supp. 1): S7 (2012), a study of the Virus Resistant Cassava Project for Africa (VIRCA), a partnership in Kenya and Uganda involving Monsanto Corporation and the Monsanto Fund (among others) employed semi-structured interviews. Interviewees in that study expressed a number of concerns. Among them, they reported "a skewed emphasis in favor of the product development component at the expense of other components (such as regulatory [issues], communication and outreach)."

102. De Schutter, "Report of the UN Special Rapporteur," (2011).

103. Modi Motswami, ed., *Public Health and the Food and Drinks Industry* (2018). With additional resources, it might be possible to scale up such an enterprise even further. Cf., Frank Hartwich et al., "Building Public-Private Partnerships for Agricultural Innovation" Washington, DC, Internal Food Policy Research Institute, 2008. http://www.foodsecurityportal.org/sites/default/files/Building%20Public-Private%20Partnerships.pdf, examining 125 agriculture partnerships in Latin America. Although the report is problematic (it contains only oblique discussion of conflicts of interest), it identifies important systemic issues: among them, the private sector tends to invest in research and development only when results can be achieved in the short-term; when those results are "appropriable" by the industry partner; and when they can be commercialized.

104. Jeff Collin et al., "Conclusions," in Motswami, *Public Health, Food, and Drink* (2018), 147.

105. Buse and Harmer, "Seven Habits," (2007), arguing that PPPs "skew" national priorities; neglect public health issues less amenable to PPPs; tend to focus on "product-oriented interventions;" that the private sector is often overrepresented; and that they promote "a diminished sense of the 'public' nature of global public health initiatives," resulting in underfunding of the WHO.

106. Kraak and Story, "A Public Health Perspective on Healthy Lifestyles," (2010), 195–196.

CHAPTER 7

1. In chapters 6 and 8, I discuss case studies and meta-analyses contradicting claims about the alleged public health benefits of PPPs. But in this chapter, I offer a theoretical objection that would still apply even if there were stronger evidence of benefits.

2. For a more detailed discussion of institutional integrity, see chapter 2.

3. A couple of scholars have come closer than others. On separation of powers in the context of conflicts of interest and institutional corruption respectively, see Stark, "Public Sector Conflict of Interest," (1992), and Teachout, *Corruption in America* (2014).

4. Montesquieu, *The Spirit of the Laws*, bk. 11, chap. 6 (1748). Michel Troper, "Separation of Powers," in *Montesquieu Dictionary*, Institut de l'Histoire de la Pensee Classique (para. 43), has argued that the Baron's main concern was balance (not separation) of powers. But cf. Teachout, "The Anti-Corruption Principle," (2009), 373, 396, arguing that the rationale for and meaning of the separation of powers principle evolves over time, and Waldron, "Separation of Powers," (2013).

5. Hamilton, *The Federalist Papers*, No. 78, "The Judiciary Department," http://avalon. law.yale.edu/18th_century/fed78.asp.

6. Hamilton, *The Federalist Papers*, No. 78.

7. Hamilton, *The Federalist Papers*, No. 78.

8. Madison, *The Federalist Papers*, No. 48, http://avalon.law.yale.edu/18th_century/ fed48.asp.

9. Madison, *Congressional Register*, June 22, 1789, http://www.gwu.edu/~ffcp/mep/ displaydoc.cfm?docid=fc111028.

10. Corwin, *The President* (1957), 171. Corwin made the observation in the context of foreign policy, but it is more broadly applicable. Cf. Lord Steyn, "Democracy, the Rule of Law and the Role of Judges," (2006), on the significance of "friction" between the executive and judiciary.

11. Mann and Ornstein, "Finding the Common Good," (2013).

12. Lessig, "What an Originalist Would Understand Corruption to Mean," (2014), 9, invoking Newton's Third Law of Motion: for every action, there is an equal and opposite reaction.

13. Masterman, *Separation of Powers* (2011), 22.

14. Masterman, *Separation of Powers* (2011). See also Steyn, "Democracy," (2006).

15. Bagehot, *The English Constitution* (1867), chap. 3.

16. HL Debs, November 25, 1997, col. 934 (Lord Irvine of Lairg, QC). See also Masterman, *Separation of Powers* (2011).

17. Lord Woolf, "Tensions Between the Executive and the Judiciary," (1998).

18. Masterman, *Separation of Powers* (2011), 220.

19. Royal Commission on Reform of the House of Lords (Wakeham Commission), *A House for the Future* (2000).

20. Wakeham Commission, *House for the Future* (2000), para. 9.6.

21. Wakeham Commission, *House for the Future* (2000), evidence of Lord Wilberforce.

22. Notably, even as the Wakeham Commission argued that the dual roles enhanced the legislative chamber, it also recognized that "similar contributions could be, and indeed are, made by other members of the second chamber with legal expertise or experience." Wakeham Commission, *House for the Future* (2000), para. 9.7.

23. *A & Others v Secretary of State for the Home Department* [2004] UKHL 56.

24. House of Lords Select Committee on the Constitution (Constitution Committee), *Relations Between the Executive, Judiciary, and Parliament* (2007), para. 95. See also Mary Riddell, "Interview: Charles Clarke," *New Statesman*, September 26, 2005, https://www. newstatesman.com/node/162888.

25. Riddell, "Charles Clarke," (2005).

26. Riddell, "Charles Clarke," (2005).

27. Constitution Committee, "Relations," para. 95.

28. Constiution Committee, "Relations," para. 34.

29. Steyn, "Democracy, the Rule of Law, and the Role of Judges," (2006), 248.

30. Constitution Committee, "Relations," para. 96.

31. Constitution Committee, "Relations," paras. 35-36. This exchange demonstrates the culture and practice of the English judiciary and the extent to which they recognize the need to protect the rule of law and guard their independence, integrity, and credibility. Ironically, it is this culture and practice that may have led some judges to believe that the proposed judicial reforms eventually introduced by the Constitutional Reform Act of 2005 were unnecessary.

32. Constitution Committee, "Relations," para. 97. See also section 3 of the Constitutional Reform Act 2005 providing that "the Lord Chancellor and other Ministers of the Crown must not seek to influence particular judicial decisions through any special access to the judiciary."

33. Constitution Committee, "Relations," para. 55.

34. Although I have focused on an example from Britain, there are several historical instances of Supreme Court justices serving as advisors to the President. See Gerard Magloicca, "The Legacy of Chief Justice Fortas," (2015), 261–262, 266. Remarkably, when Abe Fortas was a justice of the Supreme Court, he had a direct line to the White House installed in his office. He also edited President Lyndon Johnson's State of the Union Address in 1966. In a memorandum defending his decision not to recuse himself from a case in which the vice president was a party, Supreme Court Justice Antonin Scalia (who had gone duck hunting with the vice president) observed that a Supreme Court justice serving as an "advisor and confidante" to the president is a practice "so incompatible with the separation of powers" that it has been "properly abandoned." See Cheney et al. v. US District Court, 541 U.S. 913 (2004), 926.

35. Waldron, "Separation of Powers," (2013), 442.

36. Waldron, "Separation of Powers," (2013), 460.

37. For the expression of many of these rationales, see Kraak et al., "Q Methodology," *Food Policy* (2014).

38. The different kinds of "interest" are usually not teased out. For a brief discussion of public interest, in particular, see chapter 3.

39. I critique this assumption in my brief talk, "In Praise of Conflict," available at www.ted/com/talks/2730.

40. Cf. Sterckx, "Patenting and Licensing," (2011), similarly asking whether goals can be achieved in some other way.

41. See Stark, "Public Sector Conflict," (1992), 434.

42. I say more about this toward the end of this chapter. See also Lessig, *Republic, Lost* (2010).

43. In this section, I draw on Jonathan Faull and Ali Nikpay, *The EU Law of Competition*, 3rd ed. (Oxford: Oxford University Press, 2014). See also Richard Whish and David Bailey, *Competition Law*, 8th ed. (Oxford: Oxford University Press, 2015).

44. Treaty on the Functioning of the European Union, Article 101, available at http://eur-lex.europa.eu/legal-content/EN/ALL/?uri=CELEX:12008E101. The English language

text employs the term "undertakings" (rather than corporations), and "associations of undertakings." Price fixing and market sharing (among other behaviors) are singled out in these provisions as especially problematic behaviors.

45. Case 48/69 *ICI v Commission* [1972] ECR 619, para. 64; Case C-8/08 *T-Mobile Netherlands and Others* [2009] ECR I-4529, para. 26.

46. Joined Cases 40/73, etc. *Coöperatieve Vereniging "Suiker Unie and Others v. Commission* [1975] ECR 1663.

47. Joined Cases C-89/85, etc. *Ahlström Osakeyhtiö et al v. Commission (Wood Pulp II)* [1993] ECR I-1307.

48. Faull and Nikpay, *EU Competition Law* (2014), para. 3.137.

49. Faull and Nikpay, *EU Competition Law* (2014), paras. 3.131 to 3.134.

50. Faull and Nikpay, *EU Competition Law* (2014), paras. 3.147 to 3.149.

51. *Pre-Insulated Pipes,* OJ 1999 L24/1, para. 131.

52. Tesco v. OFT (UK CAT, 2012), available at http://www.catribunal.org.uk/files/1188_Tesco_Judgment_CAT_31_201212.pdf.

53. Sections 188 and 190 of the Enterprise Act, 2002 c.40 (the "cartel offence.")

54. 15 U.S.C. 1, available at https://www.law.cornell.edu/uscode/text/15/1, (prohibiting "[e]very contract . . . or conspiracy, in restraint of trade or commerce.") Accessed January 31, 2017. On the analogy between "concerted action" in the United States and concerted practices in the European Union, see F. Ghezzi and M. Maggiolino, "Bridging EU Concerted Practices with US Concerted Actions," (2014).

55. Verizon v. Trinko, 540 U.S. 398, 124 S.Ct. 872 (2004) at 408. See also Whish and Bailey, *Competition Law* (2015), 597, arguing that collusion is the "evil" at which provisions of European competition law (in particular, Art.101 of the TFEU) are directed.

56. See Lo and Field, *Conflicts of Interest* (2009) (in particular, Appendix C, "Conflict of Interest in Four Professions: A Comparative Analysis," by Michael Davis and Josephine Johnston). Cf. the US Senate Model Code of Ethics discussed in chapter 3.

57. This space encompasses hybrid public-private institutions that are created by or result from collaborations between public and private sector bodies. I acknowledge that there are, of course, other kinds of hybrid institutions that are beyond the scope of this book.

58. Although scholars in some disciplines argue that norms cease to be norms (and should not be described as such) once they are embedded in laws and policies, I do not take such a view here.

59. See, e.g., UN SCN (2006). This policy prohibited financial or in-kind contributions from the food industry.

60. Some policies employ traffic light schemes for prohibited conduct, safe harbors, and conduct in between (red, green, amber). An analogous schema may use black, white, and grey. Principles are likely to be help navigate areas designated amber or grey, respectively.

61. See WHO, "FENSA," (2016).

62. Lo and Field, *Conflict of Interest* (2009), 6.

63. Rodwin, "Attempts to Redefine Conflicts of Interest," (2017).

64. See also Judith Richter, "Conflicts of Interest and Global Health and Nutrition Governance," *BMJ* (2015).

65. See, e.g., Sah and Fugh-Berman, "Physicians Under the Influence," (2013), and Lo and Grady, "Payments to Physicians," (2017).

66. Advisors who disclose that they have conflicts of interest may "gild the lily" even further once advisees have been put on notice. See Dana and Loewenstein, "A Social Science Perspective," (2003), and Sunita Sah, "The Paradox of Disclosure," (2016) (and the studies cited therein).

67. See Krimsky, *Science in the Private Interest* (2004); Schafer, "Biomedical Conflicts," (2004); Christopher Robertson, "The Money Blind: How to Stop Industry Bias in Biomedical Science," (2011).

68. See, e.g., Nuffield Council on Bioethics, *Public Health: Ethical Issues* (2007), a report coauthored by Richard Brownsword whose scholarship employs and develops the idea of stewardship.

69. See, e.g., John Coggon, "What Help is a Steward?" (2011).

70. Travis et al., "Towards Better Stewardship," (2002).

71. I discuss this claim in more detail in chapter 3.

72. I discuss this more fully in chapter 2 discussing (among others) Dennis Thompson's claim that "[t]he pollution of the public by the private is the core of the traditional idea of political corruption."

73. Teachout, "The Anti-Corruption Principle," (2009), 373 fn. 156, arguing that, like separation of powers, the meaning of the principle is "contextual and changes over time."

74. Teachout, *Corruption in America* (2014).

75. See my discussion in chapter 2.

76. The best-known example of "principlism" is Beauchamp and Childress, *Principles of Biomedical Ethics* (2012), an approach that is all too often applied mechanistically rather than reflectively by others. Compare Ross Upshur, "Principles for the Justification of Public Health Intervention," (2002). Notably, one of Upshur's principles is reciprocity. But he uses the term to address the obligations of public health departments and other entities to assist individuals and communities with the discharge of their obligations in relation to public health. Ironically, this kind of reciprocity (which is broadly commendable rather than problematic) can be undermined by reciprocal relations between government agencies and industry actors.

CHAPTER 8

1. Dave Eggers, *The Circle* (New York: Vintage Books, 2014), 489.

2. "Partnership" is now used so broadly some scholars argue the term cannot be defined by any set of necessary and sufficient conditions. See, e.g. Johan Nystrom, "The Definition of Partnering as a Wittgenstein Family-Resemblance Concept," (2005), drawing on and adapting Wittgenstein's notion of "family resemblance" (Ludwig Wittgenstein, *Philosophical Investigations* [New York: Macmillan, 1953/1973], §67). Nystrom argues that some conditions are necessary but not sufficient for the existence of a partnership (the center of the "flower"); other conditions, "petals," must also be present but no specific petal or set of petals is required. See also my discussion of definitions and taxonomies of partnership in chapter 1.

3. Buse and Harmer, "Power to the Partners," (2004).

4. See, e.g., Richter, *Public-Private Partnerships* (2004b).

5. Partnership Act, 1890 c. 39 (England and Wales), section 1.

6. The OED similarly defines "partner" in this context as "[a]ny of a number of individuals with interests and investments in a business or enterprise, *among whom expenses, profits, and losses are shared.*" www.oed.com, accessed May 1, 2015.

7. Kraak et al., "A Q Methodology Study," (2014). For a response, see also Marks, "Toward a Systemic Ethics," (2014a).

8. Buse and Harmer, "Power to the Partners," (2004).

9. Meinhard v. Salmon 164 N.E. 545 (N.Y. 1928) (a landmark case on fiduciary obligations). In this paragraph, I critique the use of the word "partner." An alternative, "collaborator," does not avoid this peril. But "collaborator" is arguably better than "partner" since the former may possess a positive or negative valence, depending on the context, and if employed reflectively, the word "collaborator" may invite further ethical scrutiny. As Anthony Lane recently observed, "Collaboration is a murky trade, and it covers quite a range. Whether you're siding with the enemy in Nazi-occupied France or laying out the lyrics to 'Edelweiss' so that Richard Rodgers can devise a tune to match, you're a collaborator." Anthony Lane, "High Crimes," *New Yorker,* June 18, 2018, 64.

10. I draw in this section on Marks, "Toward a Systemic Ethics," (2014a).

11. Tom Vilsack employed this phrase while serving as US secretary of agriculture. See USDA, "National Strategic Partner List," http://www.choosemyplate.gov/partneringprogram/national-partners/partner-list.html, accessed December 1, 2013.

12. I briefly review some contemporary approaches in Marks, "Toward a Systemic Ethics," (2014a). See also Alexander et al., "Achieving a Framework," (2015); Rowe et al., "Principles for Building Public-Private Partnerships," (2013).

13. ILSI North America, "Who We Are," http://ilsina.org/about-us/our-story/. Its North American division has section 501(3)(c) charitable status.

14. Sheila Kaplan, "New C.D.C. Chief Saw Coca-Cola as Ally in Obesity Fight," (2017). See also O'Connor, "Coke's Chief Scientist Is Leaving," (2015).

15. Kaplan, "New C.D.C. Chief Saw Coca-Cola as Ally," (2017).

16. Rowe et al., "Principles for Building Public-Private Partnerships," (2013).

17. ILSI North America, "Who We Are," http://ilsina.org/about-us/our-story/.

18. Alexander et al., "Achieving a Framework," (2015), 1363, arguing that "a boost to the movement toward PPPs is timely and important to grow resources for nutrition, food, and health research."

19. See, e.g., Kraak et al., "Balancing the Benefits," (2011). A few public bodies and NGOs have tried to create their own institutional policies or guidelines. See, e.g., Kraak/PCPHN (2014) and World Obesity Federation (2015). The WHO recently drafted guidelines for member states addressing nutrition-related conflicts of interest (2017). Although I cannot critically assess all these approaches in detail, I highlight a few concerns with some of these approaches both in this chapter and in Appendix A.

20. Hernandez-Aguado and Zaragoza, "Support of Public-Private Partnerships," (2016).

21. See, e.g., Kraak et al., "Balancing the Benefits," (2011).

22. See, similarly, NCPHS (National Commission for the Protection of Human Subjects of Biomedical and Behavioral Research), *The Belmont Report: Ethical Principles and Guidelines for the Protection of Human Subjects of Research* (Washington, DC: Department of Health, Education, and Welfare, 1979).

23. This matrix builds on earlier work in Marks, "Toward a Systemic Ethics," (2014a). My thinking in this chapter is also informed by Galea and McKee, "Public-Private Partnerships," (2014), and Fabio, "Conflicts of Interest in Food and Nutrition," (2015).

24. Marks, "Silencing Marcellus," (2014b).

25. See, e.g., Rowe et al., "Principles for Building Partnerships," (2013). The role of industry in the origins and authorship of these guidelines is discussed more fully above.

26. See, e.g., Childress et al., "Public Health Ethics," (2002). This analytical framework draws, in turn, from international human rights law. See also Kass, "An Ethics Framework for Public Health," (2001).

27. Hernandez-Aguado and Zaragoza, "Support of Public-Private Partnerships," (2016).

28. On the promotion of gifts, see also Appendix B, "The Anatomy of the Gift."

29. Cf. Barr, "A Research Protocol to Evaluate the Effectiveness of Public–Private Partnerships," (2007).

30. This is the term employed by Austin, "Strategic Innovation," (2000) and adopted by Vivica Kraak and colleagues in the obesity context. See my discussion in chapter 1.

31. While it is not uncommon for partnership guidelines to address the need to renegotiate partnerships, they often side-step the more challenging question of withdrawal.

32. Cf. George Monbiot, "How Have These Corporations Colonised Our Public Life?," (2014).

33. See also Judith Richter, *Dialogue or Engineering of Consent? Opportunities and Risks of Talking to Industry* (2002).

34. The NIH commissioned a working group report, "Ethical Considerations for Industry Partnership on Research to Help End the Opioid Crisis," https://acd.od.nih.gov/documents/presentations/032018_opioids-draft-report.pdf (March 2018 draft report). The report recognizes the "unique challenges due to the alleged involvement of certain companies in practices that contributed to the [opioid] crisis." However, it does not articulate and address all the ethical perils discussed in this book. In several material respects, the report's recommendations are also significantly less demanding than the approach I adopt in this chapter.

35. Jessica Todd and Lisa Mancino, "Eating Out Increases Daily Calorie Intake," (2010). See also Jessica Todd, Lisa Mancino, and Biing-Hwan Lin, "The Impact of Food Away From Home on Adult Diet Quality," (2010).

36. Todd and Mancino, "Eating Out," (2010); Todd, Mancino, and Lin, "Food Away from Home," (2010).

37. This example is discussed in further detail in chapter 6.

38. See Rose, "Patient Advocacy Organizations," (2013), and Rose et al., "Patient Advocacy Organizations," (2017).

39. The WHO's program budget for 2016-17 was $4.38 billion. See WHO, *Programme Budget 2016–2017* (Geneva: WHO, 2015), http://www.who.int/about/finances-accountability/budget/PB201617_en.pdf. The 2014 advertising budget for Coca-Cola was $3.5 billion. The budget for PepsiCo was smaller but still substantial at $2.3 billion. See Investopedia, "A Look at Coca-Cola's Advertising Expenses," August 13, 2015, http://www.investopedia.com/articles/markets/081315/look-cocacolas-advertising-expenses.asp.

40. See, e.g., Elise Hu, "1 Million Net Neutrality Comments Filed, but Will They Matter?," *NPR/All Things Considered*, July 21, 2014, http://www.npr.org/blogs/alltechconsidered/2014/07/21/332678802/one-million-net-neutrality-comments-filed-but-will-they-matter. Federal net neutrality protections were repealed in June 2018.

41. Kimberly D. Krawiec, "Don't 'Screw Joe the Plummer': The Sausage-Making of Financial Reform," 55 *Arizona Law Review* 53–103 (2013).

42. Hu, "Net Neutrality," (2014).

43. Clare Panjwani and Martin Caraher, "The Public Health Responsibility Deal: Brokering a Deal for Public Health, but on Whose Terms?" (2014).

44. In its guidance to member states on conflicts of interest in nutrition programs, the WHO defines "at arm's length" to mean "independent from the other entity, does not take instructions from it and is clearly not influenced and not reasonably perceived to be influenced in its decisions and work by the other entity." The concept of arm's length has been employed in legal contexts, such as tax and competition law. In the latter case, an assessment of arm's length relationships may be made by looking for factors that "militate against" its finding. See, e.g., Faull and Nikpay, *EU Competition Law* (2014), para. 5.135 fn. 183.

45. I discuss "safe harbors" in more detail in chapter 7.

46. Since small gifts may be influential, public officials should not assume that only gifts or in-kind contributions above a certain absolute or relative value (for example, 20 percent of the recipient's budget) might render an interaction close. See chapter 4 on reciprocity and Appendix B, "The Anatomy of the Gift."

47. Pomeranz et al., "Innovative Legal Approaches to Address Obesity," (2009); Rutkow and Teret, "Role of State Attorneys General in Health Policy," (2010). Recent examples of coordinated legal action are claims brought by states against pharmaceutical companies to recover the costs of the opioid crisis. See, e.g., Mattie Quinn, "The Opioid Files: More Than 100 States and Cities Are Suing Drug Companies," Governing.com, November 13, 2017, http://www.governing.com/topics/health-human-services/gov-opioid-lawsuits-companies-states-cities.html.

CHAPTER 9

1. Given Henry Etzkowitz's use of Archimedes' triple helix as a metaphor to argue for closer relationships with industry actors, it seems fitting to draw on the words of the same ancient Greek scholar to argue the contrary. I critique Etzkowitz's position in chapter 5.

2. These strategies are increasingly described as "commercial determinants of health." See, e.g., Kickbusch, Allen, and Franz, "The Commercial Determinants of Health," (2016) ("strategies and approaches used by the private sector to promote products and choices that are detrimental to health.") For a much earlier use of the term, see Wikler, "Persuasion and Coercion," (1978).

3. White House Council of Economic Advisors, *Underestimated Costs* (2017).

4. NIH, "Public-Private Initiative to Address the Opioid Crisis," (2017).

5. HSGAC, "Fueling an Epidemic: Report Two," (2018).

6. Volkow and Collins, "The Role of Science," (2017).

7. Streeck and Thelen, "Introduction," (2005), 7–8.

8. Thompson, *Restoring Responsibility* (2004), 29.

9. See, e.g., De Schutter, "Report of the UN Special Rapporteur," (2011), calling for the overhaul of agricultural subsidies and the support of local food production, in addition to regulation and taxation.

APPENDIX A

1. WHO, "Principles Governing Relations with Non-Governmental Organizations," (1987) (this language appears in the version of the principles adopted at the World Health Assembly in 1987, WHA 40.25).

2. WHO, "NGOs in Official Relations with the WHO," http://www.who.int/civilsociety/relations/NGOs-in-Official-Relations-with-WHO.pdf, accessed December 1, 2015.

3. Official relations were later terminated with some of these bodies. See, e.g., WHO Standing Committee on Official Relations, Report to Executive Board (2014), EB134/44/, http://apps.who.int/gb/ebwha/pdf_files/EB134/B134_44-en.pdf, accessed December 1, 2015, recommending removal of International Special Dietary Foods Industries, not because of their "commercial or profit-making nature," but for failing to provide "the deliverables expected during the collaboration period."

4. WHO, "Guidelines on Working with the Private Sector to Achieve Health Outcomes," (2000), provided that donors "may not . . . seek promotion from the fact that they have made a donation" to support the WHO's work (para. 29).

5. WHO, "FENSA," (2016).

6. WHO, "FENSA," (2016), para. 7.

7. Khayatzadeh-Mahani, Ruckert, and Labonté, "WHO's Framework," (2017). See also Lida Lhotska and Arun Gupta, "Whose Health? Crucial Negotiations for the WHO's Future," 2016, http://www.gifa.org/whose-health-the-crucial-negotiations-for-the-world-health-organizations-future/

8. WHO, "Register of Non-State Actors," http://apps.who.int/register-nonstate-actors/search.aspx.

9. FAO, "Principles and Guidelines for Cooperation with the Private Sector," (2000).

10. FAO, "Organization-Wide Strategy on Partnerships," (2012).

11. FAO, "Strategy for Partnerships with the Private Sector," (2013a).

12. FAO, "Strategy," (2013a), 20–21.

13. FAO, "Strategy," (2013a), 11.

14. FAO/WHO, "World Declaration and Plan of Action for Nutrition," (ICN 1992).

15. ICN, Plan of Action (1992). See, e.g., paras. 3, 22, and 32(e).

16. ICN2, Rome Declaration 2014, para. 15(f).

17. FAO/WHO, "Report of the Joint WHO/FAO Secretariat on the Second International Conference on Nutrition," (2014).

18. FAO, "FAO considers the Private Sector to be a key ally in the fight against hunger," (2016).

19. UN General Assembly, "Political Declaration on Non-Communicable Diseases," (2011), A/RES/66/2, para. 36.

20. UNGA, NCD Declaration (2011), para. 38.

21. UNGA, NCD Declaration (2011), para. 54.

22. UN, "Outcome Document," (2014), para. 28.

23. UN, "Outcome Document," (2014), para. 29. It also expresses concern about the need for "appropriate protection from vested interests."

24. UN, Sustainable Development Goals, (2015), Target 17.17.

25. WHO Director General, Safeguarding against possible conflicts of interest in nutrition programmes: Draft approach for the prevention and management of conflicts of interest in the policy development and implementation of nutrition programmes at country level, EB 142/23 (dated December 4, 2017; presented at the January 2018 meeting of WHO Executive Board).

26. See chapter 7 in which I also critique the use of the term "risk-benefit balancing."

27. The report has been critiqued for its definition of conflict of interest. See also Rodwin, "Attempts to Redefine Conflicts of Interest," (2017).

28. During an open consultation period in September 2017, I provided a brief written response to the WHO addressing the way in which my work on integrity was employed in an earlier draft. However, personal circumstances and time constraints prevented me from commenting in detail on the whole document.

29. UN, "Progress on the prevention and control of non-communicable diseases," (2017), 1; WHO, "Preparation for the Third High-Level Meeting on NCDs," (2018a), para 11; WHO, "Time to Deliver: Report of the Independent High-Level Commission on NCDs" (2018b), 10.

30. WHO, "Montevideo Roadmap 2018–2030 on NCDs," (2017b), para 4; UN, "Progress on the prevention and control of NCDs," (2017), 9; WHO, "Preparation for the Third High-Level Meeting on NCDs," (2018a), 6 and Annex 4.

31. WHO, "Preparation for the Third High-Level Meeting on NCDs," (2018a), 5; UN, "Progress on the prevention and control of NCDs," (2017), 8.

32. WHO, "Montevideo Roadmap," (2017b), paras 27 and 29; WHO, "Time to Deliver," (2018b), 24; UN, "Political Declaration of the Third High-Level Meeting on NCDs," (2018). For concerns that the declaration is not sufficiently robust and that this too may reflect industry influence and interference, see the statement of NCD Alliance (September 27, 2018), https://bit.ly/2P8Spoo.

33. See, e.g., WHO, "Montevideo Roadmap," (2017b), para 34.

APPENDIX B

1. For scholars writing about the "biography of the gift," see Stirrat and Henkel, "The Problem of Reciprocity in the NGO World," (1997).

2. Some scholars have proposed establishing such an entity to eliminate or attenuate influence arising from industry-funded research. I discuss the limitations of these proposals in chapter 7.

3. See, e.g., the ABA's creation of a foundation to coordinate the donation of $10 million from soda companies to CHOP (discussed in chapter 6).

4. The ethical objection to eliminating or minimizing the appearance of influence without addressing the influence itself is analogous to my concern with seeking to restore trust in an

institution while failing to address the problem that reasonably led to the loss of trust. I explore the latter concern in my discussion of institutional integrity in chapter 2.

5. A major criticism of the International Life Sciences Institute (ILSI) is that its name does not make clear that the organization primarily depends on financial support from industry. A recent *New York Times* article described ILSI as "the food industry's premier research center" and noted that its past presidents included the chief science and health officer at Coca-Cola, who helped "orchestrate a strategy of funding scientists who encouraged the public to focus on exercise and worry less about how calories contribute to obesity." See Sheila Kaplan, "New C.D.C. Chief Saw Coca-Cola as Ally in Obesity Fight," (2017).

6. Comparison of tissue types involves the "histo-compatibility complex" or human leukocyte antigen (HLA) testing. I am grateful to Dr. Stephen Marks for guidance on kidney transplants. Any errors are my own.

7. Cf. Titmuss, *The Gift Relationship* (1971), 199, defining mixed externalities as "divergences between the costs borne by (or benefits accruing to) individual organizations or firms and the costs (or diswelfares) imposed upon (or benefits accruing to) the community as a whole."

8. The ABA's gift to the Children's Hospital of Philadelphia, discussed in chapter 6, arguably served to stave off a soda tax in Philadelphia for six years (although money was not, in fact, spent immediately by the hospital). See also my discussion in chapter 1 of the view that one-off gifts may constitute partnerships.

9. See my discussion in chapter 4. This is where the analogy between industry gifts and organ donations breaks down. You can only donate one kidney. In contrast, corporate gifts usually come from profitable revenue streams, so—as executives and development officers are often eager to point out—there is "more where that came from."

10. See, e.g., Mark Hrywna, "Even in Death, Lay's Gift Stirs Controversy," *Nonprofit Times*, July 1, 2006, http://www.thenonprofittimes.com/news-articles/even-in-death-lay-s-gift-stirs-controversy/ (discussing the gift made by the former CEO of Enron to the University of Missouri before his conviction for fraud and death shortly thereafter).

11. For a brief discussion of evidence regarding the influence of small gifts on physicians, see Sah and Fugh-Berman, "Physicians Under the Influence," (2013), and Lo and Grady, "Payments to Physicians," (2017).

12. Meir Dan-Cohen, "Decision Rules and Conduct Rules: On Acoustic Separation in Criminal Law," 97 *Harvard Law Review* 626, 627–31 (1984), contrasting laws that provide instructions to society about behavior, and decision rules that speak to a targeted audience (judges and prosecutors) about how to apply those conduct laws.

13. WHO, "FENSA," (2016), para. 69. See also the previous guidelines, WHO, Guidelines on interactions with commercial enterprises to achieve health outcomes, EB 107/20, Annex (2000), para. 29.

SELECTED BIBLIOGRAPHY

Aaron, Daniel, and Michael Siegel. 2017. "Sponsorship of National Health Organizations by Two Major Soda Companies." *American Journal of Preventive Medicine* 52(1): 20–30.

Ackerman, Frank, and Lisa Heinzerling. 2004. *Priceless: On Knowing the Price of Everything and the Value of Nothing.* New York: New Press.

Adams, Barbara, and Jens Martens. 2015. *Fit for Whose Purpose? Private Funding and Corporate Influence in the United Nations.* Bonn; New York: GPF.

Adams, Peter J. 2007. "Assessing Whether to Receive Funding Support from Tobacco, Alcohol, Gambling and Other Dangerous Consumption Industries." *Addiction* 102 (7): 1027–1033. doi:10.1111/j.1360-0443.2007.01829.x.

———. 2013. "Addiction Industry Studies: Understanding How Proconsumption Influences Block Effective Interventions." *American Journal of Public Health* 103 (4): e35–e38. doi:10.2105/AJPH.2012.301151.

———. 2016. *Moral Jeopardy: Risks of Accepting Money from the Alcohol, Tobacco and Gambling Industries.* New York: Cambridge University Press.

Alexander, Nick, Sylvia Rowe, Robert E. Brackett, Britt Burton-Freeman, Eric J. Hentges, Alison Kretser, David M. Klurfeld, Linda D. Meyers, Ratna Mukherjea, and Sarah Ohlhorst. 2015. "Achieving a Transparent, Actionable Framework for Public-Private Partnerships for Food and Nutrition Research." *American Journal of Clinical Nutrition* 101 (6): 1359–1363. doi:10.3945/ajcn.115.112805.

Amann, Wolfgang and Agata Stachowicz-Stanusch. 2012. *Integrity in Organizations: Building the Foundations for Humanistic Management.* New York: Springer.

American Association of University Professors (AAUP). 1940. *Statement of Principles on Academic Freedom and Tenure.* Washington, DC: AAUP. https://www.aaup.org/report/1940-statement-principles-academic-freedom-and-tenure.

———. 2014. *Recommended Principles to Guide Academy-Industry Relationships.* http://public.eblib.com/choice/publicfullrecord.aspx?p=3414326..

Aristotle. *Nicomachean Ethics. Book I.* Translated by Susan Collins. 2012. Chicago: University of Chicago Press.

Armstrong, Jim. 1997. "Stewardship and Public Service: A Discussion Paper Prepared for the Public Service Commission of Canada." http://publiccommons.ca/public/uploads/literature/stewardship_e.pdf.

Arnold, Craig Anthony. 2009. "Water Privatization Trends in the United States: Human Rights, National Security, and Public Stewardship." SSRN Scholarly Paper ID 1407720. Rochester, NY: Social Science Research Network. http://papers.ssrn.com/abstract=1407720.

Association of American Medical Colleges (AAMC), and Baylor College of Medicine. 2007. *The Scientific Basis of Influence and Reciprocity: A Symposium.* Washington, DC: Association of American Medical Colleges. https://members.aamc.org/eweb/upload/The%20Scientific%20Basis%20of%20Influence.pdf.

Atwood, Margaret. 2008. *Payback: Debt and the Shadow Side of Wealth.* Toronto: Anansi.

Austin, James E. 2000. "Strategic Collaboration Between Nonprofits and Business." *Nonprofit and Voluntary Sector Quarterly* 29 (suppl. 1): 69–97. doi:10.1177/089976400773746346.

Azétsop, Jacquineau, and Tisha R. Joy. 2013. "Access to Nutritious Food, Socioeconomic Individualism and Public Health Ethics in the USA: A Common Good Approach." *Philosophy, Ethics, and Humanities in Medicine* 8: 16. doi:10.1186/1747-5341-8-16.

Babor, Thomas F., and Katherine Robaina. 2012. "Public Health, Academic Medicine, and the Alcohol Industry's Corporate Social Responsibility Activities." *American Journal of Public Health* 103 (2): 206–214. doi:10.2105/AJPH.2012.300847.

Backholer, Kathryn, Miranda Blake, and Stefanie Vandevijvere. 2016. "Have We Reached The Tipping Point For Sugar-Sweetened Beverage Taxes?" *Public Health Nutrition* 19(17): 3057–3061.

Backholer, Kathryn, and Jane Martin. 2017. "Sugar-Sweetened Beverage Tax: The Inconvenient Truths." *Public Health Nutrition* 20(18): 3225–3227.

Backholer, Kathryn, and Stefanie Vandevijvere. 2017. "Sugar-Sweetened Beverage Taxation: An Update on the Year That Was 2017." *Public Health Nutrition* 20(18): 3219–3224.

Backholer, Kathryn, et al. 2016. "The Impact of a Tax on Sugar-Sweetened Beverages According to Socio-Economic Position: A Systematic Review of the Evidence." *Public Health Nutrition* 19(17): 3070–3084.

Bagehot, Walter. (1867) 2001. *The English Constitution.* Cambridge: Cambridge University Press.

Baghdadi-Sabeti, Guitelle, and Fatima Serhan. 2010. "WHO Good Governance for Medicines Programme: An Innovative Approach to Prevent Corruption in the Pharmaceutical Sector." Background Paper, 25. Geneva, Switzerland: WHO. http://www.who.int/healthsystems/topics/financing/healthreport/25GGM.pdf?ua=1.

Ball, Terence, James Farr, and Russell L Hanson. 1989. *Political Innovation and Conceptual Change.* Cambridge; New York: Cambridge University Press.

Barak-Erez, D. 2005. "The Doctrine of Legitimate Expectations and the Distinction Between the Reliance and Expectation Interests." *European Public Law* 11 (4): 583–601.

Barr, Donald A. 2007. "Ethics in Public Health Research: A Research Protocol to Evaluate the Effectiveness of Public–Private Partnerships as a Means to Improve Health and Welfare Systems Worldwide." *American Journal of Public Health* 97 (1): 19–25. doi:10.2105/AJPH.2005.075614.

Basu, Sanjay et al. 2013. "Relationship of Soft Drink Consumption to Global Overweight, Obesity, and Diabetes: A Cross-National Analysis of 75 Countries." *American Journal of Public Health* 103 (11): 2071–2077.

Bazerman, Max, and Ann Tenbrunsel. 2010. *Blind Spots: Why We Fail to Do What's Right and What to Do About It.* Princeton, NJ: Princeton University Press.

Beadle, Ron, and Geoff Moore. 2006. "MacIntyre on Virtue and Organization." *Organization Studies* 27 (3): 323–340. doi:10.1177/0170840606062425.

Beauchamp, Tom L., and Norman E. Bowie. 1988. *Ethical Theory and Business.* Englewood Cliffs, NJ: Prentice Hall.

Beauchamp, Tom L., and James F. Childress. 2012. *Principles of Biomedical Ethics.* 7th ed. New York: Oxford University Press.

Becker, Lawrence C. 1986. *Reciprocity.* London; Boston: Routledge and Kegan Paul.

Bekelman, J. E., Y. Li, and C. P. Gross. 2003. "Scope and Impact of Financial Conflicts of Interest in Biomedical Research: A Systematic Review." *JAMA* 289 (4): 454–465. doi:10.1001/jama.289.4.454.

Benefit Corp. 2016. "What Is a Benefit Corporation?" http://benefitcorp.net/.

Ben-Ner, Avner, and Louis Putterman. 2001. "Trusting and Trustworthiness Symposium: Trust Relationships." *Boston University Law Review* 81: 523–552.

Bes-Rastrollo, Maira, Matthias B. Schulze, Miguel Ruiz-Canela, and Miguel A. Martinez-Gonzalez. 2013. "Financial Conflicts of Interest and Reporting Bias Regarding the Association Between Sugar-Sweetened Beverages and Weight Gain: A Systematic Review of Systematic Reviews." *PLOS Med* 10 (12): e1001578. doi:10.1371/journal.pmed.1001578.

Birn, Anne-Emanuelle. 2014. "Philanthrocapitalism, Past and Present: The Rockefeller Foundation, the Gates Foundation, and the Setting of the International/Global Health Agenda." *Hypothesis* 12 (1): 1–27.

Birn, Anne-Emanuelle, and Judith Richter. 2017. "US Philanthrocapitalism and the Global Health Agenda: The Rockefeller and Gates Foundations, Past and Present." Policies for Equitable Access to Health. www.peah.it/2017/05/4019.

Block, Peter. 1993. *Stewardship: Choosing Service over Self-Interest.* San Francisco: Berrett-Koehler.

Bok, Derek Curtis. 2003. *Universities in the Marketplace. The Commercialization of Higher Education.* Princeton, NJ: Princeton University Press.

Brennan, Troyen A., David J. Rothman, Linda Blank, David Blumenthal, Susan C. Chimonas, Jordan J. Cohen, Janlori Goldman, et al. 2006. "Health Industry Practices That Create Conflicts of Interest: A Policy Proposal for Academic Medical Centers." *JAMA* 295 (4): 429–433. doi:10.1001/jama.295.4.429.

Brinkerhoff, Derick W., and Jennifer M. Brinkerhoff. 2011. "Public-Private Partnerships: Perspectives on Purposes, Publicness, and Good Governance." *Public Administration and Development* 31(1): 2–14.

Brosnan, Sarah F., and Frans B. M. de Waal. 2002. "A Proximate Perspective on Reciprocal Altruism." *Human Nature* 13 (1): 129–152. doi:10.1007/s12110-002-1017-2.

Brown, Wendy. 2015. *Undoing the Demos: Neoliberalism's Stealth Revolution.* Cambridge, MA: MIT Press/Zone Books.

Browne, Katherine E., and B. Lynne Milgram, eds. 2009. *Economics and Morality: Anthropological Approaches.* Lanham: AltaMira Press.

Brownell, Kelly D. 2012. "Thinking Forward: The Quicksand of Appeasing the Food Industry." *PLOS Med* 9 (7): e1001254. doi:10.1371/journal.pmed.1001254.

Brownell, Kelly D., and Kenneth E. Warner. 2009. "The Perils of Ignoring History: Big Tobacco Played Dirty and Millions Died. How Similar Is Big Food?" *Milbank Quarterly* 87 (1): 259–294. doi:10.1111/j.1468-0009.2009.00555.x.

Bruno, Kenny. 2000. "Perilous Partnerships: The UN's Corporate Outreach Program." *Journal of Public Health Policy* 21 (4): 388–393.

Bryden, Anna, Mark Petticrew, Nicholas Mays, Elizabeth Eastmure, and Cecile Knai. 2013. "Voluntary Agreements Between Government and Business—A Scoping Review of the Literature with Specific Reference to the Public Health Responsibility Deal." *Health Policy* 110 (2–3): 186–197. doi:10.1016/j.healthpol.2013.02.009.

Buchanan, A., and M. DeCamp. 2006. "Responsibility for Global Health." *Theoretical Medicine and Bioethics* 27 (1): 95–114.

Buse, K., and G. Walt. 2000. "Global Public-Private Partnerships: Part I: A New Development in Health?" *Bulletin of the World Health Organization* 78 (4): 549–561. doi:10.1590/S0042-96862000000400019.

Buse, Kent, and Andrew M. Harmer. 2007. "Seven Habits of Highly Effective Global Public-Private Health Partnerships: Practice and Potential." *Social Science & Medicine* 64 (2): 259–271. doi:10.1016/j.socscimed.2006.09.001.

Buse, Kent, and Sonja Tanaka. 2011. "Global Public-Private Health Partnerships: Lessons Learned from Ten Years of Experience and Evaluation." *International Dental Journal* 61: 2–10. doi:10.1111/j.1875-595X.2011.00034.x.

Byrne, John. 2015. "Chicago Soda Tax Fizzles at City Council Hearing." *Chicago Tribune*, September 5. http://www.chicagotribune.com/news/local/politics/ct-chicago-sugary-drink-tax-hearing-met-0910-20150909-story.html

Calhoun, Craig. 1998. "The Public Good as a Social and Cultural Project." In *Private Action and the Public Good*, edited by Walter Powell and Elisabeth Clemens, 20–35. New Haven, CT: Yale University Press.

Calvino, Italo. 1994. *The Road to San Giovanni*. Translated by Tim Parks. New York: Vintage.

Campbell, Eric G., Greg Koski, and David Blumenthal. 2004. "The Triple Helix: University, Government and Industry Relationships in the Life Sciences." SSRN Scholarly Paper ID 1262367. Rochester, NY: Social Science Research Network. http://papers.ssrn.com/abstract=1262367.

Campbell, Norm, Kevin J. Willis, Gavin Arthur, Bill Jeffery, Helen Lee Robertson, and Diane L. Lorenzetti. 2013. "Federal Government Food Policy Committees and the Financial Interests of the Food Sector." *Open Medicine* 7 (4): e107.

Canadian Association of University Teachers (CAUT). 2001. "The Olivieri Report." https://www.caut.ca/docs/af-reports-indepedent-committees-of-inquiry/the-olivieri-report.pdf.

———. 2012. "Guiding Principles for University Collaborations." https://www.caut.ca/docs/default-source/professional-advice/guiding-principles-for-university-collaborations-(april-2012)(1).pdf.

———. 2013. *Open for Business on What Terms?: An Analysis of 12 Collaborations Between Canadian Universities and Corporations, Donors and Governments* https://www.caut.ca/docs/default-source/academic-freedom/open-for-business-(nov-2013).pdf.

Cannon, Geoffrey. 2009. "Out of the Box." *Public Health Nutrition* 12 (9): 1584–1587. doi:10.1017/S1368980009990875.

Cardy, Robert L., and Gregory H. Dobbins. 1986. "Affect and Appraisal Accuracy: Liking as an Integral Dimension in Evaluating Performance." *Journal of Applied Psychology* 71 (4): 672–678. doi:10.1037/0021-9010.71.4.672.

Carlat, Daniel. 2007. "Dr Drug Rep." *New York Times*, November 25. www.nytimes.com/2007/11/25/magazine/25memoir-t.html.

Carmona R. H. 2006. "Foundations for a Healthier United States." *Journal of the American Dietetic Association* 106 (3): 341.

Carter, Stephen L. 1996. *Integrity*. New York: Basic Books.

Centers for Disease Control and Prevention (CDC). 2016. "Mission, Role and Pledge About CDC." http://www.cdc.gov/about/organization/mission.htm.

Chandon, Pierre, and Brian Wansink. 2007. "The Biasing Health Halos of Fast-Food Restaurant Health Claims: Lower Calorie Estimates and Higher Side-Dish Consumption Intentions." *Journal of Consumer Research* 34 (3): 301–314. doi:10.1086/519499.

Childress, James, et al. 2002. "Public Health Ethics: Mapping the Terrain." *Journal of Law, Medicine and Ethics* 30(2): 170–178.

Christakis, Nicholas A., and James H. Fowler. 2009. *Connected: The Surprising Power of Our Social Networks and How They Shape Our Lives*. New York: Little, Brown.

Choi, Candice. 2016. "How Candy Makers Shape Nutrition Science." *Associated Press*, June 2. http://bigstory.ap.org/f9483d554430445fa6566bb0aaa293d1.

Cialdini, Robert B. 2007. *Influence: The Psychology of Persuasion*. New York: Collins.

Ciccone, Dana Karen. 2010. "Arguing for a Centralized Coordination Solution to the Public-Private Partnership Explosion in Global Health." *Global Health Promotion* 17 (2): 48–51. doi:10.1177/1757975910365224.

Cladis, Mark. 2006. *Private Vision, Public Lives*. New York: Columbia University Press.

Coca-Cola. 2016. "Sustainability—The Coca-Cola Company." http://www.coca-colacompany.com/topics/sustainability/.

Cochran, Clarke E. 1978. "Yves R. Simon and 'The Common Good': A Note on the Concept." *Ethics* 88 (3): 229–239.

Coggon, John. 2011. "What Help is a Steward? Stewardship, Political Theory, and Public Health Law and Ethics." *Northern Ireland Legal Quarterly,* 62(4): 599–616.

Cole, David. 2014. "The Three Leakers and What to Do About Them." *New York Review of Books*, February 6 http://www.nybooks.com/articles/2014/02/06/three-leakers-and-what-do-about-them/.

Collin, Jeff, S. Hill, M. Kandlik Eltanani, E. Plotnikova, R. Ralston, et al. 2017. "Can Public Health Reconcile Profits and Pandemics? An Analysis of Attitudes to Commercial Sector Engagement in Health Policy and Research." *PLOS One* 12(9): e0182612. https://doi.org/10.1371/journal.pone.0182612.

Cook, Karen S., Margaret Levi, and Russell Hardin. 2005. *Cooperation Without Trust?* New York: Russell Sage Foundation.

Corwin, Edward S. 1957. *The President, Office and Powers: 1787–1957, History and Analysis of Practice and Opinion*. New York: New York University Press.

Cosgrove, Lisa, and Robert Whitaker. 2013. "Finding Solutions to Institutional Corruption: Lessons from Cognitive Dissonance Theory." Edmond J. Safra Working Paper No. 9. https://papers.ssrn.com/abstract_id=2261375

Dana, J., and G. Loewenstein. 2003. "A Social Science Perspective on Gifts to Physicians from Industry." *JAMA* 290 (2): 252–255. doi:10.1001/jama.290.2.252.

Dangour, Alan D., Zoey Diaz, and Lucy Martinez Sullivan. 2012. "Building Global Advocacy for Nutrition: A Review of the European and US Landscapes." *Food and Nutrition Bulletin* 33 (2): 92–98. doi:10.1177/156482651203300202.

Datz, Todd. 2011. "Harvard Serves Up Its Own 'Plate': Healthy Eating Plate Shows Shortcomings in Government's MyPlate." *Harvard Gazette*, September 14. http://news.harvard.edu/gazette/story/2011/09/harvard-serves-up-itsown-plate/

Dawes, Sharon S. 2010. "Stewardship and Usefulness: Policy Principles for Information-Based Transparency." *Government Information Quarterly*, 27 (4): 377–383. doi:10.1016/j.giq.2010.07.001.

DeAngelis, Catherine D. 2000. "Conflict of Interest and the Public Trust." *JAMA* 284 (17): 2237–2238. doi:10.1001/jama.284.17.2237.

Derrida, Jacques. 1992. *Given Time: I. Counterfeit Money*. Translated by Peggy Kamuf. Chicago: University of Chicago Press.

De Schutter, Olivier. 2011. "Report of the UN Special Rapporteur on the Right to Food." www.ohchr.org/Documents/HRBodies/HRCouncil/RegularSession/Session19/A-HRC-19-59_en.pdf.

Di Costanzo, Caterina. 2014. "The Dual Dimension of the Global Governance of Health." *American Journal of Public Health Research* 2 (2): 36–45. doi:10.12691/ajphr-2-2-1.

Dobel, J. Patrick. 1999. *Public Integrity*. Baltimore, MD.: Johns Hopkins University Press.

Durand, M. A. 2015. "An Evaluation of the Public Health Responsibility Deal: Informants' Experiences and Views of the Development, Implementation and Achievements of a Pledge-Based, Public-Private Partnership to Improve Population Health in England." *Health Policy* 119 (11): 1506–1514.

Edwards, Mickey. 2013. "What Is the Common Good? The Case for Transcending Partisanship." *Daedalus* 142 (2): 84–94. doi:10.1162/DAED_a_00205

Elinder, Liselotte Schäfer. 2011. "Obesity and Chronic Diseases, Whose Business?" *European Journal of Public Health* 21 (4): 402–403. doi:10.1093/eurpub/ckr086.

Entman, Robert. 1993. "Framing: Toward Clarification of a Fractured Paradigm." *Journal of Communication* 43 (4): 51–58.

Epstein, Wendy Netter. 2014. "Public-Private Contracting and the Reciprocity Norm." *American University Law Review* 64: 52.

Etzioni, Amitai. 2015. "Common Good." *Encyclopedia of Political Thought*, edited by Michael T. Gibbons. London: John Wiley and Sons.

Etzkowitz, Henry. 2008. *The Triple Helix: University-Industry-Government Innovation in Action*. New York: Routledge.

Euben, J. Peter. 1998. "Corruption," in *Political Innovation and Conceptual Change*, edited by Terrence Ball, James Farr, and Russell Hanson, 220–246. New York: Cambridge University Press.

Eyal, Nir, Samia Hurst, Ole Norheim, and Dan Wikler. 2013. *Inequalities in Health: Concepts, Measures, and Ethics*. New York: Oxford University Press.

Falbe, Jennifer, Hannah R. Thompson, Christina M. Becker, Nadia Rojas, Charles E. McCulloch, and Kristine A. Madsen. 2016. "Impact of the Berkeley Excise Tax on Sugar-Sweetened Beverage Consumption." *American Journal of Public Health* 106(10): 1865–1871.

Federal Trade Commission (FTC). 2012. "A Review of Mood Marketing to Children and Adolescents: Follow Up Report." http://www.ftc.gov/sites/default/files/documents/reports/review-food-marketing-children-and-adolescents-follow-report/121221foodmarketingreport.pdf

Fields, Jeff. 2011. "Big Beverage Gives $10 Million to CHOP." Philadelphia Inquirer, March 16. http://www.philly.com/philly/blogs/heardinthehall/118077483.html.

Fillmore, K. M., and R. Roizen. 2000. "The New Manichaeism in Alcohol Science." *Addiction* 95 (2): 188–190.

Fisher, Joseph C. 2010. "Can We Engage the Alcohol Industry to Help Combat Sexually Transmitted Disease?" *International Journal of Public Health* 55 (3): 147–148. doi:10.1007/s00038-010-0142-7.

Food and Agriculture Organization of the United Nations (FAO). 2000. "Principles and Guidelines for FAO Cooperation with the Private Sector." http://www.fao.org/3/a-x2215e.pdf.

———. 2012. "Organization-Wide Strategy on Partnerships." http://www.fao.org/fileadmin/user_upload/corp_partnership/docs/stratbrochure_en_web.pdf.

———. 2013a. "FAO Strategy for Partnerships with the Private Sector." http://www.fao.org/docrep/018/i3444e/i3444e.pdf.

———. 2013b. "The Contribution of the Private Sector and Civil Society to Improve Nutrition Global Forum on Food Security and Nutrition." http://www.fao.org/fsnforum/forum/discussions/CS-PS-Nutrition?page=1.

———. 2016. "FAO considers the Private Sector to be a key ally in the fight against hunger." http://www.fao.org/partnerships/private-sector/en/.

Food and Agriculture Organization and World Health Organization (FAO/WHO). 1992a. "International Conference on Nutrition: Final Report of the Conference." http://whqlibdoc.who.int/hq/1992/a34812.pdf

———. 1992b. "World Declaration and Plan of Action for Nutrition." http://www.fao.org/docrep/015/u9260e/u9260e00.pdf

———. 2014a. "Report of the Joint WHO/FAO Secretariat on the Second International Conference on Nutrition" (ICN2). http://www.fao.org/3/a-mm531e.pdf

———. 2014b. "Rome Declaration on Nutrition" (ICN2). http://www.fao.org/3/a-ml542e.pdf

Fooks, Gary J., and Anna B. Gilmore. 2013. "Corporate Philanthropy, Political Influence, and Health Policy." *PLOS One* 8 (11): e80864. doi:10.1371/journal.pone.0080864.

Fox, Renée C., and Judith P. Swazey. 1992. *Spare Parts: Organ Replacement in American Society*. New York: Oxford University Press.

Freedhoff, Y. 2014. "The Food Industry Is Neither Friend, nor Foe, nor Partner: Can the Food Industry Partner in Health?" *Obesity Reviews* 15 (1): 6–8. doi:10.1111/obr.12128.

Freedhoff, Yoni, and Paul C. Hebert. 2011. "Partnerships Between Health Organizations and the Food Industry Risk Derailing Public Health Nutrition." *Canadian Medical Association Journal* 183 (3): 291–292. doi:10.1503/cmaj.110085.

Freeman, R. Edward. 1984. *Strategic Management: A Stakeholder Approach*. Boston: Pitman.

Freudenberg, Nicholas. 2014. *Lethal but Legal: Corporations, Consumption, and Protecting Public Health*. New York: Oxford University Press, 2014.

Freudenberg, Nicholas, and Sandro Galea. 2008. "The Impact of Corporate Practices on Health: Implications for Health Policy." *Journal of Public Health Policy* 29 (1): 86–104.

Friedl, Karl et al. 2014. "Report of an EU–US Symposium on Understanding Nutrition-Related Consumer Behavior: Strategies to Promote a Lifetime of Healthy Food Choices." *Journal of Nutrition Education and Behavior* 46 (5): 445–50.

Friedman, Milton. 1962. *Capitalism and Freedom*. Chicago: University of Chicago Press.

Friedman, Milton. 1970. "The Social Responsibility of Business is to Increase Its Profits." *New York Times Magazine*, September 13.

Fugh-Berman, A. et al. 2011. "Closing the door on pharma? A national survey of family medicine residencies regarding industry interactions." *Academic Medicine* 86 (5): 649–654.

Fuller, Thomas, Anahad O'Connor, and Matt Richtel. 2017. "In Asia's Fattest Country, Nutritionists Take Money from Food Giants." *New York Times*, December 23. https://nyti. ms/2DBd5bW.

Fung, Archon, Mary Graham and David Weil. 2007. *Full Disclosure: The Perils and Promise of Transparency*. New York: Cambridge University Press.

Galea, Gauden, and Martin McKee. 2014. "Public-Private Partnerships with Large Corporations: Setting the Ground Rules for Better Health." *Health Policy* 115 (2–3): 138–140. doi:10.1016/j.healthpol.2014.02.003.

Galea, Sandro. 2007. *Macrosocial Determinants of Population Health*. New York: Springer.

Galston, William A. 2013. "The Common Good: Theoretical Content, Practical Utility." *Daedalus* 142 (2): 9–14. doi:10.1162/DAED_a_00199.

Gardner, Howard. 2013a. "Reestablishing the Commons for the Common Good." *Daedalus* 142 (2): 199–208. doi:10.1162/DAED_a_00213.

Gash, Alison, and Christine Trost. 2008. *Conflict of Interest and Public Life: Cross-National Perspectives*. New York: Cambridge University Press.

Ghezzi F., and M. Maggiolino. 2014. "Bridging EU Concerted Practices with US Concerted Actions." *Journal of Competition Law & Economics* 10 (3): 647–690.

Gilmore, Anna B., and Simon Capewell. 2016. "Should We Welcome Food Industry Funding of Public Health Research?" *BMJ* 353: i2161.

Gilmore, Anna B., and Gary Fooks. 2012. "Global Fund Needs to Address Conflict of Interest." *Bulletin of the World Health Organization* 90 (1): 71–72. doi:10.1590/S0042-96862012000100017.

Gilmore, Anna B., Emily Savell, and Jeff Collin. 2011. "Public Health, Corporations and the New Responsibility Deal: Promoting Partnerships with Vectors of Disease?" *Journal of Public Health* 33 (1): 2–4. doi:10.1093/pubmed/fdr008.

Glenna, Leland L., William B. Lacy, Rick Welsh, and Dina Biscotti. 2007. "University Administrators, Agricultural Biotechnology, and Academic Capitalism: Defining the Public Good to Promote University-Industry Relationships." *Sociological Quarterly* 48 (1): 141–163. doi:10.1111/j.1533-8525.2007.00074.x.

Glenna, Leland, Sally Shortall, and Barbara Brandl. 2015. "Neoliberalism, the University, Public Goods and Agricultural Innovation." *Sociologia Ruralis* 55 (4): 438–459. doi:10.1111/soru.12074.

Global Fund. 2016. "Constituencies." The Global Fund to Fight AIDS, Tuberculosis and Malaria. http://www.theglobalfund.org/en/board/constituencies/.

Godelier, Maurice. 1999. *The Enigma of the Gift*. Chicago: University of Chicago Press.

Goel, Akash, and Jeffrey L. Sturchio. 2012. "The Private-Sector Role in Public Health: Reflections on the New Global Architecture." Washington, DC: Center for Strategic and International Studies. https://csis-prod.s3.amazonaws.com/s3fs-public/legacy_files/files/publication/120131_Sturchio_PrivateSectorRole_Web.pdf

Goffman, Erving. 1974. *Frame Analysis: An Essay on the Organization of Experience*. New York: Harper and Row.

Goldstein, Josh. 2010. "Philadelphia Soft-Drink Tax Proposed." *Philadelphia Inquirer*, March 4. http://www.philly.com/philly/blogs/healthcare/Philadelphia_soft-drink_tax_proposed.html.

Gomes, Fabio. 2015. "Conflicts of Interest in Food and Nutrition," *Cadernos de Saúde Pública* 31(10): 2039–2046.

Gomes, Fabio, and Tim Lobstein. 2011. "Food and Beverage Transnational Corporations and Nutrition Policy," *SCN News* 39: 57–65.

Gómez, Luis, Enrique Jacoby, Lorena Ibarra, Diego Lucumí, Alexandra Hernandez, Diana Parra, Alex Florindo, and Pedro Hallal. 2011. "Sponsorship of Physical Activity Programs by the Sweetened Beverages Industry: Public Health or Public Relations?" *Revista de Saúde Pública* 45 (2): 423–427. doi:10.1590/S0034-89102011000200022.

Gomory, Ralph and Richard Sylla. 2013. "The American Corporation," *Daedalus*, 142(2): 102–118.

Goodin, Robert E. 1985. *Protecting the Vulnerable: A Reanalysis of Our Social Responsibilities.* Chicago: University of Chicago Press.

Goodman, Ryan, Mindy Jane Roseman, Harvard Law School, and Human Rights Program. 2009. *Interrogations, Forced Feedings, and the Role of Health Professionals: New Perspectives on International Human Rights, Humanitarian Law, and Ethics.* Cambridge, MA: Human Rights Program, Harvard Law School.

Gornall, Jonathan. 2015. "Sugar: Spinning a Web of Influence." *BMJ* 350:h231.

Gostin, Lawrence O. 2009. "FDA Regulation of Tobacco: Politics, Law, and the Public's Health." *JAMA* 302 (13): 1459–1460. doi:10.1001/jama.2009.1421.

———. 2016. "Big Food Is Making America Sick." *Milbank Quarterly* 94(3): 480–484.

Gouldner, Alvin W. 1960. "The Norm of Reciprocity: A Preliminary Statement." *American Sociological Review* 25 (2): 161–178. doi:10.2307/2092623.

Gregory, C. A. 1997. *Savage Money: The Anthropology and Politics of Commodity Exchange.* Amsterdam: Harwood Academic.

Gudeman, Stephen. 2001. *The Anthropology of Economy: Community, Market, and Culture.* Malden, MA: Blackwell.

Gunn, J. A. W. 1969. *Politics and the Public Interest in the Seventeenth Century.* London; Toronto: Routledge.

Gutmann, Amy, and Dennis F. Thompson. 2004. *Why Deliberative Democracy?* Princeton NJ: Princeton University Press.

Gutmann, Amy, and Dennis Thompson. 2013. "Valuing Compromise for the Common Good." *Daedalus* 142 (2): 185–198. doi:10.1162/DAED_a_00212.

Guyatt, Gordon et al. 2010. "The Vexing Problem of Guidelines and Conflict of Interest: A Potential Solution." *Annals of Internal Medicine* 152 (11): 738. doi:10.7326/0003-4819-152-11-201006010-00254.

Hacker, Jacob. 2004. "Privatizing Risk Without Privatizing the Welfare State: The Hidden Politics of Social Policy Retrenchment in the United States." *American Political Science Review* 98 (2): 243–260.

Hacker, Jacob, Kathleen Thelen, and Paul Pierson. 2015. "Drift and Conversion: Hidden Faces of Institutional Change." In *Comparative Historical Analysis in the Social Sciences,* edited by Kathleen Thelen and James Mahoney. New York: Cambridge Press.

Haidt, Jonathan. 2013. *The Righteous Mind: Why Good People are Divided by Politics and Religion.* New York: Vintage.

Haidt, Jonathan, and Jesse Graham. 2007. "When Morality Opposes Justice." *Social Justice Research* 20 (1): 98–116.

Halfon, Mark S. 1989. *Integrity: A Philosophical Inquiry.* Philadelphia: Temple University Press.

Ham, Chris, and K. G. M. M. Alberti. 2002. "The Medical Profession, the Public, and the Government." *BMJ* 324 (7341): 838–842. doi:10.1136/bmj.324.7341.838.

Hamilton, Alexander. 1788. *The Federalist Papers*, No. 78. "The Judiciary Department." http://avalon.law.yale.edu/18th_century/fed78.asp.

Hamlin, Alan. 1996. "Promoting Integrity and Virtue: The Institutional Dimension." *The Good Society* 6 (3): 35–40.

Hardin, Russell. 2002. *Trust and Trustworthiness*. New York: Russell Sage Foundation.

———. 2006. *Trust*. Cambridge: Polity.

Hartley, Christie, Margaret Dancy, Victoria Costa, and Joshua Gert. 2014. "Two Conceptions of Justice as Reciprocity." *Social Theory and Practice* 40 (3): 409–432.

Harvard Corporation. 2016. "President and Fellows (Harvard Corporation)." Harvard University. http://www.harvard.edu/about-harvard/harvards-leadership/president-and-fellows-harvard-corporation.

Harvey, Ann H., Ulrich Kirk, George H. Denfield, and P. Read Montague. 2010. "Monetary Favors and Their Influence on Neural Responses and Revealed Preference." *Journal of Neuroscience* 30(28): 9597–9602. doi:10.1523/JNEUROSCI.1086-10.2010.

Hawkes, Corinna, and Kent Buse. 2011. "Public-Private Engagement for Diet and Health: Addressing the Governance Gap." *SCN News* 39: 6–10.

Hawkes, Corinna, and Kent Buse. 2011. "Public Health Sector and Food Industry Interaction: It's Time to Clarify the Term 'Partnership' and Be Honest About Underlying Interests." *European Journal of Public Health* 21(4): 400–401.

Heclo, Hugh. 2008. *On Thinking Institutionally*. New York: Oxford University Press.

Held, Virginia. 1970. *The Public Interest and Individual Interests*. New York: Basic Books.

Hénaff, Marcel, 2010. *The Price of Truth: Gift, Money, and Philosophy*. Translated by and Jean-Louis Morhange. Stanford, CA: Stanford University Press.

Hernández-Aguado, Ildefonso, and Blanca Lumbreras Lacarra. 2014. "Crisis and the Independence of Public Health Policies." *Gaceta Sanitaria* 28 (June): 24–30. doi:10.1016/j.gaceta.2014.03.005.

Hernandez-Aguado, Ildefonso, and G. A. Zaragoza. 2016. "Support of Public-Private Partnerships in Health Promotion and Conflicts of Interest." *BMJ Open* 6:e009342.

Herxheimer, Andrew. 2005. "Public-Private Partnerships and International Health Policy-Making: How Can Public Interests Be Safeguarded?" *Journal of the Royal Society of Medicine* 98 (10): 476–477.

Heugens, Pursey P. M. A. R., Muel Kaptein, and J. (Hans) van Oosterhout. 2006. "The Ethics of the Node Versus the Ethics of the Dyad? Reconciling Virtue Ethics and Contractualism." *Organization Studies* 27 (3): 391–411. doi:10.1177/0170840606062428.

Hirschman, Albert O. 1998. *Crossing Boundaries: Selected Writings*. New York: Zone Books.

Hoffman, Beth. 2013. *Behind the Brands: Food Justice and the "Big 10" Food and Beverage Companies*. Oxford: Oxfam International. https://policy-practice.oxfam.org.uk/publications/behind-the-brands-food-justice-and-the-big-10-food-and-beverage-companies-270393

Hofman W., J. De Houwer, M. Perugini, F. Baeyens, and G. Crombez. 2010. "Evaluative Conditioning in Humans: A Meta-Analysis," *Psychological Bulletin* 136(3): 390–421. doi: 10.1037/a0018916.

House of Lords Select Committee. House of Lords Select Committee on the Constitution (Constitution Committee). 2007. *Relations Between the Executive, Judiciary, and Parliament*. https://publications.parliament.uk/pa/ld200607/ldselect/ldconst/151/151.pdf

Hughes, Laura. 2016. "More Spent on Treating Obesity-Related Conditions Than on the Police or Fire Service, Says NHS Chief." *The Telegraph*, June 7. http://www.telegraph.co.uk/news/2016/06/07/more-spent-on-treating-obesity-related-conditions-than-on-the-po/.

Hyde, Justin. 2008. "GM's 'Engine Charlie' Wilson Learned to Live with a Misquote." *Detroit Free Press*, September 14. http://archive.freep.com/article/20080914/BUSINESS01/809140308/GM-s-Engine-Charlie-Wilson-learned-live-misquote

Institute of Medicine (US), Committee on Opportunities in the Nutrition and Food Sciences, Paul R. Thomas, and Robert O. Earl. 1994. *Opportunities in the Nutrition and Food Sciences: Research Challenges and the Next Generation of Investigators*. Washington, DC: National Academy Press.

Institute of Medicine (US), Committee on Food Marketing and Diets of Children and Youth. 2005. *Food Marketing to Children and Youth: Threat or Opportunity*. Washington DC: National Academies Press.

Internal Revenue Service (IRS). 2016. "Exemption Requirements—501(c)(3) Organizations." https://www.irs.gov/charities-non-profits/charitable-organizations/exemption-requirements-section-501-c-3-organizations.

Jacobs, Andrew, and Matt Richtel. 2017. "How Big Business Got Brazil Hooked on Junk Food." *New York Times*, September 16. https://www.nytimes.com/interactive/2017/09/16/health/brazil-obesity-nestle.html.

Jacobs, Jane. 1992. *Systems of Survival: A Dialogue on the Moral Foundations of Commerce and Politics*. New York: Random House.

Jacobson, Michael, and Kelly Brownell. 2000. "Small Taxes on Soft Drinks and Snack Foods to Promote Health." *American Journal of Public Health* 90(6): 854–857.

Jahiel, René I. 2008. "Corporation-Induced Diseases, Upstream Epidemiologic Surveillance, and Urban Health." *Journal of Urban Health* 85 (4): 517–531. doi:10.1007/s11524-008-9283-x.

———. 2009. "The Global Alcohol Industry: An Overview." *Addiction* 104 (Feb.): 6–12. doi:10.1111/j.1360-0443.2008.02430.x.

Jennings, Bruce, Daniel Callahan, and Susan Wolf. 1987. "The Professions: Public Interest and the Common Good." *Hastings Center Report*, 17 (1): 3–10.

Johnson and Johnson. 2013. "The Writing of Our Credo." Kilmer House. December 18. http://www.kilmerhouse.com/2013/12/the-writing-of-our-credo/.

Johnston, Lee M., and Diane T. Finegood. 2015. "Cross-Sector Partnerships and Public Health: Challenges and Opportunities for Addressing Obesity and Noncommunicable Diseases Through Engagement with the Private Sector." *Annual Review of Public Health* 36 (1): 255–271. doi:10.1146/annurev-publhealth-031914-122802.

Kaplan, Sheila. 2017. "New C.D.C. Chief Saw Coca-Cola as Ally in Obesity Fight." *New York Times*, July 22. https://www.nytimes.com/2017/07/22/health/brenda-fitzgerald-cdc-coke.html

Kappeler, Andreas, and Mathieu Nemoz. 2010. "Public-Private Partnerships—Before and During the Recent Financial Crisis." European Investment Bank Economic and Financial Report. 2010. http://www.eib.org/epec/resources/efr_epec_ppp_report1.pdf

Kass, Henry D. 1988. "Stewardship as a Fundamental Element in Images of Public Administration." *Dialogue* 10 (2): 2–48.

Kass, Nancy. 2001. "An Ethics Framework for Public Health," *American Journal of Public Health Ethics* 91(11):1776–1782.

Kass, Nancy, Kenneth Hecht, Amy Paul, and Kerry Birmbach. 2014. "Ethics and Obesity Prevention: Ethical Considerations in 3 Approaches to Reducing Consumption of Sugar-Sweetened Beverages." *American Journal of Public Health* 104 (5): 787–793.

Kaul, Inge, Isabelle Grunberg, and Marc A. Stern. 1999. *Global Public Goods: International Cooperation in the 21st Century*. New York: Oxford University Press.

Keast, Debra R., Theresa A. Nicklas, and Carol E. O'Neil. 2010. "Snacking Is Associated with Reduced Risk of Overweight and Reduced Abdominal Obesity in Adolescents: National Health and Nutrition Examination Survey (NHANES) 1999–2004." *American Journal of Clinical Nutrition* 92 (2): 428–435.

Kearns, Cristin E., Dorie Apollonio, and Stanton A. Glantz. 2017. "Sugar Industry Sponsorship of Germ-Free Rodent Studies Linking Sucrose to Hyperlipidemia and Cancer: An Historical Analysis of Internal Documents." *PLoS Biology* 15(11): e2003460.

Kearns, Crisitin E., S. A. Glantz, and L. A. Schmidt. 2015. "Sugar Industry Influence on the Scientific Agenda of the National Institute of Dental Research: A Historical Analysis of Internal Documents." *PLoS Med.* 12(3): e1001798.

Kearns, Cristin E., L. A. Schmidt, and S. A. Glantz. 2016. "Sugar Industry and Coronary Heart Disease: A Historical Analysis of Internal Industry Documents." *JAMA Internal Medicine* 176(11): 1680–1685.

Keefe, Patrick Radden. 2017. "The Family That Built an Empire of Pain." *New Yorker*, October 31. https://www.newyorker.com/magazine/2017/10/30/the-family-that-built-an-empire-of-pain.

Kempshall, M. S. 1999. *The Common Good in Late Medieval Political Thought*. Oxford; New York: Clarendon Press; Oxford University Press.

Khayatzadeh-Mahani, Akram, Arne Ruckert, and Ronald Labonté. 2017. "Could the WHO's Framework on Engagement with Non-State Actors (FENSA) Be a Threat to Tackling Childhood Obesity?" *Global Public Health,* published online June 24, http://dx.doi.org/10.1080/17441692.2017.1342852

Kickbusch I., Luke Allen, and Christian Franz. 2016. "The Commercial Determinants of Health." *The Lancet Global Health* 4(12): e895–e896.

Kickbusch, I., and J. Quick. 1997. "Partnerships for Health in the 21st Century." *World Health Statistics Quarterly* 51 (1): 68–74.

Knai, Cécile, Mark Petticrew, Mary Alison Durand, Elizabeth Eastmure, and Nicholas Mays. 2015. "Are the Public Health Responsibility Deal Alcohol Pledges Likely to Improve Public Health? An Evidence Synthesis." *Addiction* 110 (8): 1232–1246. doi:10.1111/add.12855.

Knai, Cécile, Mark Petticrew, Mary Alison Durand, Courtney Scott, Lesley James, Anushka Mehrotra, Elizabeth Eastmure, and Nicholas Mays. 2015. "The Public Health Responsibility Deal: Has a Public-Private Partnership Brought About Action on Alcohol Reduction?" *Addiction* 110 (8): 1217–1225. doi:10.1111/add.12892.

Knai, Cecile, et al. 2015. "Has a Public-Private Partnership Resulted in Action on Healthier Diets in England?" *Food Policy* 54: 1–10.

Kolm, Serge-Christophe. 2006. "Reciprocity: Its Scope, Rationales and Consequences." In Kolm and Ythier, *Handbook of the Economics of Giving*. Vol. 1, 371–544.

Kolm, Serge-Christophe, and Jean Mercier Ythier. 2006. *Handbook of the Economics of Giving, Altruism and Reciprocity*. Vols. 1 & 2. Amsterdam; Boston; Paris: Elsevier.

Koplan, J. P., and Brownell K. D. 2010. "Response of the Food and Beverage Industry to the Obesity Threat." *JAMA* 304 (13): 1487–1488. doi:10.1001/jama.2010.1436.

Korn, David. 2000. "Conflicts of Interest in Biomedical Research." *JAMA* 284 (17): 2234–2237. doi:10.1001/jama.284.17.2234.

Kotchen, Matthew, and J.J. Moon, "Corporate Social Responsibility for Irresponsibility." *B.E. Journal of Economic Analysis & Policy* 12 (1), art. 55.

Kraak, Vivica I. 2015. "Guiding Principles and a Decision-Making Framework for Stakeholders Pursuing Healthy Food Environments." *Health Affairs* 34 (11): 1972–1978. doi:10.1377/hlthaff.2015.0635.

Kraak, Vivica I., Paige B Harrigan, Mark Lawrence, Paul J Harrison, Michaela A. Jackson, and Boyd Swinburn. 2012. "Balancing the Benefits and Risks of Public-Private Partnerships to Address the Global Double Burden of Malnutrition." *Public Health Nutrition* 15(3): 503–517. doi:10.1017/S1368980011002060.

Kraak, Vivica I., Shiriki K. Kumanyika, and Mary Story. 2009. "The Commercial Marketing of Healthy Lifestyles to Address the Global Child and Adolescent Obesity Pandemic: Prospects, Pitfalls and Priorities." *Public Health Nutrition* 12 (11): 2027–2036. doi:10.1017/S1368980009990267.

Kraak, Vivica I., and Mary Story. 2010. "A Public Health Perspective on Healthy Lifestyles and Public-Private Partnerships for Global Childhood Obesity Prevention." *Journal of the American Dietetic Association* 110 (2): 192–200. doi:10.1016/j.jada.2009.10.036.

Kraak, Vivica I., Mary Story, Ellen A. Wartella, and Jaya Ginter. 2011. "Industry Progress to Market a Healthful Diet to American Children and Adolescents." *American Journal of Preventive Medicine* 41 (3): 322–333. doi:10.1016/j.amepre.2011.05.029.

Kraak, Vivica I., Boyd Swinburn, Mark Lawrence, and Paul Harrison. 2011. "The Accountability of Public-Private Partnerships with Food, Beverage and Quick-Serve Restaurant Companies to Address Global Hunger and the Double Burden of Malnutrition." *SCN News* 39 (Jan.): 11–24.

Kraak, Vivica I., Boyd Swinburn, Mark Lawrence, and Paul Harrison. 2014. "An Accountability Framework to Promote Healthy Food Environments." *Public Health Nutrition* 17(11): 2467–2483

Kraak, Vivica I. et al. 2014. "A Q Methodology Study of Stakeholders' Views About Accountability for Promoting Healthy Food Environments in England Through the Responsibility Deal Food Network." *Food Policy*, 49:207–218.

Kraak, Vivica, and Pan-Canadian Public Health Network (PCPHN). 2014. Public Health and Food and Beverage Industry Engagement: A Tool to Guide Partnership Opportunities and Challenges. Ontario, Canada. https://www.paho.org/hq/dmdocuments/2015/ppptg-guide.PDF

Krimsky, Sheldon. 2004. *Science in the Private Interest: Has the Lure of Profits Corrupted Biomedical Research?* New York: Rowman and Littlefield.

Kronman, Anthony. 2008. *Education's End: Why Our Colleges and Universities Have Given Up on the Meaning of Life.* New Haven, CT: Yale University Press.

Kuypers, Jim A. 2006. *Bush's War: Media Bias and Justifications for War in a Terrorist Age.* Lanham, MD.: Rowman and Littlefield.

———. 2009. *Rhetorical Criticism: Perspectives in Action.* Lanham, MD: Lexington Books.

Laing, R. D. 1969. *The Divided Self.* New York: Pantheon Books.

Lalazarian, Kathy. 2001. "Comparative Approaches to Conflict of Interest: The United States, Canada and the United Kingdom." The World Bank. http://documents.worldbank.org/curated/en/301681468227950841/Comparative-approaches-to-conflict-of-interest-The-United-States-Canada-and-the-United-Kingdom.

Lang, Tim, and Geof Rayner. 2010. "Corporate Responsibility in Public Health." *BMJ* 341 (January): c3758. doi:10.1136/bmj.c3758.

Lawrence, Felicity. 2010. "McDonald's and PepsiCo to Help Write UK Health Policy: Department of Health Putting Fast Food Companies at Heart of Policy on Obesity, Alcohol and Diet-Related Disease." *The Guardian*, November 12. http://www.theguardian.com/politics/2010/nov/12/mcdonalds-pepsico-help-health-policy

———. 2010. "Who Is the Government's Health Deal with Big Business Really Good For? Do Andrew Lansley's 'Responsibility Deals' Mean Food Firms' Dream of Writing Public Health Policy Has Come True?" *The Guardian*, November 12. http://www.theguardian.com/politics/2010/nov/12/government-health-deal-business.

Lee, Jaeah, and Alex Park. 2013. "The Gates Foundation's Hypocritical Investments," *Mother Jones*, December 6. http://www.motherjones.com/environment/2013/12/gates-foundations-24-most-egregious-investments

Lemmens, Paul H. H. M. 2016. "Critical Independence and Personal Integrity Revisited." *The International Journal of Alcohol and Drug Research*. doi:10.7895/ijadr.v0i0.230.

Lemmens, Trudo, and Benjamin Freedman. 2000. "Ethics Review for Sale? Conflict of Interest and Commercial Research Review Boards." *Milbank Quarterly* 78 (4): 547–584. doi:10.1111/1468-0009.00185.

Leon, Kenneth S. and Ivy Ken. 2017. "Food Fraud and the Partnership for a 'Healthier' America: A Case Study in State-Corporate Crime." *Critical Criminology* 25: 393–410.

Lesser, Lenard I., Cara B. Ebbeling, Merrill Goozner, David Wypij, and David S. Ludwig. 2007. "Relationship Between Funding Source and Conclusion Among Nutrition-Related Scientific Articles." *PLOS Med* 4 (1): e5. doi:10.1371/journal.pmed.0040005.

Lessig, Lawrence. 2009. "Against Transparency." *New Republic,* October 9, 2009.

———. 2011. *Republic, Lost: How Money Corrupts Congress—and a Plan to Stop It.* New York: Twelve Books.

———. 2013a. "Institutional Corruption Defined." *Journal of Law, Medicine and Ethics* 41: 553.

———. 2013b. "Institutional Corruptions." Edmond J. Safra Working Paper No. 1. http://papers.ssrn.com/abstract_id=2233582

———. 2014. "What an Originalist Would Understand Corruption to Mean." *California Law Review* 102: 1.

Levine, Jane, Joan Dye Gussow, Diane Hastings, and Amy Eccher. 2003. "Authors' Financial Relationships with the Food and Beverage Industry and Their Published Positions on the Fat Substitute Olestra." *American Journal of Public Health* 93 (4): 664–669. doi:10.2105/AJPH.93.4.664.

Lévi-Strauss, Claude. 1969. *The Elementary Structures of Kinship [Les structures élémentaires de la parenté]*. Boston: Beacon Press.

Lewis, Steven, Patricia Baird, Robert G. Evans, William A. Ghali, Charles J. Wright, Elaine Gibson, and Françoise Baylis. 2001. "Dancing with the Porcupine: Rules for Governing the University-Industry Relationship." *Canadian Medical Association Journal* 165 (6): 783–785.

Lincoln, Paul, Patti Rundall, Bill Jeffrey, et al. 2011. "Conflicts of Interest and the UN High-Level Meeting on Non-Communicable Diseases." *The Lancet* 378: e6.

Lo, Bernard and Marilyn J. Field. 2009. *Conflict of Interest in Medical Research, Education, and Practice*. Washington, DC: National Academies Press.

Lo, Bernard and Christine Grady. 2017. "Payments to Physicians: Does the Amount of Money Make a Difference?" *JAMA* 317 (17):1719–1720.

Lowenstein, Daniel Hays. 1986. "For God, for Country, or for Me?" *California Law Review* 74 (4): 1479–1512. doi:10.2307/3480368.

Luban, David. 2003. "Integrity: Its Causes and Cures." *Fordham Law Review* 72: 279–310.

———. 2007. *Legal Ethics and Human Dignity*. Cambridge; New York: Cambridge University Press.

Luhmann, Niklas. 1988. "Familiarity, Confidence, Trust: Problems and Alternatives." In *Trust: Making and Breaking Cooperative Relations*, edited by Diego Gambetta, 94–107. Oxford: Basil Blackwell.

Ludwig D. S., and Nestle M. 2008. "Can the Food Industry Play a Constructive Role in the Obesity Epidemic?" *JAMA* 300 (15): 1808–1811. doi:10.1001/jama.300.15.1808.

Lyles A. 2005. "Must an Interest Be a Conflict?" *Clinical Therapeutics* 27 (3): 344–345.

MacIntyre, Alasdair C. (1981) 2007. *After Virtue: A Study in Moral Theory*. Notre Dame, IN: University of Notre Dame Press.

Macintyre, Sally. 2012. "Evidence in the Development of Health Policy." *Public Health* 126 (3): 217–219. doi:10.1016/j.puhe.2012.01.026.

Madison, James. 1788. "These Departments Should Be So Far Separated as to Have No Constitutional Control Over Each Other." February 1. http://avalon.law.yale.edu/18th_century/fed48.asp.

———. 2016. *The Congressional Register*. Accessed April 4. http://www.gwu.edu/~ffcp/mep/displaydoc.cfm?docid=fc111028.

———. 2016b. *The Federalist Papers*, No. 47. The Particular Structure of the New Government and the Distribution of Power Among Its Different Parts." Accessed April 4. http://avalon.law.yale.edu/18th_century/fed47.asp.

Magloicca, Gerard. 2015. "The Legacy of Chief Justice Fortas." *Green Bag 2d* 18: 261–269.

Maharaj, S. V. M. 2015. "A New Method for Scoring Financial Conflicts of Interest." *International Journal of Occupational and Environmental Health* 21 (1): 49–52. doi:10.1179/2049396714Y.0000000097.

Malinowski, Bronislaw. 1922. *Argonauts of the Western Pacific: An Account of Native Enterprise and Adventure in the Archipelagoes of Melanesian New Guinea*. London; New York: G. Routledge and Sons; E.P. Dutton.

———. 1932. *Crime and Custom in Savage Society*. New York; London: Harcourt, Brace.

Malmendier, Ulrike, and Klaus Schmidt. 2012. "You Owe Me." Working Paper No. 18543. National Bureau of Economic Research. http://www.nber.org/papers/w18543.

Mann, Thomas E., and Norman J Ornstein. 2013. "Finding the Common Good in an Era of Dysfunctional Governance." *Daedalus* 142 (2): 15–24.

Mansbridge, Jane. 1998. "On the Contested Nature of the Public Good." In *Private Action and the Public Good*, edited by Walter Powell and Elisabeth Clemens, 3–19. New Haven, CT: Yale University Press.

Marks, Jonathan H. 2008. "Expedited Industry-Sponsored Translational Research: A Seductive but Hazardous Cocktail?" *American Journal of Bioethics* 8 (3): 56–58. doi:10.1080/15265160802109363.

———. 2011. "On Regularity and Regulation." *Hastings Center Report* 41 (4): 11–12.

———. 2012. "Toward a Unified Theory of Professional Ethics and Human Rights." *Michigan Journal of International Law* 33: 215.

———. 2013a. "The Undocumented Unwell." *Hastings Center Report* 43 (1): 10–11. doi:10.1002/hast.124.

———. 2013b. "What's the Big Deal?" Edmond J. Safra Working Paper No. 11. https://papers.ssrn.com/abstract=2268079.

———. 2014a. "Toward a Systemic Ethics of Public-Private Partnerships Related to Food and Health." *Kennedy Institute of Ethics Journal* 24 (3): 267–299. doi:10.1353/ken.2014.0022.

———. 2014b. "Silencing Marcellus: When the Law Fractures Public Health." *Hastings Center Report* 44 (2): 8–10. doi:10.1002/hast.278.

———. 2014c. "Nutrition and Global Health Policy: A Critical Moment" *BMJ* 349: g5457.

———. 2016. "The Ethics of Compromise: Third Party, Public Health and Environmental Perspectives" *Journal of Medical Ethics* 11. doi:10.1136/medethics-2015-103279

———. 2017. "Caveat Partner: Sharing Responsibility for Health with the Food Industry?" *American Journal of Public Health* 107 (3): 360–361.

Marmot, Michael. 2004. *Status Syndrome: How Your Social Standing Directly Affects Your Health*. London: Bloomsbury.

Marmot Review. 2010. *Fair Society, Healthy Lives: Strategic Review of Health Inequalities in England Post-2010*. London: The Marmot Review.

Masterman, Roger. 2011. *The Separation of Powers in the Contemporary Constitution: Judicial Competence and Independence in the United Kingdom*. Cambridge, UK; New York: Cambridge University Press.

Mauss, Marcel. (1925) 1990. *The Gift: Forms and Functions of Exchange in Archaic Societies*. Translated by W.D. Halls. New York: W. W. Norton.

McCambridge, Jim, Benjamin Hawkins, and Chris Holden. 2014. "Vested Interests in Addiction Research and Policy. The Challenge Corporate Lobbying Poses to Reducing Society's Alcohol Problems: Insights from UK Evidence on Minimum Unit Pricing: Corporate Lobbying in the UK." *Addiction* 109 (2): 199–205. doi:10.1111/add.12380.

McCartney, Margaret. 2014. "Is Coca-Cola's Antiobesity Scheme the Real Thing?" *BMJ* 349: g4340. http://www.bmj.com/content/349/bmj.g4340.

McComas K. A. 2008. "Session 5: Nutrition Communication. The Role of Trust in Health Communication and the Effect of Conflicts of Interest Among Scientists." *The Proceedings of the Nutrition Society* 67 (4): 428–436. doi:10.1017/S0029665108008689

McCreanor, Tim, Sally Casswell, and Linda Hill. 2000. "ICAP and the Perils of Partnership." *Addiction* 95 (2): 179–185. doi:10.1046/j.1360-0443.2000.9521794.x.

McFall, Lynne. 1987. "Integrity." *Ethics* 98 (1): 5–20.

McKinnon, Robert, et al. 2009. "A Case for Public-Private Partnerships in Health: Lessons from an Honest Broker." *Prevention of Chronic Disease* 6 (2): A72.

McLeod, Carolyn. 2006. "Trust." *Stanford Encyclopedia of Philosophy*, edited by Edward N. Zalta, revised spring 2011. http://plato.stanford.edu/archives/spr2011/entries/trust/.

McPherson, Klim. 2013. "Can We Leave Industry to Lead Efforts to Improve Population Health? No." *BMJ* 346 (Apr.): f2426. doi:10.1136/bmj.f2426.

McQueen, David V. 2013. *Global Handbook on Noncommunicable Diseases and Health Promotion*. New York: Springer.

Meghani, Zahra, and Jennifer Kuzma. 2010. "The 'Revolving Door' Between Regulatory Agencies and Industry: A Problem That Requires Reconceptualizing Objectivity." *Journal of Agricultural and Environmental Ethics* 24 (6): 575–599. doi:10.1007/s10806-010-9287-x.

Mello, Michelle M., Jennifer Pomeranz, and Patricia Moran. 2008. "The Interplay of Public Health Law and Industry Self-Regulation: The Case of Sugar-Sweetened Beverage Sales in Schools." *American Journal of Public Health* 98 (4): 595–604. doi:10.2105/AJPH.2006.107680.

Michaels, David. 2008. *Doubt Is Our Product*. New York: Oxford University Press.

Miller, David, and Claire Harkins. 2010. "Corporate Strategy, Corporate Capture: Food and Alcohol Industry Lobbying and Public Health." *Critical Social Policy* 30 (4): 564–589. doi:10.1177/0261018310376805.

Monbiot, George. 2014. "How Have These Corporations Colonised Our Public Life? Our Politicians Have Delegated Power to Global Giants Engineering a World of Conformity and Consumerism." *The Guardian*, April 7. http://www.theguardian.com/commentisfree/2014/apr/08/corporations-public-life-unilever.

Montefiore, Alan, and David Vines. 1999. *Integrity in the Public and Private Domains*. New York: Routledge.

Monteiro, Carlos A., and Geoffrey Cannon. 2012. "The Impact of Transnational 'Big Food' Companies on the South: A View from Brazil." *PLOS Med* 9 (7): e1001252. doi:10.1371/journal.pmed.1001252.

Moodie, Rob, David Stuckler, Carlos Monteiro, Nick Sheron, Bruce Neal, Thaksaphon Thamarangsi, Paul Lincoln, and Sally Casswell. 2013. "Profits and Pandemics: Prevention of Harmful Effects of Tobacco, Alcohol, and Ultra-Processed Food and Drink Industries." *The Lancet* 381 (9867): 670–679. doi:10.1016/S0140-6736(12)62089-3.

Mosko, Mark S. 2000. "Inalienable Ethnography: Keeping-While-Giving and the Trobriand Case." *Journal of the Royal Anthropological Institute* 6 (3): 377–396. doi:10.1111/1467-9655.00022.

Moss, Michael. 2010. "While Warning About Fat, U.S. Pushes Cheese Sales." *New York Times*, November 6. http://www.nytimes.com/2010/11/07/us/07fat.html.

Motswami, Modi. 2018. *Public Health and the Food and Drinks Industry: The Governance of Ethics and Interaction. Lessons from Research, Policy and Practice*. London: UK Health Forum.

Mozaffarian, Darius. 2014. "The Health Weight Commitment Foundation Trillion Calorie Pledge: Lessons from a Marketing Ploy." *American Journal of Preventive Medicine* 47(4): e9–10.

Mudd, Michael. 2013. "How to Force Ethics on the Food Industry." *New York Times*, March 17. http://www.nytimes.com/2013/03/17/opinion/sunday/how-to-force-ethics-on-the-food-industry.html.

Multilateral Investment Guarantee Agency (MIGA). 2016. "Institutional Integrity." Accessed September 27. https://www.miga.org/projects/institutional-integrity.

Murray, Alan. 2005. "The Profit Motive Has a Limit: Tragedy." *Wall Street Journal*, September 8, sec. News, http://www.wsj.com/articles/SB112605268602433438.

Murray, J. Haskell. 2013. "Social Enterprise Innovation: Delaware's Public Benefit Corporation Law." *Harvard Business Law Review*, 4: 345–371.

Murray, Thomas H., and Josephine Johnston, eds. 2010. *Trust and Integrity in Biomedical Research: The Case of Financial Conflicts of Interest*. Baltimore, MD: Johns Hopkins University Press.

Nadolny, Tricia. 2016. "Soda Tax Passes; Philadelphia Is First Big City in Nation to Enact One." *Philadelphia Inquirer*, June 18. http://articles.philly.com/2016-06-18/news/73844306_1_philadelphia-city-council-tax-credit-first-such-tax.

National Conference of State Legislators. 2016. "For-Profit Colleges and Universities." Accessed September 14. http://www.ncsl.org/research/education/for-profit-colleges-and-universities.aspx.

National Research Council. 2005. *Food Marketing to Children and Youth: Threat or Opportunity?* Washington, DC: National Academies Press.

Nestle, Marion. 2007. *Food Politics: How the Food Industry Influences Nutrition and Health.* Berkeley: University of California Press.

———. 2015. *Soda Politics: Taking on Big Soda (and Winning).* New York: Oxford University Press.

———. 2016. "Corporate Funding of Food and Nutrition Research: Science or Marketing?" *JAMA Internal Medicine* 176 (1): 13–14.

———. 2016 "Food Industry Funding of Nutrition Research: The Relevance of History for Current Debates." *JAMA Internal Medicine* 176 (11): 1685–1686. doi:10.1001/jamainternmed.2016.5400

Neuman, William. 2010. "Save the Children Breaks with Soda Tax Effort." *New York Times,* December 14. http://www.nytimes.com/2010/12/15/business/15soda.html.

Newhouse, Marie. 2014. "Institutional Corruption: A Fiduciary Theory" *Cornell Journal of Law and Public Policy* 23: 553–594.

Ng, Marie, et al. 2014. "Global, Regional, and National Prevalence of Overweight and Obesity in Children and Adults During 1980–2013: A Systematic Analysis for the Global Burden of Disease Study 2013." *The Lancet* 384 (9945): 766–781.

Nicklas T. A., W. Karmally, and C. E. O'Neil. 2011. "Nutrition Professionals Are Obligated to Follow Ethical Guidelines When Conducting Industry-Funded Research." *Journal of the American Dietetic Association* 111 (12): 1931–1932.

Nuffield Council on Bioethics. 2007. *Public Health: Ethical Issues.* http://nuffieldbioethics.org/wp-content/uploads/2014/07/Public-health-ethical-issues.pdf.

Nystrom, Johan. 2005. "The Definition of Partnering as a Wittgenstein Family-Resemblance Concept." *Construction Management and Economics* 23 (5): 473–481.

Obama, Barack. 2010. "Remarks by the President in State of the Union Address." January 27. https://www.whitehouse.gov/the-press-office/remarks-president-state-union-address.

O'Connor, Anahad. 2015. "Coca-Cola Funds Scientists." *New York Times,* August 9. http://well.blogs.nytimes.com/2015/08/09/coca-cola-funds-scientists-who-shift-blame-for-obesity-away-from-bad-diets/.

———. 2015. "Coke's Chief Scientist, Who Orchestrated Obesity Research, Is Leaving." *New York Times,* November 24. https://well.blogs.nytimes.com/2015/11/24/cokes-chief-scientist-who-orchestrated-obesity-research-is-leaving/.

———. 2015. "University Returns $1 Million Grant to Coca-Cola." *New York Times,* November 6. http://well.blogs.nytimes.com/2015/11/06/university-returns-1-million-grant-to-coca-cola/.

———. 2016. "How the Sugar Industry Shifted Blame to Fat." *New York Times,* September 12. https://www.nytimes.com/2016/09/.../how-the-sugar-industry-shifted-blame-to-fat.html

———. 2016. "Coke and Pepsi Give Millions to Public Health, Then Lobby Against It." *New York Times,* October 10. https://www.nytimes.com/2016/10/10/well/eat/coke-and-pepsi-give-millions-to-public-health-then-lobby-against-it.html

———. 2016. "Studies Linked to Soda Industry Mask Health Risks." *New York Times,* October 31. https://www.nytimes.com/2016/11/01/well/eat/studies-linked-to-soda-industry-mask-health-risks.html

———. 2016. "Study Tied to Industry Tries to Discredit Sugar Guidelines." *New York Times,* December 19. https://www.nytimes.com/2016/12/19/well/eat/a-food-industry-study-tries-to-discredit-advice-about-sugar.html

———. 2017. "Sugar Industry Long Downplayed Potential Harms." *New York Times,* November 21. https://www.nytimes.com/2017/11/21/well/eat/sugar-industry-long-downplayed-potential-harms-of-sugar.html

O'Connor, Anahad and Margot Sanger-Katz. 2016. "As Soda Taxes Gain Wider Acceptance, Your Bottle May Be Next." *New York Times*, November 26. http://www.nytimes.com/2016/11/26/well/eat/as-soda-taxes-gain-wider-acceptance-your-bottle-may-be-next.html

Organization for Economic Co-operation and Development (OECD). 2009. "OECD Principles for Integrity in Public Procurement." http://www.oecd.org/gov/ethics/48994520.pdf.

———. 2014. "The Rationale for Fighting Corruption." https://www.oecd.org/cleangovbiz/49693613.pdf.

Orlowski, James P., and Leon Wateska. 1992. "The Effects of Pharmaceutical Firm Enticements on Physician Prescribing Patterns: There's No Such Thing as a Free Lunch." *Chest* 102 (1): 270–273. doi:10.1378/chest.102.1.270.

Ormiston, M. E., and E. M. Wong. 2014. "License to Ill: The Effects of Corporate Social Responsibility and CEO Moral Identity on Corporate Social Irresponsibility." *Personnel Psychology* 66:861–893.

Oshaug, Arne. 2009. "What Is the Food and Drink Industry Doing in Nutrition Conferences?" *Public Health Nutrition* 12 (7): 1019–1020. doi:10.1017/S136898000900593X.

Panjwani, Clare, and Martin Caraher. 2014. "The Public Health Responsibility Deal: Brokering a Deal for Public Health, but on Whose Terms?" *Health Policy* 114 (2–3): 163–173. doi:10.1016/j.healthpol.2013.11.002.

Park, Alex, and Lee Jaeah. 2016. "You Won't Believe the Companies Bill Gates' Foundation Invests In." *Mother Jones*. Accessed September 21. http://www.motherjones.com/environment/2013/12/gates-foundations-24-most-egregious-investments.

Parry, Jonathan P, and Maurice Bloch. 1989. *Money and the Morality of Exchange*. New York: Cambridge University Press.

Pellegrino, Edmun D. 1986. "Rationing Health Care: The Ethics of Medical Gatekeeping." *Journal of Contemporary Health Law and Policy* 2: 23.

Penders, Bart, and Annemiek P. Nelis. 2011. "Credibility Engineering in the Food Industry: Linking Science, Regulation, and Marketing in a Corporate Context." *Science in Context* 24 (4): 487–515. doi:10.1017/S0269889711000202.

Penn State University. 2013. "Penn State's New Natural Gas Center to Keep Pa. at Forefront of Industry Penn State University." *Penn State News*, March 6. http://news.psu.edu/story/267496/2013/03/06/impact/penn-states-new-natural-gas-center-keep-pa-forefront-industry.

Pham-Kanter, Genevieve. 2014. "Revisiting Financial Conflicts of Interest in FDA Advisory Committees." *Milbank Quarterly* 92 (3): 446–470. doi:10.1111/1468-0009.12073.

Plerhoples, Alicia. 2013. "Representing Social Enterprise." SSRN Scholarly Paper ID 2214954. Rochester, NY: Social Science Research Network. http://papers.ssrn.com/abstract=2214954.

———. 2014. "Delaware Public Benefit Corporations 90 Days Out: Who's Opting In?" *UC Davis Business Law Journal*, 14: 247–280.

Pomeranz, Jennifer, Stephen Teret, Stephen Sugarman, Lainie Rutkow, and Kelly Brownell. 2009. "Innovative Legal Approaches to Address Obesity." *Milbank Quarterly* 87 (1): 185–213.

Porter, Andrew. 2008. "David Cameron Launches 'Moral Neutrality' Attack on Obese, Idle and Poor." *The Telegraph*, July 7, sec. News. http://www.telegraph.co.uk/news/politics/conservative/2263521/David-Cameron-launches-moral-neutrality-attack-on-obese-idle-and-poor.html.

Putnam, Ruth A. 1988. "Reciprocity and Virtue Ethics." *Ethics*, 98 (2): 379–389.

Raheja, Gloria Goodwin. 1988. *The Poison in the Gift: Ritual, Presentation, and the Dominant Caste in a North Indian Village*. Chicago: University of Chicago Press.

Raw, Martin. 2000. "Real Partnerships Need Trust." *Addiction* 95(2): 196

Rawal, Sanjay. 2016. *Food Chains*. http://www.foodchainsfilm.com.

Rawls, John. 1971. *A Theory of Justice*. Cambridge, MA: Belknap Press of Harvard University Press.

Rayner, Geof, and Tim Lang. 2011. "Is Nudge an Effective Public Health Strategy to Tackle Obesity? No." *BMJ* doi:10.1136/bmj.d2177.

Reczek, Peter R. 2004. "Research and the Bayh-Dole Act." *Science* 303 (5654): 40. doi:10.1126/science.303.5654.40a.

Reich, Robert B. 2007. *Supercapitalism: The Transformation of Business, Democracy, and Everyday Life*. New York: Alfred A. Knopf.

———. 2018. *The Common Good*. New York: Alfred A. Knopf.

Reynolds, Susan. 2010. *Before Eminent Domain Toward a History of Expropriation of Land for the Common Good*. Chapel Hill: University of North Carolina Press.

Rhode, Deborah L. 2003. "If Integrity Is the Answer, What Is the Question?" *Fordham Law Review* 72: 333–344.

Richter, Judith. 2002. *Dialogue or Engineering of Consent? Opportunities and Risks of Talking to Industry*. Geneva: GIFA/IBFAN. http://www.gifa.org/wp-content/uploads/2016/05/JRichter_2002_Dialogue_or_Engineering_of_Consent.pdf.

———. 2004a. "Public-Private Partnerships for Health: A Trend with No Alternatives?" *Development* 47 (S2): 43–48. doi:10.1057/palgrave.development.1100043.

———. 2004b. *Public-Private Partnerships and International Health Policy-Making*. Helsinki: GASPP. http://formin.finland.fi/public/download.aspx?ID=12360&GUID=%7B3556FE5F-6CBC-4000-86F3-99EBFD2778FC%7D.

———. 2012. "WHO Reform and Public Interest Safeguards: An Historical Perspective." *Social Medicine* 6 (3): 141–150.

———. 2014. "Time to Turn the Tide: WHO's Engagement with Non-State Actors and the Politics of Stakeholder Governance and Conflicts of Interest." *BMJ* 348: g3351. doi:10.1136/bmj.g3351.

———. 2015. "Conflicts of Interest and Global Health and Nutrition Governance—The Illusion of Robust Principles." *BMJ*. http://www.bmj.com/content/349/bmj.g5457/rr

Riordan, Patrick. 2008. *A Grammar of the Common Good: Speaking of Globalization*. London: Continuum.

Robbins, A., and M. Nestle. 2011. "Obesity as Collateral Damage: A Call for Papers on the Obesity Epidemic." *Journal of Public Health Policy* 32 (2): 143–145.

Robertson, Christopher. 2011. "The Money Blind: How to Stop Industry Bias in Biomedical Science, Without Violating the First Amendment." *American Journal of Law & Medicine* 37: 358–387.

Rodwin, Marc. 2011. *Conflicts of Interest and the Future of Medicine*. New York: Oxford University Press.

———. 2018. "Attempts to Redefine Conflicts of Interest." *Accountability in Research* 25 (2): 67–78.

Roehrich, Jens K., Michael A. Lewis, and Gerard George. 2014. "Are Public-Private Partnerships a Healthy Option? A Systematic Literature Review." *Social Science & Medicine* 113 (July): 110–119. doi:10.1016/j.socscimed.2014.03.037.

Roizen, Ron, and Kaye Fillmore. 2000. "Commentaries on McCreanor et al.'s ICAP and the Perils of Partnership." *Addiction* 95 (2): 187–198. doi:10.1080/09652140031856.

Roosevelt, Theodore. 1901. "Theodore Roosevelt: First Annual Message." http://www.presidency.ucsb.edu/ws/?pid=29542.

Rose, Susannah L. 2013. "Patient Advocacy Organizations: Institutional Conflicts of Interest, Trust, and Trustworthiness." *Journal of Law, Medicine & Ethics* 41 (3): 680–687. doi:10.1111/jlme.12078.

Rose, Susannah L., et al. 2017. "Patient Advocacy Organizations, Industry Funding, and Conflicts of Interest." *JAMA Internal Medicine* 177(3): 1–7.

Rosenthal, Benjamin, Michael Jacobson, and Mary Bohm. 1976. "Professors on the Take: Financial Ties to Huge Food Corporations May Shade the 'Expert Testimony' of Nutritionists." *The Progressive,* November, 42–47.

Rothman, David J., Walter J. McDonald, Carol D. Berkowitz, Susan C. Chimonas, Catherine D. DeAngelis, Ralph W. Hale, Steven E. Nissen. 2009. "Professional Medical Associations and Their Relationships with Industry: A Proposal for Controlling Conflict of Interest." *JAMA* 301 (13): 1367–1372. doi:10.1001/jama.2009.407.

Rowe, Sylvia, Nick Alexander, Alison Kretser, Robert Steele, Molly Kretsch, Rhona Applebaum, and Fergus Clydesdale. 2013. "Principles for Building Public-Private Partnerships to Benefit Food Safety, Nutrition, and Health Research." *Nutrition Reviews* 71 (10): 682–691. doi:10.1111/nure.12072.

Royal Commission on the Reform of the House of Lords (Wakeham Commission). 2000. *A House for the Future.* London: Stationery Office. https://www.gov.uk/government/publications/a-house-for-the-future-royal-commission-on-the-reform-of-the-house-of-lords

Ruckert, Arne, and Ronald Labonté. 2014. "Public-Private Partnerships (PPPs) in Global Health: The Good, the Bad and the Ugly." *Third World Quarterly* 35 (9): 1598–1614. doi:10.1080/01436597.2014.970870.

Rutkow, Lainie, and Stephen Teret. 2010. "Role of State Attorneys General in Health Policy." *JAMA* 304(12):1377–1378.

Sacks, Gary et al. 2017. "How Food Companies Influence Evidence and Opinion—Straight from the Horse's Mouth." *Critical Public Health.* http://dx.doi.org/10.1080/09581596.2017.1371844.

Sah, Sunita. 2016. "The Paradox of Disclosure." *New York Times,* July 8. https://www.nytimes.com/2016/07/10/opinion/sunday/the-paradox-of-disclosure.html

Sah, Sunita, and Adriane Fugh-Berman. 2013. "Physicians Under the Influence: Social Psychology and Industry Marketing Strategies." *Journal of Law, Medicine & Ethics* 41 (3): 665–672. doi:10.1111/jlme.12076.

Sahlins, Marshall. 1968. *Tribesmen.* Englewood Cliffs, NJ: Prentice-Hall.

———. 1972. *Stone Age Economics.* Chicago: Aldine-Atherton.

Salter, Malcolm S. 2013. "Short-Termism at Its Worst: How Short-Termism Invites Corruption . . . and What to Do About It." Edmond J. Safra Working Paper No. 5. http://papers.ssrn.com/sol3/papers.cfm?abstract_id=2247545.

Saltman, Richard B., and Odile Ferroussier-Davis. 2000. "The Concept of Stewardship in Health Policy." *Bulletin of the World Health Organization* 78 (6): 732–739. doi:10.1590/S0042-96862000000600005.

Samuelson, Paul A. 1954. "The Pure Theory of Public Expenditure." *The Review of Economics and Statistics* 36 (4): 387–389. doi:10.2307/1925895.

Sansone, Robert, et al. 2015. "Cocoa Flavanol Intake Improves Endothelial Function and Framingham Risk Score in Healthy Men and Women: A Randomised, Controlled, Double-Masked Trial: The Flaviola Health Study." *British Journal of Nutrition,* 114: 1246–1255.

Schafer, A. 2004. "Biomedical Conflicts of Interest: A Defence of the Sequestration Thesis—Learning from the Cases of Nancy Olivieri and David Healy." *Journal of Medical Ethics* 30 (1): 8–24. doi:10.1136/jme.2003.005702.

Schwartz, Barry. 1967. "The Social Psychology of the Gift." *American Journal of Sociology* 73 (1): 1–11.

Scott, W. Richard. 2014. *Institutions and Organizations: Ideas, Interests, and Identities.* New York: Sage.

Searcey, Dionne, and Matthew Richtel. 2017. "Obesity Was Rising as Ghana Embraced Fast Food. Then Came KFC." *New York Times*, October 2. https://www.nytimes.com/2017/10/02/health/ghana-kfc-obesity.html

Seward, Christopher. 2015. "Bill and Melinda Gates' Trust Sheds Coca-Cola, Adds UPS to Holdings." The Biz Beat Blog, February 17. http://business.blog.myajc.com/2015/02/17/bill-and-melinda-gates-trust-sheds-coca-cola-add-ups-to-holdings/#__federated=1.

Sharma, Lisa L., Stephen P. Teret, and Kelly D. Brownell. 2010. "The Food Industry and Self-Regulation: Standards to Promote Success and to Avoid Public Health Failures." *American Journal of Public Health* 100(2): 240–246.

Shields, Jeff. 2011. "Big Beverage Gives $10 Million to CHOP." *Philadelphia Inquirer*, March 18. https://web.archive.org/web/20110318100909/http://www.philly.com/philly/blogs/heardinthehall/118077483.html.

Shuchman, Miriam. 2007. "Commercializing Clinical Trials—Risks and Benefits of the CRO Boom." *New England Journal of Medicine* 357(14):1365–1368.

Simm, Kadri. 2011. "The Concepts of Common Good and Public Interest: From Plato to Biobanking." *Cambridge Quarterly of Healthcare Ethics* 20 (4): 554–562. doi:10.1017/S0963180111000296.

Simon, Caitlin, S. Lawrence Kocot, and Willliam H. Dietz. 2017. "Partnership for a Healthier America: Creating Change Through Private Sector Partnerships." *Current Obesity Reports* 6: 108–115.

Simon, Michelle. 2013. *And Now a Word from Our Sponsors: Are America's Nutrition Professionals in the Pocket of Big Food?* http://www.eatdrinkpolitics.com/wp-content/uploads/AND_Corporate_Sponsorship_Report.pdf

Simon, Yves R. 1960. "Common Good and Common Action." *The Review of Politics* 22 (2): 202–244. doi:10.1017/S0034670500008214.

Sinclair, Upton. (1935) 1994. *I, Candidate for Governor: And How I Got Licked.* Berkeley: University of California Press.

Singer, Peter A., Sean Ansett, and Isabella Sagoe-Moses. 2011. "What Could Infant and Young Child Nutrition Learn from Sweatshops?" *BMC Public Health* 11: 276. doi:10.1186/1471-2458-11-276.

Six, Frédérique E., and Leo W. J. C. Huberts. 2008. "Judging a Public Official's Integrity." In *Ethics and Integrity of Governance: Perspectives Across Frontiers*, edited by Leo W. J. C. Huberts, Jeroen Maesschalk, and Carole L. Jurkiewicz, 66–74. Cheltenham, UK: Edward Elgar.

Smith, Adam. 1776. *An Inquiry into the Nature and Causes of the Wealth of Nations.* London: W. Strahan and T. Cadell.

Snow, David A., E. Burke Rochford, Steven K. Worden, and Robert D. Benford. 1986. "Frame Alignment Processes, Micromobilization, and Movement Participation." *American Sociological Review* 51 (4): 464–481. doi:10.2307/2095581.

Soares, Andréia A. 2016. "Putting Taxes into the Diet Equation," *Bulletin of the World Health Organization* 94: 239–240.

Solomon, David, and Bingxiang Luo. 2014. *The Common Good: Chinese and American Perspectives.*

Sorkin, Andrew Ross. 2009. *Too Big to Fail: The Inside Story of How Wall Street and Washington Fought to Save the Financial System from Crisis—and Lost.* New York: Viking.

Stark, Andrew. 1992. "Public Sector Conflict of Interest at the Federal Level in Canada and the U. S.: Differences in Understanding and Approach." *Public Administration Review* 52 (5): 427–437. doi:10.2307/976802.

———. 2001. "Public Integrity." *American Political Science Review* 95 (1): 203–204.

Stenius, Kerstin, and Thomas F. Babor. 2010. "The Alcohol Industry and Public Interest Science." *Addiction* 105(2): 191–198

Sterckx, Sigrid. 2011. "Patenting and Licensing of University Research: Promoting Innovation or Undermining Academic Values?" *Science and Engineering Ethics* 17 (1): 45–64. doi:10.1007/s11948-009-9168-8.

Stevenson, Michael A. 2016. "The Relevance of the Public-Private Partnership Paradigm to the Prevention of Diet-Associated Non-Communicable Diseases in Wealthy Countries." *Global Public Health* 10 (8): 930–946.

Steyn, Lord. 2006. "Democracy, the Rule of Law and the Role of Judges." *European Human Rights Law Review* 3: 243.

Stiglitz, Joseph E., and Arjun Jayadev. 2010. "Medicine for Tomorrow: Some Alternative Proposals to Promote Socially Beneficial Research and Development in Pharmaceuticals." *Journal of Generic Medicines* 7 (3): 217–226. doi:10.1057/jgm.2010.21.

Stirrat, R.L., and Heiko Henkel. 1997. "The Development Gift: The Problem of Reciprocity in the NGO World." *Annals of the American Academy of Political and Social Science* 554: 66–80.

Streeck, Wolfgang, and Kathleen Ann Thelen. 2005. *Beyond Continuity: Institutional Change in Advanced Political Economies.* New York: Oxford University Press.

Strom, Stephanie. 2012. "Has 'Organic' Been Oversized? Organic Food Purists Worry About Big Companies' Influence." *New York Times*, July 7. http://www.nytimes.com/2012/07/08/business/organic-food-purists-worry-about-big-companies-influence.html.

Stuckler, David, Sanjay Basu, and Martin McKee. 2011. "Global Health Philanthropy and Institutional Relationships: How Should Conflicts of Interest Be Addressed?" *PLOS Med* 8 (4): e1001020. doi:10.1371/journal.pmed.1001020.

Stuckler, David, and Marion Nestle. 2012. "Big Food, Food Systems, and Global Health." *PLOS Med* 9 (6): e1001242. doi:10.1371/journal.pmed.1001242.

Stuckler, David, and Karen Siegel. 2011. *Sick Societies: Responding to the Global Challenge of Chronic Disease.* Oxford; New York: Oxford University Press.

Suchak, Malini, and Frans B. M. de Waal. 2012. "Monkeys Benefit from Reciprocity Without the Cognitive Burden." *Proceedings of the National Academy of Sciences* 109 (38): 15191–15196. doi:10.1073/pnas.1213173109.

Sulmasy, Daniel. 2001. "Four Basic Notions of the Common Good." *St. John's Law Review* 303.

Sunstein, Cass R. 2014. *Why Nudge?: The Politics of Libertarian Paternalism.* New Haven, CT: Yale University Press.

———. 2016. *The Ethics of Influence: Government in the Age of Behavioral Science.* New York: Cambridge University Press.

Swinburn, Body. 2015. "Strengthening of Accountability Systems to Create Healthy Food Environments and Reduce Global Obesity." *The Lancet* 385(9986): 2534–2545.

Tachibana, Chris. 2013. "Opening Industry-Academic Partnerships." *Science*, April 12. doi:10.1126/science.opms.r1300132.   http://www.sciencemag.org/features/2013/04/opening-industry-academic-partnerships

Tang, Shi et al. 2017. "Taste Moral, Taste Good: The Effects of Fairtrade Logo and Second Language on Product Taste Evaluation." *Food Quality and Preference*, 50: 152–156.

Taubes, Gary. 2016. *The Case Against Sugar.* New York: Alfred Knopf.

Taylor, Paul C. 2014. "Institutional Corruption: From Purpose to Function." Edmond J. Safra Working Paper No. 40, March 2014, http://papers.ssrn.com/abstract=2417066.

Teachout, Zephyr. 2009. "The Anti-Corruption Principle," *Cornell Law Review* 94 (341): 342–413.

———. 2014. *Corruption in America: From Benjamin Franklin's Snuff Box to Citizens United.* Cambridge, MA: Harvard University Press.

Tjidde Tempels, Marcel Verweij, and Vincent Blok. 2017. "Big Food's Ambivalence: Seeking Profit and Responsibility for Health." *American Journal of Public Health* 107(3): 402–406. doi: 10.2105/AJPH.2016.303601

Thaler, Richard H., and Cass R. Sunstein. 2008. *Nudge: Improving Decisions About Health, Wealth, and Happiness.* New Haven, CT: Yale University Press.

Thomas, Bryan, and Lawrence O. Gostin. 2013. "Tackling the Global NCD Crisis: Innovations in Law and Governance." *Journal of Law, Medicine & Ethics* 41 (1): 16–27. doi:10.1111/jlme.12002.

Thompson, Clive. 2009. "Are Your Friends Making You Fat?" *New York Times*, September 10. http://www.nytimes.com/2009/09/13/magazine/13contagion-t.html.

Thompson, Dennis F. 1987. *Political Ethics and Public Office.* Cambridge, MA: Harvard University Press.

———. 1993. "Understanding Financial Conflicts of Interest." *NEJM.* 329:573–576 (8).

———. 2005. *Restoring Responsibility: Ethics in Government, Business, and Healthcare.* Cambridge, UK; New York: Cambridge University Press.

———. 2013. "Two Concepts of Corruption." SSRN Scholarly Paper ID 2304419. Rochester, NY: Social Science Research Network. http://papers.ssrn.com/abstract=2304419.

Thompson, Jon, Jocelyn Downie, P. Baird, and Canadian Association of University Teachers. 2001. *The Olivieri Report: The Complete Text of the Report of the Independent Inquiry Commissioned by the Canadian Association of University Teachers.* Toronto: J. Lorimer. https://www.caut.ca/docs/af-reports-indepedent-committees-of-inquiry/the-olivieri-report.pdf

Thursby, Jerry G., and Marie C. Thursby. 2003. "University Licensing and the Bayh-Dole Act." *Science* 301 (5636): 1052. doi:10.1126/science.1087473.

Titmuss, Richard Morris. 1971. *The Gift Relationship: From Human Blood to Social Policy.* New York: Pantheon Books.

Todd, Jessica, and Lisa Mancino. 2010. "Eating Out Increases Daily Calorie Intake." USDA/Amber Waves, June 1. http://www.ers.usda.gov/amber-waves/2010-june/eating-out-increases-daily-calorie-intake.aspx#.U86zTlaO7VI.

Todd, Jessica, Lisa Mancino, and Biing-Hwan Lin. 2010. "The Impact of Food Away from Home on Adult Diet Quality." www.ers.usda.gov/publications/err90

Transparency International. 2016. "What Is Corruption?" https://www.transparency.org/what-is-corruption/#define.

Travis, Phyllida, Dominique Egger, Philip Davies, and Abdelhay Mechbal. 2002. "Towards Better Stewardship: Concepts and Critical Issues." Geneva: WHO. http://www.who.int/entity/healthinfo/paper48.pdf.

Trivers, Robert L. 1971. "The Evolution of Reciprocal Altruism." *The Quarterly Review of Biology* 46 (1): 35–57.

Troper, Michel. 2013. "Separation of Powers." Translated by Philip Stewart, in *A Montesquieu Dictionary*, edited by Catherine Volpilhac-Auger. http://dictionnaire-montesquieu.ens-lyon.fr/en/article/1376427308/en/.

Trost, Christine, and Alison Gash. 2008. *Conflict of Interest and Public Life*. New York: Cambridge University Press.

United Kingdom Committee on Standards in Public Life (Nolan Committee). 1995. "The 7 Principles of Public Life." https://www.gov.uk/government/publications/the-7-principles-of-public-life/the-7-principles-of-public-life--2.

United Nations (UN). 2006. "SNC Private Sector Engagement Policy." March, revised June 19. http://www.unsystem.org/scn/Publications/html/FinalSCNPrivateSectorEngagementPolicyAgreed-June2006.doc.

———. 2011. "Political Declaration on Non-Communicable Diseases," A/RES/66/2, http://www.who.int/nmh/events/un_ncd_summit2011/political_declaration_en.pdf.

———. 2011. "Report of the Secretary-General: Personal Conflict of Interest." http://www.un.org/en/ga/search/view_doc.asp?symbol=A/66/98.

———. 2013. "Enhanced Cooperation Between the United Nations and All Relevant Partners, in Particular the Private Sector." August 15. http://repository.un.org/bitstream/handle/11176/272580/A_68_326-EN.pdf

———. 2014. "Outcome Document of the High-Level Meeting of the General Assembly on the Comprehensive Review and Assessment of the Progress Achieved in the Prevention of and Control of Non-Communicable Diseases." July 17. http://www.un.org/en/ga/search/view_doc.asp?symbol=A/RES/68/300

———. 2015. "Sustainable Development Goals." https://sustainabledevelopment.un.org.

———. 2017. "Progress on the prevention and control of NCDs." A/72/662. https://undocs.org/A/72/662.

———. 2018. "Political Declaration of the Third High-Level Meeting on NCDs." http://www.un.org/en/ga/73/resolutions.shtml.

Upshur, Ross. 2002. "Principles for the Justification of Public Health Intervention." *Canadian Journal of Public Health* 93 (2): 101–103.

Vartanian, Lenny R., Marlene B. Schwartz, and Kelly D. Brownell. 2007. "Effects of Soft Drink Consumption on Nutrition and Health: A Systematic Review and Meta-Analysis." American Journal of Public Health 97 (4): 667–675. doi:10.2105/AJPH.2005.083782.

Vickerstaff, Sarah, Jan Macvarish, Peter Taylor-Gooby, Wendy Loretto, and Tina Harrison. 2012. "Trust and Confidence in Pensions: A Literature Review." Department for Work and Pensions Working Paper No.108. http://research.dwp.gov.uk/asd/asd5/WP108.pdf.

Waal, Frans B.M. de. 2000. "Attitudinal Reciprocity in Food Sharing among Brown Capuchin Monkeys." *Animal Behaviour* 60 (2): 253–261. doi:10.1006/anbe.2000.1471.

Wakeham Commission. 2000. "The Laws Lords and the Judicial Functions of the Second Chamber." https://www.gov.uk/government/uploads/system/uploads/attachment_data/file/266072/chap9.pdf

Waldron, Jeremy. 2013. "Separation of Powers in Thought and Practice." 54 *Boston College Law Review* 433–468.

Wallace, David Foster. 2009. *This Is Water*. New York: Little, Brown.

Walt, Gill, Ruairi Brugha, and Andy Haines. 2002. "Working with the Private Sector: The Need for Institutional Guidelines." *BMJ* 325 (7361): 432–435.

Wansink, Brian, and Pierre Chandon. 2006. "Can 'Low-Fat' Nutrition Labels Lead to Obesity?" *Journal of Marketing Research* 43 (4): 605–617. doi:10.1509/jmkr.43.4.605.

Warner, Bob. 2011. "City Turns Down Beverage-Industry Funds from Children's Hospital for Anti-Obesity Program." *Philadelphia Inquirer*, September 13. http://articles.philly.com/2011-09-13/news/30149740_1_antiobesityprogram-funding-million-grant.

Washburn, Jennifer. 2006. *University Inc.: The Corruption of Higher Education*. New York: Basic Books.

Watson-Capps, Jana J., and Thomas R. Cech. 2014. "Academia and Industry: Companies on Campus." *Nature*, October 15. http://www.nature.com/news/academia-and-industry-companies-on-campus-1.16127.

Weiner, Annette B. 1992. *Inalienable Possessions the Paradox of Keeping-While-Giving*. Berkeley: University of California Press.

White, Jenny and Lisa Bero. 2010. "Corporate Manipulation of Research: Strategies are Similar Across Five Industries." 21 *Stanford Law and Policy Review* 105–134.

Wikler, Daniel. 1978. "Persuasion and Coercion for Health: Ethical Issues in Government Efforts to Change Life-Styles." *Milbank Quarterly* 56 (3): 303–338.

———. 2002. "Personal and Social Responsibility for Health." *Ethics and International Affairs*.16 (2): 47–55.

Wood, Susan F., and Jillian K. Mador. 2013. "Uncapping Conflict of Interest?" *Science* 340 (6137): 1172–1173. doi:10.1126/science.1231955.

Woolf, Lord. 1998. "Master of the Rolls, Judicial Review—the Tensions Between the Executive and the Judiciary." 114 *Law Quarterly Review* 579.

World Bank. 2016a. "Helping Countries Combat Corruption: The Role of the World Bank." Accessed August 25. http://www1.worldbank.org/publicsector/anticorrupt/corruptn/cor02.htm#define.

———. 2016b. "Integrity Vice Presidency." Accessed September 27. http://www.worldbank.org/en/about/unit/integrity-vice-presidency

World Health Organization. (1946) 2005. "WHO Constitution." http://apps.who.int/gb/bd/PDF/bd47/EN/constitution-en.pdf.

———. (1987) 2015. "Principles Governing Relations with Non-Governmental Organizations." Accessed December 1. http://www.who.int/civilsociety/relations/principles/en/.

———. 2000. "Guidelines on Working with the Private Sector to Achieve Health Outcomes." http://apps.who.int/iris/bitstream/10665/78660/1/ee20.pdf.

———. 2013. "Public-Private Partnerships for Health." Accessed January 2. http://www.who.int/trade/glossary/story077/en.

———. 2014. *Basic Documents*, 48th edition. http://apps.who.int/gb/bd/PDF/bd48/basic-documents-48th-edition-en.pdf.

———. 2015. "Addressing and Managing Conflicts of Interest in the Planning and Delivery of Nutrition Programmes at Country Level." http://apps.who.int/iris/bitstream/10665/206554/1/9789241510530_eng.pdf.

——. 2016. "Framework of Engagement with Non-State Actors (FENSA)." http://apps.who. int/gb/ebwha/pdf_files/WHA69/A69_R10-en.pdf.

——. 2017a. "Safeguarding against possible conflicts of interest in nutrition programmes." http://apps.who.int/gb/ebwha/pdf_files/EB142/B142_23-en.pdf.

——. 2017b. "Montevideo Roadmap 2018–2030 on NCDs as a Sustainable Development Priority." http://apps.who.int/gb/ebwha/pdf_files/WHA71/A71_R2-en.pdf.

——. 2018a. "Preparation for the Third High-Level Meeting on NCDs." http://apps.who.int/ gb/ebwha/pdf_files/WHA71/A71_14-en.pdf.

——. 2018b. "Time to Deliver: Report of the Independent High-Level Commission on NCDs." http://apps.who.int/iris/bitstream/handle/10665/272710/9789241514163-eng.pdf.

World Obesity Federation. 2015. "World Obesity's Financial Relationship Policy." http://www. worldobesity.org/site_media/uploads/WOF_Financial_Relationship_Policy_June2015.pdf.

Wright, Robert. 1994. *The Moral Animal: The New Science of Evolutionary Psychology.* New York: Pantheon Books.

Yach, D. 2016. "Food Industry: Friend or Foe?" *Obesity Reviews* 15 (1): 2–5.

Yach, Derek, Zoë A. Feldman, Dondeena G. Bradley, and Mehmood Khan. 2010. "Can the Food Industry Help Tackle the Growing Global Burden of Undernutrition?" *American Journal of Public Health* 100 (6): 974–980. doi:10.2105/AJPH.2009.174359.

Yach, Derek, Mehmood Khan, Dondeena Bradley, Rob Hargrove, Stephen Kehoe, and George Mensah. 2010. "The Role and Challenges of the Food Industry in Addressing Chronic Disease." *Globalization and Health* 6: 10. doi:10.1186/1744-8603-6-10.

Yang, Jia Lynn. 2013. "Maximizing Shareholder Value: The Goal That Changed Corporate America." *The Washington Post*, August 26. https://www.washingtonpost.com/business/ economy/maximizing-shareholder-value-the-goal-that-changed-corporate-america/2013/08/ 26/26e9ca8e-ed74-11e2-9008-61e94a7ea20d_story.html.

Yank V., D. Rennie, and L. A. Bero. 2007. "Financial Ties and Concordance Between Results and Conclusions in Meta-Analyses." *BMJ* 335(7631): 1202–1205.

Yoon, Sungwon, and Tai-Hing Lam. 2013. "The Illusion of Righteousness: Corporate Social Responsibility Practices of the Alcohol Industry." *BMC Public Health* 13: 630. doi:10.1186/ 1471-2458-13-630.

Young, I. M. 1997. "Asymmetrical Reciprocity: On Moral Respect, Wonder, and Enlarged Thought." *Constellations* 3 (3): 340–363.

Zachwieja, Jeffrey, Eric Hentges, James O. Hill, Richard Black, and Maria Vassileva. 2013. "Public-Private Partnerships: The Evolving Role of Industry Funding in Nutrition Research." *Advances in Nutrition: An International Review Journal* 4 (5): 570–572. doi:10.3945/an.113.004382.

Zacka, Bernardo. 2017. "Are Bureaucracies a Public Good?." In *The President's House Is Empty: Losing and Gaining Public Goods,* edited by Joshua Cohen. Boston: Boston Review.

INDEX

Figures and notes are indicated by "f" and "n" following page numbers

Printed in the USA/Agawam, MA
January 2, 2020

746684.001